Content Knowledge in English Language Teacher Education

Also available from Bloomsbury

Initial English Language Teacher Education, edited by Darío Luis Banegas
Language Learning Strategies and Individual Learner Characteristics, edited by
Rebecca L. Oxford and Carmen M. Amerstorfer
Sustainable English Language Teacher Development at Scale, edited by Ian Eyres,
Robert McCormick and Tom Power

Content Knowledge in English Language Teacher Education

International Experiences

Edited by Darío Luis Banegas

BLOOMSBURY ACADEMIC
LONDON • NEW YORK • OXFORD • NEW DELHI • SYDNEY

BLOOMSBURY ACADEMIC
Bloomsbury Publishing Plc
50 Bedford Square, London, WC1B 3DP, UK
1385 Broadway, New York, NY 10018, USA

BLOOMSBURY, BLOOMSBURY ACADEMIC and the Diana logo
are trademarks of Bloomsbury Publishing Plc

First published in Great Britain 2020

Cover design: Adriana Brioso
Cover image © JohnnyGreig/iStock

A catalogue record for this book is available from the British Library.

ISBN: HB: 978-1-3500-8462-9
ePDF: 978-1-3500-8463-6
eBook: 978-1-3500-8464-3

Typeset by Deanta Global Publising Services, Chennai, India
Printed and bound in Great Britain

To find out more about our authors and books visit www.bloomsbury.com
and sign up for our newsletters.

Contents

Illustrations

Figures

Tables

Contributors

Liliana Anglada is a translator and teacher of English from the Facultad de Lenguas, Universidad Nacional de Córdoba. She holds an MA in Applied Linguistics (Ohio University) and a PhD in English (Texas Tech University). She has taught EFL/ESL undergraduate and graduate courses on language, grammar and linguistics and is currently the head of the doctoral programme at Facultad de Lenguas. Her research interests include systemic functional linguistics and EFL writing instruction.

Darío Luis Banegas is a lecturer in TESOL (University of Strathclyde), a curriculum developer and teacher educator with the Ministry of Education of Chubut, Argentina, and an associate fellow with the University of Warwick, UK. He coordinates an IELTE programme in Esquel and facilitates professional development courses. He is also an online tutor at an online IELTE programme in Argentina. Darío is the founding editor of the *Argentinian Journal of Applied Linguistics*. His main interests are content and language integrated learning, IELTE and action research.

Cristina Banfi is a linguist and educator who has taught English at primary and secondary levels and is currently a teacher educator. She teaches linguistics and second language acquisition at different institutions, including the University of Buenos Aires. She holds an MPhil from the University of Cambridge and a PhD from University College London, both in linguistics, and a postgraduate diploma in higher education policy from the University of Buenos Aires. Her most recent books are *El Aprendizaje de Idiomas: Cómo Habla la Mente* and *Exorcising Grammar* (co-edited).

Malba Barahona is an associate lecturer in TESOL at Instituto de Literatura y Ciencias del Lenguaje, Pontificia Universidad Católica de Valparaíso, Chile. Malba Barahona holds a PhD from the Australian National University, a master in Linguistics from the Universidad de Chile and a degree in the teaching of English from Universidad Metropolitana de Ciencias de la Educación (Pedagógico). Malba has been teaching in higher education institutions over the last twenty years in the fields of foreign language learning, second language teacher education, applied linguistics, language and identity and cultural historical activity theory.

Ricardo Benítez is an associate professor at the Institute of Literature and Language Sciences, Pontificia Universidad Católica de Valparaíso, Chile, where he has been teaching English language and second language writing for over thirty-five years. He received his master's degree in Teaching English as a second language from Arizona State University, USA, in 1992, and was a visiting professor at both Spelman College, Atlanta (2003), and Colorado State University, Colorado (2008). His academic duties also include being action research adviser for pre-service teachers.

Bettiana A. Blázquez is a teacher of English (Universidad Nacional del Comahue, UNCO) and has an MA in English Language Teaching and Applied Linguistics (King's College London University). She is a professor of English Phonetics and Phonology and co-director of a research project on prosody and meaning at UNCO. She is currently finishing her PhD in Applied Linguistics at Universidad Internacional Iberoamericana, México.

Phil Chappell is a senior lecturer and deputy head of the Department of Linguistics at Macquarie University. He conducts research in a variety of areas of TESOL, supervises research students at masters and PhD levels, and teaches on the applied linguistics and TESOL programme. Phil has taught and managed in Southeast Asia and in Australia in a variety of language and literacy programmes.

Mónica Campos Espinoza is a teacher educator with experience in the Chilean educational system at different levels. At present, she is working at Universidad Católica de Temuco and is responsible for courses in English language, methodology and practicum for the English Teacher Education Programme at Universidad Católica de Temuco. She has a master's in curriculum and evaluation.

Gonzalo E. Espinosa is a teacher of English (Universidad Nacional del Comahue, UNCO) and has a PhD in linguistics (Universidad de Buenos Aires). He is a teaching assistant in English Phonetics and Phonology at UNCO. He does postdoctoral studies on English and Spanish prosody and on second language acquisition thanks to a grant awarded by the National Scientific and Technical Research Council in Argentina.

Müzeyyen Nazlı Güngör, PhD, is a research assistant at Gazi University, Foreign Languages Teaching Department. She works as INGED board member and IATEFL associate committee member. She completed her dissertation on educating teachers of young learners. She has organized Erasmus+, US Embassy and scientific research projects, and delivered seminars for language teachers. Her research interests are teaching English to young learners, teacher identity and sociocultural teacher education.

Bahiyyih Hardacre, PhD, is an assistant professor in the MA in TESOL Programme at California State University, Los Angeles. She is originally from Brazil where she worked as an EFL teacher for twelve years at binational centres. She has lived in the United States for the past ten years, where she has been an active member of professional organizations such as TESOL, CATESOL and AAAL, has served as editor-in-chief for the peer-reviewed journal *Issues in Applied Linguistics*, has coordinated ESL programmes working as Director of Education and Teacher Trainer at language schools, coordinated and participated in state-wide and university level language assessment programmes, and taught international students in credit and non-credit programmes at the University of California, Los Angeles, and Santa Monica College. Besides teaching, her main research interests in TESOL and Applied Linguistics are language processing and cognition, language assessment, language evolution, and neurobiology of language learning and language use.

Gerardo Esteban Heras is an instructor and researcher at the University of Cuenca, Ecuador. He is part of the English Major Faculty at the Philosophy Department. He teaches pragmatics, sociolinguistics, conversation, and English as a foreign language. He is a PhD candidate at the Universidad Nacional de la Plata, Argentina. He is mainly interested in the area of pragmatics and sociolinguistics as chief components of second and foreign language teaching and learning.

Makoto Ikeda is a professor in English in the Department of English Literature at Sophia University. He received his MA in Applied Linguistics and ELT from King's College London and his PhD in English Philology from Sophia University. He has published a number of books and articles on ELT (particularly CLIL) and historical linguistics (mainly prescriptive grammar), including *CLIL:*

New Challenges in Foreign Language Education at Sophia University (Sophia University Press, 2016) and *Competing Grammars: Noah Webster's Vain Efforts to Defeat Lindley Murray* (Shinozaki-shorin, 1997).

Pamela Saavedra Jeldres is an English teacher with a master's degree in Educational Technology. She has taught English language and culture for the English Teacher Education Programme and English grammar and a seminar for the English-Spanish Translation Programme at Universidad Católica de Temuco. Her areas of interest are information literacy, academic writing, written feedback and teaching English as a foreign language.

Leopoldo O. Labastía is a teacher of English (INSP Joaquín V. González), has an MA in Linguistics (Universidad Nacional del Comahue, UNCO) and a PhD in Linguistics (UNED). He is a professor of English language and phonetics and phonology and director of a research project on prosody and meaning at UNCO. He has made contributions to *Procedural Meaning: Problems and Perspectives* (2011) and *Intonational Grammar in Ibero-Romance* (2016).

Ricardo Martín Ramírez has specialized in education and new technologies (FLACSO) and holds an MA in TEFL (Universidad Europea del Atlántico, Spain). Ricardo is a teacher educator (UADER), IVLP scholar (US Embassy Department of State), an ARTESOL (Argentina TESOL) board member, and is doing an MA in American Literature at Washington State University (USA) under the sponsorship of the Fulbright scholarship. His main research interests include teacher education, reading and writing in academic contexts, literary and cultural studies, rhetorics and composition, language policy, technology-enhanced language lessons, distance/blended learning, game-based learning.

T. Leo Schmitt has lived in seven countries and visited dozens more. He has extensive experience in intercultural communication and can communicate in multiple languages. He has used this knowledge to enhance his work with international students both as an administrator and faculty member in a wide variety of environments over twenty-five years. He has an MA and MPhil in linguistics from the CUNY Graduate Center and is currently completing his doctorate. He currently works as an assistant professor in the MA TESOL programme at the New School, New York. His research interests include second language development, sociolinguistics, corpus linguistics, intercultural communication, language and power, and the interaction between these and other linguistic phenomena.

Araceli Salas Serrano holds a PhD in Language Science and an MA in TESOL. She has been involved in ELT and teacher education for a long time. Her research interests include discourse analysis, English for specific purposes and teacher education. At Benemérita Universidad Autónoma de Puebla, Araceli collaborates as a professor and researcher where she is also a co-editor of *Lenguas en Contexto*. She has written several articles in the field and has presented in national and international forums.

Marguerite Ann Snow, PhD, is a professor at California State University, Los Angeles, where she teaches in the TESOL MA programme. She is co-author/co-editor of eleven books, including her two most recent: *Teaching English as Second or Foreign* Language (4th ed.) (2014) (with Marianne Celce-Murcia and Donna Brinton) and *The Content-Based Classroom: New Perspectives on Integrating Language and Content* (2017) (with Donna Brinton). She serves as a series editor for *Q: Skills for Success* for Oxford University Press, a twelve-book ESL/EFL textbook series. She is a co-recipient of the Pimsleur Award for the best research article in foreign language education, and, at CAL State LA, received the Outstanding Professor and the President's Distinguished Professor Award. She was a Fulbright scholar in Hong Kong (1985) and Cyprus (2009). In addition to working closely with public school teachers in the United States, she has made over fifty trips to consult or teach in international settings.

María Alejandra Soto is a teacher educator at the Universidad Autónoma de Entre Ríos, where she teaches English and foreign language didactics and coordinates a language skills workshop for Year 1 student-teachers. She also teaches ESP/EAP courses at the Universidad Nacional de Entre Ríos and has worked as a curriculum developer for the local Ministry of Education. Alejandra holds an MA in TESOL Teacher Education (University of Leeds, UK) and is currently undertaking a specialization in reading, writing and education at FLACSO (Argentina). Her main areas of interest include IELTE, context-sensitive curriculum innovations, teacher cognitions and their impact on classroom practices.

Blanca Adriana Téllez Méndez holds a master's degree on Language Sciences and a Bachelor on Modern Languages. She has been involved on academic and administrative areas and projects. Her research interests include discourse analysis particularly from systemic linguistics theory and more recently legitimacy code theory and curriculum design. She has been Tutorial Coordinator, Planning and

Evaluation Department Coordinator and at present coordinates the Bachelor Teaching English Language program at BUAP.

Rining Wei (Tony), PhD, teaches courses related to bilingualism and research methods at undergraduate and postgraduate levels, at the Department of English, Xi'an Jiaotong-Liverpool University. He has supervised masters and doctoral dissertation projects concerning bilingual education, content and language integrated learning (CLIL), and Teaching English to speakers of other languages (TESOL). He has published in journals including *Bilingualism: Language & Cognition, English Today,* and *World Englishes.* He serves on the editorial board of the *TESOL International Journal.*

Yi Zhang earned an MA TESL degree in the Pennsylvania State University and a PhD in Second Language Acquisition and Instructional Technology in the University of South Florida. His main research interests include sociolinguistics, discourse analysis, multilingualism, language and globalization, and computer-mediated communication. He has published papers in *language@internet* and *Discourse, Context & Media.* He has also presented studies and research projects in various international conferences such as American Association for Applied Linguistics (AAAL).

Abbreviations and Acronyms

AR	Action research
BA	Bachelor's program
BBC	British Broadcasting Company
BNC	British National Corpus
BUAP	Benemérita Universidad Autónoma de Puebla
CAE	Cambridge English Advanced
CBI	Content-based instruction
CDA	Critical discourse analysis
CDST	Complex dynamic systems theory
CEFR	Common European Framework of Reference for Languages
CLIL	Content and language integrated learning
CNN	Cable News Network
CoHE	Council of Higher Education
CRADLE	Curriculum reform aimed at the development of the learning of English
DA	Discourse analysis
DAC	Discourse analysis course
DCT	Discourse completion task
EALD	English as an additional language or dialect
EAR	Exploratory action research
EFL	English as a foreign language
EIL	English as an international language
ELF	English as a Lingua Franca
ELL	English language learner
ELP	English language proficiency
ELT	English language teaching
ELTE	English language teacher education
EMI	English-medium instruction

EP	Exploratory practice
ESL	English as a second language
FL	Foreign language
GPK	General pedagogical knowledge
GVS	Great vowel shift
HEL	History of English language
IATEFL	International Association of Teachers of English as a Foreign Language
IEL	Introduction to the English language
IELTE	Initial English language teacher education
INGED	English Language Education Association in Turkey
IPA	International phonetic alphabet
L2	Foreign/second language
LEI	Licenciatura en lengua inglesa
MA	Master's degree
MA TESOL	Master of arts in teaching English to speakers of other languages
NNEST	Non-native English-speaking teachers
NNS	Non-native speaker
NS	Native speaker
PCK	Pedagogical content knowledge
PUCV	Pontificia Universidad Católica de Valparaíso
RP	Received pronunciation
SCI	Student-centred instruction
SFG	Systemic functional grammar
SFL	Systemic functional linguistics
TBL	Task-based learning
TESOL	Teaching English to speakers of other languages
TIHL	Taller Integrador de Habilidades Lingüísticas
UNCO	Universidad Nacional del Comahue
WE	World Englishes
XJTLU	Xi'an Jiaotong-Liverpool University

Introduction

Darío Luis Banegas

Let me start with a few questions: How much English should a teacher of English know to teach it effectively as another language? How much knowledge about English should a teacher have to be a good teacher? Should they know about syntax, phonology and discourse analysis? How does that affect a teacher's professional identity?

Now, let me share two different stories that are connected to the questions posed above.

Story 1: I was interviewing a group of teenage learners about their teachers' practices in secondary education. They criticized some of their teachers for various reasons, but they also praised others for how much they knew about the subject they taught. One example specifically referred to their EFL teacher:

> Sandra rocks! She knows so much about English. She gives us all kinds of feedback, like when something is OK, when something is wrong, what other possibilities we can use. Or she teaches us jokes and expressions, or makes us note differences in meaning according to intonation, or pronunciation. I now know that we can't say that British English is purer than American English because she gave us this explanation about languages, dialects, and how they evolve. That makes her an excellent teacher!

Story 2: I was doing research on EFL teachers' perceptions as regards the impact that the pre-service ELTE programme they had completed had made on them (Banegas 2009). Most participants coincided in stressing the importance of content knowledge – that is, knowledge of and about English. For example, one teacher said:

> We must learn how to use the language. Mastery of English is absolutely necessary to be a model. After all, we have to know what we teach. Of course the *how* is important, but perhaps the *what* is a priority because this is what we actually teach: English.

Judging by the stories shared above, it is clear that subject-matter knowledge may define teachers of English in terms of their professional identity not only in the eyes of their learners but also in the eyes of colleagues. Language teaching as a sociocultural activity is embedded in complex and dynamic contexts (Cross 2010), where both teachers and learners are engaged in learning as a long-lasting process. If we take teaching as a sociocultural activity, ELTE programmes need to provide (future) teachers with opportunities to imagine and develop their professional identity and agency socially and critically constructed, which could be supported by experienced teachers (Donnini Rodrigues, de Pietri, Sanchez, & Kuchah 2018). In this regard, teachers' knowledge of their subject as a component of their professional identity should be axiomatic (Cross 2018).

The aim of this edited collection is to understand how tutors/lecturers approach English-language-as-content knowledge in ELTE programmes. In this regard, the volume does not aspire to make a significant contribution at research and theoretical levels by renowned experts. Rather, it seeks to illustrate how tutors deliver modules which represent content knowledge in a diversity of programmes and settings. While in a previous volume I focused on the intersection between ELTE and pedagogical knowledge (Banegas 2017a), in this volume, the lens is on how teacher educators, lecturers or tutors, depending on contextual circumstances, help (future) teachers develop and configure knowledge of and about the English language. Accordingly, in their chapters contributors have chosen to share descriptive and reflective accounts of their practices and modules they teach or present findings based on researching their own practices. As in Banegas' (2017a), experiences come from a wide range of geographical settings, some of them underrepresented in the international literature: Argentina, Australia, Chile, China, Ecuador, Japan, Mexico, Turkey and the United States.

Content knowledge in ELTE

Widdowson (2002) has been categorical about the importance of teachers' knowledge:

> It seems reasonable to expect that teachers should know their subject. This knowledge provides the grounds for their authority, and gives warrant to the idea that they are practising a profession. Without this specialist knowledge, they have no authority, and no profession. (p. 67)

Widdowson's quote seems to respond to what legitimizes teachers of English and what their knowledge base should consist of. Following Shulman's (1986, 1987) widespread conception of the knowledge base, ELTE programmes particularly at pre-service level usually organize what teachers should know around three broad and interrelated areas, which, according to König et al. (2016), are (1) content or subject-matter knowledge (CK), (2) pedagogical content knowledge (PCK), and (3) general pedagogical knowledge (GPK). In this edited volume, our interest is in exploring CK and how it is approached in ELTE programmes as it has been largely ignored in the literature (but see Bartels 2005). In line with Borg (2013), we agree that the teacher knowledge base should incorporate knowledge created by teachers out of their own beliefs, personal theories and trajectories.

In the educational rhetoric, it is usually agreed that CK refers to 'the knowledge of the specific subject and related to the content teachers are required to teach. CK is shaped by academic disciplines underlying the subject' (König et al. 2016: 321). In the case of ELTE, academics and curriculum developers (e.g. Richards & Farrell 2011; Roberts 1998; Widdowson 2002; Woodgate-Jones 2008) agree that CK includes knowledge of the English language as a system of subsystems and proficiency in using English. The latter is of paramount importance since English may be both the object of study and the medium of instruction in ELTE programmes (Bale 2016). König et al. (2016) add that 'language teachers are also required to develop a high level of language awareness, language learning awareness, and of intercultural competencies' (p. 322). Thus, CK may be summarized under two contextually dimensions embedded in mutual dialogue: (1) English as a system and (2) English language proficiency. These dimensions show that in this volume we take a broad conceptualization of CK as it is what may actually happen in practice around the world; however, we must acknowledge the pre-eminent role that linguistics plays throughout the chapters.

English as a system

Knowledge about language refers to understanding, in this volume, English as a system. Drawing on the fundamental concepts introduced by linguist Saussure, language is often regarded as a system of signs. Language is a human artefact made up of symbolic and iconic signs which involve the pairing of form, phonetic and orthographic, and meaning (McGregor 2009). A system means that such signs coexist in paradigmatic and syntagmatic relationships; therefore, from a limited number of signs, language users can create an unlimited number of meaningful units such as words, phrases, clauses and entire texts to make sense of their experience, past, present and future.

Linguistics is the scientific study of language. It studies language by describing the languages spoken around the world (Bauer 2007; Brown 2006; Department of Linguistics 2016; McGregor 2009). Therefore, linguistics plays a central role in content knowledge in ELTE. However, Widdowson (2002) has noted that EFL/ESL teachers do not need to study language but the language they teach. Thus, content knowledge, according to Widdowson, should be primarily concerned with English as a system. In a publication about the relevance of understanding language variation among so-called non-native teachers in English language classrooms, Mahboob (2017) is categorical:

> Given that the key role of English language teachers (ELTs) is to teach *language*, it is essential that language teachers have a more technical understanding of what language and grammar are. And, more specifically, since NNESTs are teachers of English, teacher education programs need to help pre- and in-service teachers develop an understanding of 'English' in today's world. (p. 14; emphasis in original)

Linguistics provides ELTE programmes with the technical understanding Mahboob (2017) stresses in the quote above. ELTE programmes usually include modules or content related to the following branches of linguistics: grammar, syntax, morphology, phonetics, phonology, psycholinguistics, sociolinguistics, language acquisition, pragmatics, discourse analysis, stylistics, semantics, applied linguistics and cognitive linguistics among others. Such modules and topics are usually delivered in English, thus converting ELTE programmes into instantiations of EMI in settings where English is not the mainstream language (e.g. Macaro 2018; Macaro, Purle, Cun, & An 2018). In this volume, contributors offer their insights and experiences with teaching some of the branches listed above.

Whether teacher educators in ELTE programmes follow a formal, functional or no particular theory or approach to understanding language, they seek to ensure that there are strong correlations between linguistic understanding and ELT. In other words, in what ways does, for example, sociolinguistics, explicitly inform language teachers' situated practices? Such a question signals that in ELTE, linguistics-related modules and topics should be pursued following a pedagogical intent since, as Richards (2017a) rightly argues, 'content knowledge in itself does not provide a sufficient basis for the teaching of a language' (p. 12). This is not to say that there should be an instrumentalist view of linguistic knowledge, but rather a holistic perspective which shows that ELTE programmes are not educating, at least in principle, linguists but language teachers. The integration of linguistics-driven content knowledge with language pedagogy contributes to the realization of the content pedagogical knowledge dimension of ELTE programmes. In so doing, teachers may develop informed decisions based on their knowledge of linguistics (i.e. knowledge about the language) which may, for example, guide their selection of teaching resources (Tomlinson 2013) or inform the feedback they provide their learners. Furthermore, as I have stated elsewhere (Banegas 2017b), linguistics learning may become more meaningful when it is framed by tutors in the same teaching approaches that future teachers are expected to enact in their own professional practices. In this regard, Borg (2013) calls for more research and informed accounts which describe how knowledge about language can be developed through ELTE in ways that enable future teachers to support learning.

English language proficiency

Knowledge of the language is how proficient teachers are in the language they teach or the language through which they teach as it may be the case of EMI or CLIL. Although it has been suggested that language proficiency is a rather elusive concept (Tsang 2017), Harsch (2017: 250) has broadly defined it as follows: 'Proficiency in a second or foreign language comprises the aspects of being able to do something with the language ("knowing how") as well as knowing about it ("knowing what").'

In ELTE programmes, English language proficiency may be developed not only through modules built around English as a system which are delivered in English but also through specific modules on written and oral language practices. In Argentina, for example, student-teachers must complete modules which focus on academic reading and writing, oral skills, the four skills, or language development (skills, grammar, and vocabulary) usually organized around topics which aim at integrating content and language learning (Fortanet-Gómez 2013; Nikula, Dafouz, Moore, & Smit 2016). Teacher educators and tutors in charge of these modules often frame their teaching practices around learning theories such as sociocultural theory (Lantolf & Poehner 2014), critical theory in language education (e.g. Hawkins & Norton 2009) or cognitivism (Golombek 2015). Other perspectives also included are interculturality (Porto & Byram 2017), EIL and ELF. These last perspectives may also be embraced by linguistics-related modules such as sociolinguistics or discourse analysis or overall ELTE programmes, for example, at masters level (e.g. Nguyen 2017) to challenge the so-called native-speaker model (Holliday 2006). Further, I will return to this concept.

English language proficiency plays out a major role in teachers' professional identity and is said to exert a direct influence on teacher efficacy. In relation to identity, Pennington and Richards (2016; also Richards 2010) suggest that teachers' perception of their English language proficiency is linked to teaching confidence and perceptions of teaching efficacy. Richards (2017a) has later remarked that in teaching English through English, teachers must be proficient users of English before, during and after teaching. As in Widdowson's quote above, teachers' authority somehow rests on English language proficiency, but proficiency should be understood as a process, and teachers may need to develop a personal disposition as life-long learner of English to navigate that process.

However, the construct of English language proficiency in ELTE has given rise to a few concerns. For example, Freeman (2017) challenges the syllogism 'the more fluent in English, the more effective the teacher' since teacher language proficiency as determinant of effective teaching is based on the highly criticized native-speaker model because it promotes an ideological position of superiority of native-speaker teachers over non-native-speaker teachers (Martínez Agudo 2017). This view seems to indicate that only content knowledge, or in fact, language use, is more important than teaching competency or pedagogical content knowledge in ELTE.

In terms of proficiency and what counts as acceptable, teachers may have different bars depending on whether learners or teachers are involved. Through a mixed-methods study, Nguyen (2017) studied engagement with the native-speaker model among a group of Vietnamese ELT teachers completing a master's programme. Results showed that while the programme and the teachers agreed on promoting linguistic diversity, multilingualism and interculturalism, teachers' language proficiency, particularly oral, was still dominated by a native-speaker model.

With the aim of offering an alternative approach to the native-speaker model, Freeman (2017) suggests the construct of English-for-teaching which

> identifies the English language that teachers can use in the classroom to do their work. In so doing, the construct bounds this set of language resources within the broader sweep of general English proficiency. The bounding is grounded by the situations and circumstances in which the teacher uses (may use; needs to use) English in the activity of teaching. (pp. 41–2)

Two studies lend support to the syllogism criticized above. In a qualitative study, Tsang (2017) examined the relationship between teachers' general language proficiency and teaching effectiveness operationalized by learners' engagement. Data showed that those teachers with higher language proficiency were more flexible in the use of English and promoted metalinguistic knowledge among learners. In addition, learners paid more attention to those teachers who were seen as 'very good' language models. However, when these learners were asked to choose the most effective teachers, they selected those who were not the most proficient in English. Instead, they chose teachers who displayed different teaching techniques, were more inspiring or had some personal characteristics such as a good sense of humour.

While this English-for-teaching construct may find traction in ELTE, it may be difficult to predict the English language teachers may use in their potential teaching posts. In times of approaches which highlight communication, cognition, socioconstructivism, competencies, problem-solving techniques and the integration of curriculum content and language, teachers may need more English than just a few structures and survival vocabulary. That said, it is also true that ELTE programmes, particularly in pre-service education, cannot possibly 'teach it all' and therefore they need to define what aspects of the English language will be addressed and included in relation to the teaching degree they offer.

It may be concluded that content knowledge in ELTE poses challenges, debates and questions around the knowledge of and about the English language that EFL/ESL teachers need in order to carry out successful teaching practices. In a reflective chapter on teacher identity in second language teacher education, Richards (2017b) once again stresses that when teachers ask themselves where they are in their professional development, there are two components that will contribute to their sense of identity: language proficiency and content knowledge. In this volume, the interest lies in taking a look at what teacher educators do and think in relation to such complex components in ELTE.

Structure of the book

The chapters in this edited volume lie at the intersection between exploring English as a semiotic system and improving English language proficiency among student-teachers in ELTE. While Chapters 1 to 9 concentrate on English as a system, the remaining chapters give more importance to English language proficiency. However, it should be noted that English language proficiency and language awareness run across the volume. Below, readers will find an overview of each chapter. Each chapter summary has a different format given that some of the chapters are reflective (e.g. Chapter 1), descriptive (e.g. Chapter 2) or primary data based (e.g. Chapter 11).

In Chapter 1, Ikeda reflects on the value and usefulness of history of English (HEL) in the teaching and learning of English at a teaching programme in Japan. The chapter also presents a sample HEL lesson using CLIL in order to show the possibility and problem of developing both disciplinary knowledge and language skills at the same time.

In Chapter 2, Chappell describes a unit of study that student-teachers take when undertaking either a Graduate Certificate of TESOL or a Master of Applied Linguistics and TESOL programme in an Australian university. This unit of study, *Linguistics and Language Teaching*, introduces student-teachers to a functional model of language based on SFL, SFG and genre theory and pedagogy.

Chapter 3 comes from Argentina. Anglada describes two prevalent approaches to the teaching of English grammar in IELTE: (1) a formal model and (2) a systematic functional model. The chapter characterizes both teaching models by describing their aims, showing their foci and including some activities as examples. The traditional approach, which focuses on the teaching of formal aspects of language sometimes neglecting the role of meaning, has been losing ground lately.

In Chapter 4, Hardacre and Snow describe a graduate-level pedagogical grammar class offered at California State University in the TESOL MA programme. It describes foundational concepts used in the course such as descriptive and prescriptive usage; the form, meaning, use framework (Celce-Murcia & Larsen-Freeman 2016); how to use corpora to show teachers-in-training authentic usage patterns; strategies for giving feedback when teaching grammar; and examples of grammar activities drawn from content- and task-based projects developed by the teachers-in-training in the MA programme.

In Chapter 5, Schmitt outlines approaches to incorporating other languages in the classroom based on a module taught at an ELTE programme in the United States. The author explains that the use of other languages can enhance the classroom experience, improve empathy for learners and empower non-native speakers of English. It additionally offers an appropriate context for translingual and contrastive linguistic practice.

In Chapter 6, Zhang and Wei describe the learning experience of five MA TESOL students in a world Englishes module entitled *English as a Global*

Language at the largest Sino-UK international collaborative university in China. Interviews with the MA TESOL student-teachers revealed that they experienced 'knowledge shock' in learning that (1) English can be in the plural form, (2) users can claim ownership of a particular variety of the English language and (3) challenges for teachers wishing to apply ideas (e.g. world Englishes) from the pluralistic paradigm to teaching English at primary and secondary levels.

Chapter 7 shows how Heras has addressed the teaching of pragmatics at an IELTE programme in Ecuador. Heras demonstrates that pragmatics is an important part of language teaching and learning. Therefore, the teacher plays a big role in the enhancement of students' pragmatic competence. The author argues that the use of film is one of the best techniques when attempting to teach pragmatics in the classroom.

Chapter 8, set in Mexico, presents the way a traditional DA module in IELTE was updated in order to allow student-teachers not only to gain knowledge on discourse and several approaches on its analysis but also to experience doing DA. Salas Serrano and Téllez Méndez discuss how their student-teachers became aware of the relationship between discourse and their social and cultural reality.

In Chapter 9, Blázquez, Espinosa and Labastía describe the rationale in the teaching, learning, contents and assessment of a phonetics and phonology module taught at an IELTE programme at Universidad Nacional del Comahue, Argentina. This module, designed for a mixed-ability group of freshmen, follows an eclectic approach by focusing on both segmentals and suprasegmentals from the very beginning. Student-teachers are engaged in an inductive way of learning with consciousness-raising activities, paving the way for autonomous learning.

In Chapter 10, Banfi, drawing on her vast experience in Argentinian IELTE, discusses her approach in teaching a module called *English Language IV* in different IELTE programmes in the City of Buenos Aires. The innovative approach provides an integrated scheme that incorporates contents and skills learnt and developed by student-teachers in prior courses, and requires them to apply them to different tasks that involve linguistic, intercultural, academic and professional skills.

In Chapter 11, Saavedra Jeldres and Campos Espinoza discuss how developing writing skills in student-teachers is a task sometimes neglected due to time constraints. In this chapter it is shown that the writing portfolio has proven to be an effective tool for improving writing production in an IELTE programme in Chile. This mixed study pursues to improve student-teachers' writing skills and develop their reflective skills using a year-long portfolio.

Chapter 12, authored by Barahona and Benítez, explores the implementation of a thematic advanced English module in a Chilean ELTE programme that contributes to student-teachers' development of their knowledge of the English language. This module enhances practical learning experiences which allow students to explore current controversial issues in such a way that it helps put into practice the competency-based curriculum on which it is based.

Chapter 13 takes us to Turkey. Güngor discusses the knowledge base that enhances non-native student-teachers' English proficiency levels in IELTE programmes. Drawing on the results of international and national studies, constraints and affordances are analysed in the IELTE curriculum in Turkey. In addition, the chapter focuses on the ways content knowledge is approached and how non-native student-teachers are scaffolded to develop knowledge of and about the English language in Turkey.

Chapter 14 discusses how Soto and Ramírez have incorporated a cultural element into a reading and writing workshop to enhance student-teachers' English language proficiency. In addition, the workshop seeks to raise intercultural awareness so that student-teachers' self-expression of their lived experiences disrupts and enriches their language-learning process. Their chapter is based on their teaching experience at an IELTE programme in Argentina.

Readers will find that Chapters 1– 14 include what we call questions for change. The aim of these questions is to generate reflections and open roads of interdisciplinary dialogue and collaboration with other teacher educators based around the world.

In the Conclusion, I highlight the common threads running across the chapters in terms of topics, experiences, strategies and research potential. In addition, I put forward possible future directions in IELTE programmes as regards subject-matter knowledge at the intersection of pedagogy and linguistic preparation.

On behalf of the contributors and myself, I sincerely hope that you find the volume helpful for ELTE in your context. We have made every effort to represent different contexts and realities along with the voices of both student-teachers and teacher educators.

Before I go I would like to thank Maria Brauzzi from Bloomsbury for believing in me (once more!). I would also like to thank the anonymous reviewers who provided helpful comments and suggestions. I would like to thank the following colleagues, student-teachers and friends who have made this volume possible: Robert Wright, Fernando Mongiardino, Grisel Roberts and Sophie Breen. I would finally like to thank Daniel Borelli and Oinky. We know why.

1

Applied English Philology in CLIL with TESOL Student-Teachers

Makoto Ikeda

Introduction

Although interest in language for speculation, reflection and discussion dates back to philosophers in ancient Greece, truly scientific investigation into language started with philologers (now called historical linguists) in the early-nineteenth-century Germany, who tried to reconstruct the proto-Indo European language by systematically comparing languages from the Indian subcontinent to those in the Iberian peninsula (Crystal 2010: 302, 428). This diachronic approach to language analysis is the outset of modern linguistics, followed by synchronic disciplines such as phonetics and phonology, morphology and syntax, semantics and lexis, pragmatics and discourse, generative grammar and functional grammar, and corpus linguistics and cognitive linguistics. Turning our attention from the past development of language studies in the academic world to the current coverage of language systems in language teacher education, HEL is at best peripherally treated in pre-service teacher training or at worst completely ignored. Taking, for example, popular books about the English language written for ELT practitioners, no references to HEL are found (e.g. Harmer 2012; Thornbury 2017). This tendency is true of MA TESOL programmes, where student-teachers are expected to learn about the English language systems but very rarely about HEL.

Here arises a fundamental question: Is the knowledge of HEL useless to the teaching and learning of English? For someone who knows both HEL and ELT well, the answer is definitely in the negative and indeed there exist monographs, book chapters and articles addressing this issue. The most comprehensive treatment is provided by Schmitt and Marsden (2006), which is collaboratively written by an applied linguist and a historical linguist with teaching applications in mind. What makes this book unique and useful is its practicality: to help teachers utilize the historical background knowledge of English, 'applications to teaching' columns and reproducible 'classroom activity' task sheets are provided in each chapter. Yule (1998), in his chapter on indirect objects (pp. 187–209), makes use of HEL when explaining the after-verb position of indirect objects, which was the most common in the earliest English and is therefore mainly possible for native words but not necessarily so for Latin borrowings (e.g. 'They'll give *the library* some old books' vs. '*They'll donate *the library* some books'). More recently and locally, in Iyeiri's edited volume (2016), seven Japanese philologists discuss the advantages of HEL-ELT fusion in various perspectives ranging from the micro-pedagogical level (lexis, semantics, orthography, morphology, syntax) to the macro-conceptual level (teacher education, second language acquisition, awareness of linguistic change and diversity).

This chapter takes the same stance and argues that knowing about HEL broadens and deepens the understanding of English, making it possible to learn and teach the language much more systematically, intellectually and effectively. In the following, I will first discuss the rationale for offering an HEL module in the undergraduate ELT teacher preparation programme and introduce my BA students' ideas about the use of HEL knowledge in learning, using and teaching English. Then I will describe what knowledge of HEL can help enhance English language learning. And finally I will present my own practice in teaching HEL lessons using CLIL. In the conclusion I will propose the idea of applied English philology in order to conceptualize the utilization of historical linguistics in English language education.

Why should TESOL student-teachers study HEL?

I am teaching in the department of English literature at a private university in Tokyo, which is well known in Japan for its FL education. Each academic year, the department accepts 100 new BA students and about 20 of them register for the teaching certificate programme, where they learn how English is structured (phonetics, phonology, lexis, morphology, syntax, discourse, HEL), used (pragmatics, sociolinguistics), learnt (second language acquisition) and taught (teaching methodologies). HEL is a mandatory module in the programme for the following reasons.

The first reason lies in its holistic and cross-disciplinary nature, as Hayes and Burkette (2017) put it:

> Over the course of a single semester, an HEL course may incorporate material from history, geography, lexicography, philology, literature, grammar, and linguistics, the last of which includes the subfields of phonology, morphology, syntax, semantics, and sociolinguistics. (p. 3)

In other words, the HEL module provides student-teachers with an opportunity to integrate what they have learnt in other compartmentalized language and literature courses. The second rationale comes from SLA (Second Language Acquisition). In explaining how language learning takes place, Lightbown and Spada (2013) present four perspectives: the behaviourist perspective (i.e. language is learnt by mimicry and memorization), the innatist perspective (i.e. both first language and second language are naturally acquired through exposure to comprehensible input), the cognitive perspective (i.e. language learning involves conscious mental activities such as understanding, analysing, problem solving) and the sociocultural perspective (i.e. language development arises from social interactions). HEL, with its heavy focus on lexical, structural and phonological forms, contributes to the third aspect of FL acquisition by helping learners consciously understand, notice and organize linguistic features of English, which nurtures their declarative knowledge (ability to explain language explicitly) and assists the development of their procedural knowledge (ability to use language implicitly) (Nava & Pedrazzini 2018). And the last obvious reason is offered by ELT itself, which is composed of teaching language knowledge (vocabulary, grammar, pronunciation, discourse) and teaching the four skills (speaking, listening, writing, reading). When working on the former, some knowledge of HEL helps teachers and learners in various ways as described in the subsequent sections.

What benefits can BA in English students derive from HEL?

My students receive fourteen 90-minute lectures about HEL with occasional references to ELT. Table 1.1 is the outline of my HEL module.

In order to know the impact of this HEL module on my students as EFL learners, I asked them to answer the following question in writing at the end of the spring semester of 2018:

> Please describe how your understanding of English has changed or how your knowledge of the language has increased after learning about the history of the

Table 1.1 Outline of My History of English Module

1. Why English?
2. The Indo-European language family
3. Old English 1: Outer history (Germanic invasion, Viking settlement, etc.)
4. Old English 2: Phonology, lexis, morpho-syntax
5. Old English 3: Reading the Lord's prayer
6. Middle English 1: Outer history (Norman Conquest, Black Death, etc.)
7. Middle English 2: Phonology, lexis, morpho-syntax
8. Middle English 3: Reading the General Prologue of Canterbury Tales
9. Early Modern English 1: Outer history (Renaissance, Reformation, etc.)
10. Early Modern English 2: Phonology, lexis, morpho-syntax
11. Early Modern English 3: Reading Shakespeare's plays
12. Late Modern English 1: Outer history (Age of Reason, Industrial Revolution, etc.)
13. Late Modern English 2: Reading prescriptive grammars
14. Present-day English and World Englishes

English Language (HEL). When you write your response, please explain how you are going to make use of your HEL knowledge for the learning, using or teaching of English.

In total, eighty-five students responded to this question. They were all undergraduate English majors (English literature, American literature or linguistics) including student-teachers who registered for the teaching certificate programme. This means that all the respondents were learners of English and some of them were future language teachers.

The most popular comment was that they understood the overall structure and fundamental nature of English better and liked the language more. One student even said, 'I no longer see English just as a language but as a product of history spun out by many people.' Below is a list of what the students pointed out as benefits to the learning, using and teaching of English.

Benefits to learning

1. HEL makes learners realize the importance of learning synonyms.
2. HEL offers answers to some of the puzzles about irregularities in English.
3. HEL stimulates interest in language.
4. HEL helps language knowledge to stay in long-term memory.
5. HEL makes noticing happen.
6. HEL provides learners with opportunities to compare their L1 (first language) and English.

Benefits to using

1. HEL raises students' awareness of registers according to contexts.
2. HEL gives practical tips in language use (e.g. careful articulation of idiosyncratic English phonemes).
3. HEL provides some knowledge transferrable to L1 use (e.g. attitudes towards prescriptive grammar).

Benefits to teaching

1. HEL enables more persuasive explanations about English.
2. HEL provides 'a sort of spice' in teaching.
3. HEL enhances teachers' confidence.

Although there are some overlaps, what the students are saying is that HEL contributes to their acquisition and use of English in terms of language knowledge regarding vocabulary, grammar, pronunciation and spelling, each of which is described in detail in the next section.

How is HEL knowledge useful for ELT?

The English language came into existence in the middle of the fifth century with the arrival of Germanic tribes (first the Jutes, then the Angles, the Saxons and the Frisians) in Britannia, who were requested by the then British king to fight with the barbarians from the north in exchange for some land. Since then, the Germanic dialect originally spoken in the south of the Jutland peninsula has experienced centuries of military, religious and intellectual raids from the continent and dramatically changed its appearance, making it distinct from other Germanic tongues (e.g. Dutch, German, Scandinavian languages). As this chapter is not about HEL per se, a table outlining the relationships between external history (social events), internal history (linguistic changes) and eternal influences on English in each of the HEL periods is provided (Table 1.2), instead of narratively tracing the whole chronological path of the English language.

Broadly speaking, what Table 1.2 tells us is that, as the result of going through a series of significant events in the past centuries, English as we have today is characterized by at least three distinct features: rich vocabulary derived from various sources (i.e. Germanic, French, Latin, Greek), simple grammar due to the loss of word endings (e.g. no distinctions between nominative, dative and

Table 1.2 History of English at a Glance

Period in HEL	External history (Cause)	Internal history (Effect)	Eternal influence (Trace)
Pre-English (3500 BC?–450)	-Birth of the Indo-Europeans -Migration of the Indo-Europeans -Celtic settlement -Roman invasion	-Birth of the proto-Indo-European language -Development into different languages -Place and person names -Place names	-Similarities to other European languages
Old English (450–1100)	-Germanic settlement -Arrival of Christianity -Viking raids	-Birth of English -Introduction of Roman alphabets -Borrowings from Latin -Borrowings from Old Norse -Beginning of simplified morphology	-Adoption of Roman alphabets -Enrichment of vocabulary -Enrichment of vocabulary -'Drift' towards a synthetic language
Middle English (1100–1500)	-Norman Conquest -Instalment of the first printing press in London	-Borrowings from French -Simplified morphology -Beginning of standard spellings	-Enrichment of vocabulary -Development into a synthetic language -Germination of Standard English
Early Modern English (1500–1700)	-Renaissance -(Unknown causes) -Age of Discovery	-Borrowings from Latin and Greek -Etymological spellings -Retention of conventional spellings -Great Vowel Shift -Beginning of world Englishes	-Enrichment of vocabulary -Sounds and spellings discrepancy -Sounds and spellings discrepancy -Sounds and spellings discrepancy -British English and American English
Late Modern English (1700–1900)	-Age of Reason -Industrial Revolution -Imperialism	-Publication of dictionaries and prescriptive grammars -Spread of English	-Establishment of Standard English -Social dialects
Present-day English (1900–today)	-Globalization -Internet society	-Expansion of Englishes	-Varieties of English -English as a lingua franca

accusative cases in nouns) and occasionally inconsistent relationships between sounds and letters (e.g. t*i*me /aɪ/ vs. pol*i*ce /iː/, rece*i*pt /ø/ vs. acce*p*t /p/). Keeping these basic characteristics of English in mind gives teachers insights into language knowledge instruction. What follows are more details about the linguistic features, historical background and pedagogical suggestions regarding English lexis, morpho-syntax, phonology and orthography.

Vocabulary

The most conspicuous trait of English would be the size and variety of vocabulary. The total number of words could range from hundreds of thousands to millions, depending on how lexical items are counted (Crystal 2003). When English originated in the fifth century, it only had Germanic words (native words) brought from the continent, with some exceptions. However, as early as its 'toddler' stage of Old English (450–1100), it already started to borrow lexical items from other languages: some Latin words concerning religion and monastery life after the conversion to Christianity (e.g. angel, mass, priest), and everyday words from Old Norse (e.g. egg, ill, get) after the Vikings' attack, settlement and assimilation in the north eastern part of England. In its 'childhood' stage of the Middle English period (1100–1500), a large number of French vocabulary flowed into English after the Norman Conquest (1066) and the subsequent consequence of French as the official language in Britain for almost three centuries. Then, in its 'adolescent' years of the Early and Late Modern periods (1500–1900), with the arrival of the Renaissance, a tremendous number of Latin and Greek words were used to translate ancient writings into English, together with the custom of word coinage by combining stems, prefixes and suffixes. This long tradition of borrowings and word formation still continues today, the 'adulthood' in the development of the English language, bringing loan words from other languages and coining new words by affixation.

Knowing the historical background and present constituents of the English lexicon above, teachers can offer, for example, the following tips to students for their vocabulary building and appropriate use of words.

Synonyms and registers

English is a language with abundant examples of synonyms at three levels: native words (e.g. kingly, rise, time) are 'popular', vocabulary from French (e.g. royal, mount, age) are 'literary' and borrowings from Latin and Greek (e.g. sovereign, ascend, epoch) are 'learned' (Baugh & Cable 2013). The bad news for students is that users of English are expected to cope with such synonyms in writing as well as in speech, meaning it is more important for learners of English to acquire a large amount of vocabulary than for students of other languages. What is more, this affects registers: in informal/casual/everyday communication (e.g. conversation with family and friends, tweeting and text messaging), Germanic words are more often used, while in formal/academic/professional discourse (e.g. plenaries, government documents, scientific papers), French, Latin and Greek lexis tend to be employed more frequently. It is therefore beneficial for learners to know that the origins of words are related to the appropriacy of English language use according to purposes and contexts.

Etymological approach

As formal words of French, Latin and Greek origins are basically composed of stems (roots) and affixes (prefixes and suffixes), they can be acquired analytically and systematically. For example, the word 'incredible' is made up of *in* (not) + *cred* (believe, trust) + *ible* (possible), hence its basic meaning of 'impossible to believe' and its figurative use of 'extremely good'. This analytic approach to learning formal vocabulary makes it easier for learners to remember, retain and guess the meanings of those words. Besides, as English has artificially coined abstract, conceptual and technical terms in this way since the early Modern English period, this is, in a way, a scientific approach to vocabulary building. Indeed, drawing on the previous studies, Nation (1990: 171) carries a list of 'the fourteen words (keys to the meanings of over 14,000 words)', which are composed of the most productive fourteen stems and twenty prefixes (e.g. *mistranscribe*: *mis* [wrong] + *trans* [across, beyond] + *scribe* [write]). Nation (2013: 403–4) also provides some general principles for teachers who intend to teach vocabulary utilizing this linguistic knowledge. Let me summarize a few:

1. This word learning strategy works better with students who have a decent size of complicated vocabulary because the words they already know contain some important word parts which can be applied to unfamiliar words.
2. Students should be taught useful affixes one by one as they are required, instead of being given a long list of word elements to study at a time.
3. Students need to know the regular form and meaning patterns that underlie the use of word parts.

Grammar

A key word to understanding the internal history of English grammar is simplification. This means that the English language has lost most of its word forms and endings. For example, nouns in Old English had as many as eight forms according to cases (nominative, genitive, dative, accusative) and numbers (singular, plural), but present-day English only distinguishes two (genitive ending -'s as in boy's and plural ending -s as in boys). This is, again, beneficial to English language learning, as beginners are alleviated from the burden of memorizing a daunting number of different noun forms as well as various forms in adjectives, verbs and even definite and indefinite articles. To borrow Edward Sapir's classical metaphor (1955: 147–70), the 'drift' towards simplified inflections already started in the Old English period, when the Anglo-Saxons and Vikings communicated with each other using mutually intelligible Germanic languages with somewhat different word endings, which blurred strict distinctions in morphology (Gramley 2012). Since then, English has continued to reduce its inflectional complexity, saving today's language teachers and students a lot of work. Such being the case, they would benefit from sharing the subsequent views that HEL provides regarding grammar.

Noun declensions

Noun forms are simple. Learners of current English are not troubled with numerous noun inflections: all they should know is to put -'s to make a possessive form and -(e)s to make a plural form. There are, however, some exceptional plural forms such as *men, mice* and *feet*. They are actually the remains of regular plural making patterns in Old English and still used today as irregular forms because these words have been too frequently used in everyday life to be replaced by regular word formation. This means that these rare plural forms are more likely to appear in the classroom at the elementary level, which could discourage beginners of English. Teachers are advised to tell their students: 'These exceptions are limited to some everyday words and can be easily learnt in your first years of studying English.'

Verb conjugations

Verbs forms are also simple. Again, the so-called irregular past and past participle forms are the remnants of conjugation patterns in Old English and restricted to frequently used everyday words such as *bind, drink* and *write*. Teachers can assure their students by saying: 'These irregular patterns just appear in some basic verbs. You can easily remember them in a year or two without too much effort as they are so often used.'

Syntax

Word order and prepositions are important. To use technical terms, English has changed its linguistic character from an analytical language (i.e. grammatical relations are determined by word forms and endings) to a synthetic one (i.e. they are shown by word orders and prepositions). Awareness of such linguistic typology is helpful for learners whose native language allows flexible word sequences without changing meaning. For example, in Japanese ネコは捕まえるネズミを (*neko-wa tsukamaeru nezumi-o*: 'cats catch mice'), ネコはネズミを捕まえる (*neko-wa nezumi-o tsukamaeru*: 'cats mice catch'), and ネズミを捕まえるネコは (*nezumi-o tsukamaeru neko-wa*: 'mice catch cats') are all possible in structure (though the first and third sentences sound a bit awkward) and identical in meaning (it is always cats that are chasing and it is always mice that are running away), whereas in English 'cats catch mice' and 'mice catch cats' describe completely different scenes! The good news about English being a synthetic language is that learners do not have to memorize complicated paradigms but just pick up a handful rules for word arrangements. However, the bad news in exchange for simplified paradigms is that prepositions came to be employed so more frequently in so more diverse ways that students need to know which prepositions to use depending on accompanying words and contexts (e.g. *provide* somebody *with* something vs. *offer* something *to* somebody). As these fundamental features of English syntax are crucial in learning and using English, students should be encouraged to work on them attentively.

Pronunciation

There exist idiosyncratic English phonemes that date back to Old English. In order to represent those distinct sounds, new letters were created from the Roman alphabet brought by Christian monks or borrowed from the Runic alphabet, the original writing system common to the Germanic languages: *æ* (ash) for the front open vowel /æ/ and Þ (thorn) for the dental fricatives /θ/ and /ð/ (Hasenfratz & Jambeck 2011; Schmitt & Marsden 2006). Indeed, these vowel and consonant are still particularly important for English learners today because they are unlikely to appear in their mother tongues. Another important feature of English pronunciation is long vowels and diphthongs. Although we do not know exactly how this systematic change in vowel values happened, the so-called Great Vowel Shift (GVS) from roughly 1400 to 1600 is responsible for the phenomenon. This refers to a comprehensive rising shift of front long vowels (/æ:/, /ɛ:/, /e:/ became /ɛ:/, /e:/, /i:/ respectively with the highest /i:/ turning into /əɪ/ and later /aɪ/) and back long vowels (/ɔ:/ and /o:/ came to be pronounced /o:/ and /u:/ respectively with the highest /u:/ realized as /əʊ/ and eventually as /aʊ/). Examples in modern spellings include n*a*me (/æ:/>/ ɛ:/>/ɛɪ/), br*ea*k (/ɛ:/>/e:/>/ɛɪ/), gr*ee*n (/e:/>/i:/), t*i*me (/i:/>/əɪ/>/aɪ/), b*oa*t (/ɔ:/>/o:/>/əʊ/), m*oo*n (/o:/>/u:/) and h*ou*se (/u:/>/əʊ/>/aʊ/) (Schmitt & Marsden 2006: 130). This understanding of the features peculiar to English phonemes leads to the subsequent informed practice in pronunciation instruction.

Vowels and consonants

Long vowels and diphthongs are the salient attributes of today's English and therefore should be differentiated articulately. Only in English remain the Germanic dental fricatives /θ/ and /ð/, which, therefore, should be pronounced consciously.

Spelling

Seemingly chaotic discrepancies between English sounds and spellings emerged in the early Modern English period after William Caxton (*c.* 1422–91) set up the first printing workshop in England in 1475. For one thing, there were no orthographical standards, so the printers used arbitrary and inconsistent spellings. For another, English pronunciation kept changing with the GVS being the most considerable (Crystal 2012a,b; Stirling 2011). To this unfortunate disagreement between phonology and orthography, progressive intellectuals argued that spellings should reflect actual sounds, whereas conservatives insisted that conventional spellings should be kept with some modifications in order to avoid uncertainty and confusion. After all, influenced by Francis Bacon (1561–1626), who said that amending spellings according to sound changes would make it impossible to read written works and that conventional spellings would deter the further changing of sounds, the latter position determined the trend (Watanabe 1983). Also, humanists in those days proposed that words from Latin such as *det/dette*, *dote/dute* and *rcceit* should be spelt de*b*t, dou*b*t and recei*p*t, respectively, because in Latin these words were written that way, though the italicized letters were not pronounced even at that time. This is called Renaissance or etymological spellings. Treating spellings like these brought somewhat messy situations into English spellings. What advice can teachers give to their students then? Here are a couple of suggestions.

Conventional and etymological spellings

Just like irregular conjugations of everyday verbs and the exceptional declensions of basic nouns, discrepancies between sounds and spellings basically occur in words which had already existed before the GVS and are still used very frequently in everyday life (mainly native words and some French borrowings). It is therefore true that beginners of English are likely to come across those disorderly spellings, which they cannot but remember as they are, but those are not large in number and words encountered after the elementary level are basically spelt as they are sounded. Teachers are advised to tell this to their students in order not to demotivate them at the beginning of their learning.

The sound-spelling disagreements arising from Renaissance spellings are limited to a handful of words from Latin and therefore may not demand too much effort on the part of learners.

How can HEL be taught in CLIL?

In teaching some of the HEL lessons, I use CLIL to develop my students' language skills in reading, writing, listening and speaking. In a nutshell, CLIL is a holistic educational approach where not only content (subject matter) and communication (language knowledge and skills) but also cognition (critical thinking) and culture (collaborative learning and global awareness) are intentionally, organically and simultaneously integrated (Coyle, Hood, & Marsh 2010). Taking, as an example, the second session of my HEL course in Table 1.2 (i.e. the Indo-European language family), I will describe how HEL can be taught in CLIL to maximize students' content, English, thinking and intercultural proficiencies.

The ninety-minute lesson is composed of four tasks. In the first task, the students read a text about the Indo-European languages (Schmitt & Marsden

2006: 18–19) and answer the questions below (the verbatim answers from the text are shown in parentheses):

Q1. What is the Indo-European language family?
   ('The family from which most present European languages, including English, is [are] derived.')

Q2. Where did the Indo-European people originally live?
   ('Around the Black and Caspian seas')

Q3. When did they start migrating westward and eastward?
   ('3,500 BC')

Q4. Why did they do so?
   ('As a result of overpopulation')

Q5. If dialects are separated from each other for 1,500 years, what may happen to them?
   ('They can develop into distinct languages.')

I usually give two options regarding how to answer comprehension questions: either quoting directly from the text or paraphrasing part or all of the original phrases/clauses. When checking the answers, I intentionally use simple grammar and vocabulary such as 'the family most European languages come from' (Q1), 'because there were too many people' (Q4), 'they become different languages' (Q5), and explicitly explain that it is very important for English learners to shuttle between formal/academic and informal/colloquial use in order to enrich their expressions and use the language appropriately according to purposes and contexts. This language awareness and accompanying 'visible language pedagogy' (Leung & Morton 2016: 236–7) differentiate CLIL from other content-based approaches such as immersion and EMI, where teachers arguably believe that language learning takes care of itself.

After the students gain a big picture of the Indo-European language family, they work on the second task and go more into details: completing a language family tree with the help of a map of Europe and the following list of the languages to be placed at the end of the tree diagram (Cable 2013: 17 and 19):

Albanian Armenian Breton Bulgarian Czech Danish Dutch English French Greek German Icelandic Irish Italian Latvian Lithuanian Norwegian Persian Polish Portuguese Romanian Russian Scottish Gaelic Spanish Swedish Welsh.

I have italicized the vowels which many Japanese learners of English have difficulty discerning: diphthongs (/ei/ in Albanian, Danish, Lithuanian, Gaelic;

/eə/ in Bulgarian; /ou/ in Polish) and long vowels (/iː/ in Armenian, Norwegian, Swedish). This is another example of 'visible language pedagogy' or the intentional integration of language and content.

Now that the students know concretely what the present Indo-European languages are and how they relate to each other (e.g. English, Dutch, German and Scandinavian languages belong to the Germanic group; French, Spanish, Portuguese, Italian and Romanian to the Italic group), they make use of the newly acquired knowledge and work on a more cognitively demanding task. In this third task, they analyse a statistical table of the TOEFL-iBT scores classified by examinees' native country (Educational Testing Service 2018: 14–15) and discuss in groups if there are any relationships between test scores and language groups or geographic regions. The following are the expected observations:

1. Countries with Germanic languages have the highest scores (e.g. the Netherlands, Austria, Germany, Scandinavian countries).
2. Countries with Italic languages have the second highest scores (e.g. Portugal, Italy, Spain, France).
3. Former British colonies also have high scores (e.g. Singapore, Malaysia, Hong Kong).
4. Small advanced countries have high scores (e.g. Finland, Israel).

These findings are based on linguistic, historical or socio-economic factors. It can also be pointed out that a few developing countries such as Indonesia and Vietnam take relatively good scores as allegedly only elite students can afford such expensive standardized tests, meaning the test results do not precisely represent the overall English proficiency level of individual countries (this is actually warned by the testing organization in the TOEFL-iBT data brochure).

The final task is given to the students as homework, which reads: 'Apart from the linguistic distance between English and Japanese, do you think there are any other reasons why the Japanese are not generally good speakers of English? Write a short essay, paying attention to the three-part structure of the English paragraph.' Here again, the fusion of language instruction and content knowledge is explicitly intended.

The overall flow of this lesson follows an adapted framework of Meyer's 'CLIL core elements' (2010: 10): input (Task 1), processing (Tasks 2 and 3) and output (Task 4). In terms of the 4C's of CLIL described before, content is obviously the Indo-European language family, but both declarative knowledge (linguistic concepts) and procedural knowledge (application to real life) are also addressed

(Ball 2015). For communication, all the four skills (listening, reading, speaking and writing) are fully activated while working on the tasks. Cognition covers the four thinking skills of Bloom's taxonomy (Anderson et al. 2001): understanding (Task 1), applying (Task 2), analysing and evaluating (Tasks 3 and 4). Culture is realized by pair or group work and consideration of geographical, historical and socio-economic influences on English acquisition.

As exemplified in this HEL lesson, CLIL offers a dense learning opportunity to the students. In order to explore some of the perceptions about their CLIL experience, I administered a questionnaire at the end of the lesson. The questions and results (shown in parentheses) are as follows (N=80):

Q1. Have you ever had lessons which intentionally integrated subject matter and language learning?
(1) Yes (26.2 per cent)   (2) I don't know (15.0 per cent)   (3) No (58.8 per cent)

Q2. Do you want to have such integrated lessons more?
(1) Yes (75.0 per cent)   (2) I don't know (22.5 per cent)   (3) No (2.5 per cent)

Q3. Do you think CLIL lessons are effective in improving your English proficiency?
(1) Yes (87.5 per cent)   (2) I don't know (7.5 per cent)   (3) (No 5.0 per cent)

Q4. Do you think CLIL lessons are effective in learning academic subjects?
(1) Yes (56.3 per cent)   (2) I don't know (31.2 per cent)   (3) No (12.5 per cent)

The overall tendency is that only a quarter of the students have received CLIL lessons before (Q1), but three quarters of them now want to have them more (Q2), probably because the majority of them feel that CLIL lessons are effective in developing their English skills (Q3). However, when it comes to the efficacy of content learning, they seem to have mixed feelings about it (Q4).

I have selected a few favourable comments about CLIL for teaching HEL:

It made me think in English rather than just listen to lectures in English. I think it is a good way to learn English practically.

I was able to understand content deeply as well as learn English expressions. Besides, I didn't get bored because the lesson was two dimensional.

As the content was related to the English language, I found it easier and more effective to learn disciplinary knowledge in English than in Japanese.

And sceptical opinions about CLIL:

It is hard to grasp the main points of the lesson as the components of language learning and those of discipline knowledge appear alternatively.

> Addressing both content and language takes time, which may affect the depth of content learning.

> As far as disciplinary learning is concerned, I think it would be more effective to learn in Japanese because subtleties and nuances in explaining concepts can be fully transmitted.

It is understandable that students want to learn academic subjects deeply, precisely and extensively as that is the main aim of university education. In that case, studying in their native tongue might be advantageous. In contrast, the benefits of CLIL lie in the maximization of learning: students can develop their communicative, cognitive and cultural competences in English on top of content knowledge.

Conclusion

In this chapter, I have argued that HEL gives teachers and student-teachers history-based tips of teaching language knowledge and helps learners study and use English with historical insights in mind. Admittedly HEL can only partially contribute to learners' English acquisition (i.e. gaining explicit knowledge of limited lexicogrammatical items); it still has a place in ELT in that it informs both teachers and students of the 'genius' of the English language as exemplified in this chapter. What I have also tried to show is that if student-teachers whose L1 is not English learn academic disciplines such as HEL through CLIL, they are provided with opportunities to improve their English skills as well. For further and future developments in this area, informed principles of applied English philology (i.e. application of HEL knowledge to ELT) as is realized in Schmitt and Marsden (2006) should be explored more. This chapter is intended to be one of such endeavours.

Questions for change

1. What are the conspicuous features of the English language? Where do they come from?
2. Do you think historical background knowledge about English is necessary for language teachers and learners? Why, or why not?

3. Do you think CLIL is effective in teaching knowledge about English and at the same time improving student-teachers' language skills? Why, or why not?
4. Is there any room in your teacher education curriculum to include HEL? If not, what are possible obstacles?
5. What are theoretical and practical limitations of applied English philology?

2

A Functional Model of Language for Language Teacher Education

Phil Chappell

Introduction

ELTE in Australia involves student-teachers who will be working in a diverse range of ELT settings, both in Australia and in many international contexts. These student-teachers have assorted ELT experiences, including none at all, and come from various linguistic and cultural backgrounds. This chapter describes a particular unit of study that student-teachers take when enrolled in either a Graduate Certificate of TESOL or a Master of Applied Linguistics and TESOL course in an Australian university. This unit of study introduces student-teachers to a functional model of language based on SFL theory, SFG and genre theory and pedagogy.

The course

The unit of study described in this chapter is named *Linguistics and Language Teaching*. It is part of the Graduate Certificate of TESOL course, which is embedded in the Master of Applied Linguistics and TESOL course, offered in the Linguistics Department at Macquarie University, Sydney, Australia. The Graduate Certificate of TESOL is a four-unit course that qualifies graduates to teach in a variety of Australian contexts, including English as an Additional Language or Dialect (EALD) programmes in schools (for qualified teachers), migrant and refugee English language programmes, university English language colleges and private English language colleges. It also prepares students to teach in numerous international contexts.

The other units of study in the certificate course are a teaching methodology unit aimed primarily at designing and implementing tasks and activities in the classroom, with a significant amount of peer teaching (Spratt & Leug 2000) and micro teaching (He & Yan 2011); a programming and planning unit concerned with principles and practices of planning lessons and units of work, as well as covering, assessment and evaluation; and a practicum unit, where students spend most of the semester at an ELT institution observing and teaching lessons. The course has been designed via curriculum mapping principles so that weekly topics in one unit often complement a topic in another unit. Mapping of assessment tasks is done at course and unit level to ensure all course and unit learning outcomes are assessed. This also ensures a variety of learning and assessment tasks and activities across the course.

The course can be taken full-time over one semester or part-time over two to four semesters. Domestic students are eligible to be enrolled either as online or on-campus students. On-campus students attend a two- or three-hour seminar for each unit per week over thirteen weeks. Online students participate asynchronously via Macquarie University's multimedia online learning environment. Mini-lectures in seminars are recorded and automatically stored in each online unit, and all learning and teaching resources for weekly topics (including fully written lecture notes) are accessed by all students through the online learning environment. Structured online discussions are moderated either by the instructor or the students. Students in this course are mainly Australian domestic students.

The Master of Applied Linguistics and TESOL is a sixteen-unit course that takes two years to complete. With its dual focus, the course offers a variety of units of study centred around the theme of the complex relationship between language use and context, as well as a strong theoretical and practical foundation in the field of ELT. It is particularly attractive to international students, as successful completion of the course allows for a variety of pathways for additional post-study work experience in Australia. All students take the three coursework units described above in their first semester and then carry out the practicum unit later in their studies. The student cohort enrolled in this masters' course usually comprises around 60 per cent domestic students and 40 per cent international students from a range of countries.

A systemic functional model of language

The *Linguistics and Language Teaching* unit is underpinned by SFL. Michael Halliday, who developed the systemic functional model of language, famously described language learning as such: 'There are, I think, three facets to language development: learning language, learning through language, and learning about language' (2004: 308). There is much to consider in this statement. For Halliday, language is unequivocally social in nature, functioning as 'the creature and creator of human society' (Halliday 2002: 6). Language learning is also inherently social (Halliday 1993). We develop the ability to use language only in interaction with others. While doing so, we use language to learn about the world around us and within us – that is, the physical world and the world of our imagination and consciousness. At the same time, and especially in instructed second language learning, we learn about the nature of language and how it functions as a tool for making meanings (Halliday 2004).

The systemic functional model of language deems language a resource for making meaning. It is a three-level construct, whereby meanings are encoded into wordings which are recoded into expressions. Wordings are what we might traditionally call vocabulary and grammar but which are referred to as lexicogrammar in SFL. Lexicogrammar is what allows us to make infinite meanings with a finite number of units of expression (whether written, spoken, gestural or multimodal). This presents a unique perspective on grammar for language learning:

> For educational purposes we need a grammar that is functional rather than formal, semantic rather than syntactic in focus, oriented towards discourse rather than towards sentences, and represents language as a flexible resource rather than as a rigid set of rules. (Halliday 2004: 323)

It is this linguistic perspective that is the point of departure for planning the unit of study discussed in this chapter. However, before going into further detail about the content and pedagogical approach taken to deliver the unit to student-teachers, let's unpack this claim of Halliday's.

A functional orientation to grammar

In Australia, for many decades there have been debates about whether a traditional or a functional grammar is best for educational purposes. Traditional grammar is most often associated with a formal grammar, where form labels are assigned to parts of speech. Functional grammar, of which there are many theories (Steiner 1997), is associated with the communicative functions of language – the different ways of using language to make meanings. When pitted against each other, the debates over whether a functional or a formal grammar is preferable can become a distraction (Derewianka & Jones 2010), resulting in an *either/or* argument that is exclusive in nature. However, what Halliday (2004) is arguing for is a functional orientation to grammar, yet his systemic functional grammar by necessity includes both form and function.

Traditional grammar, with its formal orientation, emphasizing syntax and parts of speech, tends to use a mix of formal and functional labels. The subject of a sentence tells us what it is and what it does; therefore, we can say something about its form and its function. A noun, on the other hand, is a formal label that does not say anything about what it does, that is, what its function in a sentence is. SFG, in a sense, builds a bridge between form and function (Derewianka & Jones 2010), showing relations between grammatical classes and their functions in spoken, written and multimodal texts.

In ELT, we should be concerned with supporting our students to successfully communicate across a range of different communicative events, for example, enjoying a casual conversation with a visitor to their country, presenting their work in a seminar, collaborating with university peers on a research project, writing an email to a customer, and writing a report for a school assignment. This necessitates more than knowledge about the different forms language takes. It requires understandings of how different combinations of language forms function to make particular meanings in particular social and cultural contexts. The functional orientation of SFG allows us to do just this.

Language as a semantic system

This orientation to language is based on the premise that the reason language exists is to allow people to make meanings. Language is a tool that helps people make meanings with each other (Halliday 1985). Whenever we use language, we make three simultaneous meanings: ideational meanings to relate experience; interpersonal meanings to relate to others; and textual meanings to create cohesive and coherent stretches of language, that is, text (Halliday & Matthiessen 2014). In the above quote, Halliday (2004) calls for a semantic (meaning-based) focus rather than a syntactic (rule-based) focus. Rather than looking at language from the point of view of what part of speech goes together with which other parts of speech, the view is one of choice. What could be said in this particular social situation, and what are the alternatives? This perspective, technically referred to as paradigmatic, rather than syntagmatic (Halliday & Matthiessen 2014), underscores the view of language as a semantic system, rather than language as simply a set of structures. As Halliday and Matthiessen argue, 'Language is a resource for making meaning, and meaning resides in systemic patterns of choice' (Halliday & Matthiessen 2014: 23).

Language use as a matter of choice

Choice underpins systemic functional theory. It allows us to analyse language use by considering the choices from the language system a speaker or writer makes in order to mean something. It allows us to consider how the meaning would differ had another choice from the language system been made instead. It allows us to consider whether a second language learner has a sufficient repertoire of language to make appropriate choices. Finally, it allows us to consider what cultural and social factors constrain what choices are possible in order to successfully construct ideational, interpersonal and textual meanings simultaneously. This is what Halliday means in the above quotation, where he calls for a grammar that reflects language as being flexible rather than rule bound.

Language in cultural and social context

Consider that you have been tasked with writing a story – a narrative – about a boy and his father, a deep, dark forest and a big, wild bear. Pause for a moment and jot down or think about how you might answer these questions:

1. How does the story begin?
2. What main living and non-living participants will you introduce into the story?
3. What actions do the living participants carry out?
4. What are the main parts to the story?
5. How does the story end?

Depending on your own social, cultural, linguistic and educational background, your answers to these questions will differ from other readers. However, it is quite likely that the beginning of the story sets the scene and introduces the main characters. It is also probable that the actions you choose for the story are physical ones, involving walking, running and possibly hiding. There is also likely to be some events involving the participants saying things to each other and possibly a roaring of the bear. The main stages would be something like the following:

1. Set the scene.
2. Narrate a series of events.

3. Introduce a complicating factor.
4. Introduce a resolution.

The ending might include an evaluation of the outcome by the boy and/or his father. Of course, there may be other stages in the story, or there may be some stages that fulfil different functions, or some may be left out. However, if the story successfully achieves its social purpose within an Australian cultural context, it is most likely to reflect what I have described above.

Finally, how might we state what the social purpose of this story is? Stories entertain. Narratives often entertain by introducing a complication, and then a resolution, and then an evaluation of that resolution. We might state the social purpose as being: to entertain through narrating a series of events that include a complication and resolution, and to evaluate the final outcome. This is the role of narratives in many cultures (Martin & Rose 2008).

The reason that this task was probably not very difficult for readers is that we are able to quite readily predict what language will be used based on the cultural context in which it is set. Once we know the social purpose, we can predict how meanings will unfold in stages, and thus we can predict the genre, namely, the 'staged, goal-oriented, purposeful activity in which speakers engage as members of our culture' (Martin 1984: 25). In the example above, we have identified the stages of a particular genre of storytelling, namely a narrative.

If genres are ways of categorizing activities within a culture, texts are instances of a genre. In the above example, the activity of storytelling has resulted in a particular type of text, a narrative. The text type, narrative, is a representation – an instantiation – of the storytelling genre. Given a slightly different purpose, the genre could have been instantiated by a news story or by an autobiographical recount.

We study genres through the texts that are produced during the activity. This textual analysis allows us to understand what people do with language, and how language works to help people achieve their purposes. We examine how the text unfolds in stages, with each stage being characterized by a particular set of key language features. Among these language features, we can analyse the language that has been chosen to make ideational meanings about experience, interpersonal meanings to relate to others and textual meanings to create cohesive and coherent stretches of language. To do this with an instantiation of a genre, we analyse the context of situation and its register, which comprises language that construes ideational meanings (the field of discourse), interpersonal meanings (the tenor of discourse) and textual meanings (the mode of discourse). The

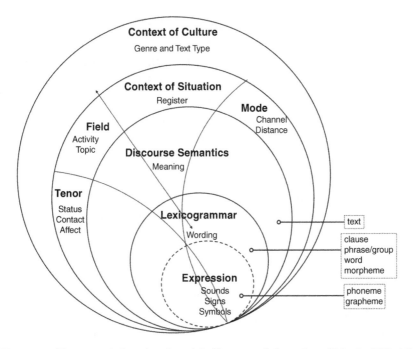

Figure 2.1 The systemic functional model of language (adaptation of Martin 2009: 12)

grammar of field, tenor and mode, together with the relation between context of situation and context of culture, is summarized in Figure 2.1.

The expression level

Figure 2.1 depicts a systemic model of language, including all levels of language use, from the more abstract context of culture, through to the lexicogrammatical resources used to construe ideational, interpersonal and textual meanings, down to the level where we use sounds (phonology) and symbols (graphology) to physically express our language choices. This makes it an attractive model of language for ELT. Depending on language learners' proficiency levels and particular language-learning needs, interventions for individual students can be planned based on assessments of their understandings and control over the various levels described above. In addition, whole units of study can be planned for delivery in language classrooms that integrate all levels of language across the four macro skills of reading, writing, listening and speaking. Indeed, this is an important aspect of the unit of study described in this chapter, to which we now turn.

Pedagogic grammar

Halliday's introduction to linguistics was through his initial FL learning and teaching experiences, when, not long after learning Chinese, he began to teach the language to military personnel during the Second World War. His motivation for working with linguistics has always been his conviction of the need for practical outcomes of this work (Halliday 1985). Thus, SFL is considered an 'appliable linguistics' (Mahboob & Knight 2010) that comes with a pedagogic grammar highly suited for second and FL teaching and learning. An effective pedagogic grammar should be descriptive rather than prescriptive, focusing on appropriate language use in different contexts rather than focusing on rules of use (McCabe 2017).

The unit of study

Linguistics and Language Teaching is a four-credit unit which explores the nature of language, language in context, register, text structure, sentence- and text-level grammar, spoken and written English, phonology and a genre-based approach to second language teaching and learning. The unit considers applications of the above aspects of language to ESOL contexts within Australia and internationally. The unit complements the *Language Teaching Methodologies* unit, the *Planning and Programming in TESOL* unit and the *Practicum in TESOL* unit, by introducing a model of language relevant for second language teaching. Successful completion of these units qualifies participants for the Graduate Certificate of TESOL award.

Teacher knowledge

The unit is primarily aimed at developing student-teachers' linguistic content knowledge, and aspects of their GPK and PCK (Figure 2.2). By doing this, it contributes to student-teachers' wisdom of practice of second language teaching and learning, which I have argued elsewhere constitutes the deep-seated philosophical orientations towards the nature of language and language learning that 'bind together everything that goes on in the classroom' (Chappell 2017: 435). Thus, an important part of the early stages of the unit is to pick apart different perspectives on the nature of language, and encourage student-teachers to articulate, and then reflect upon, compare and

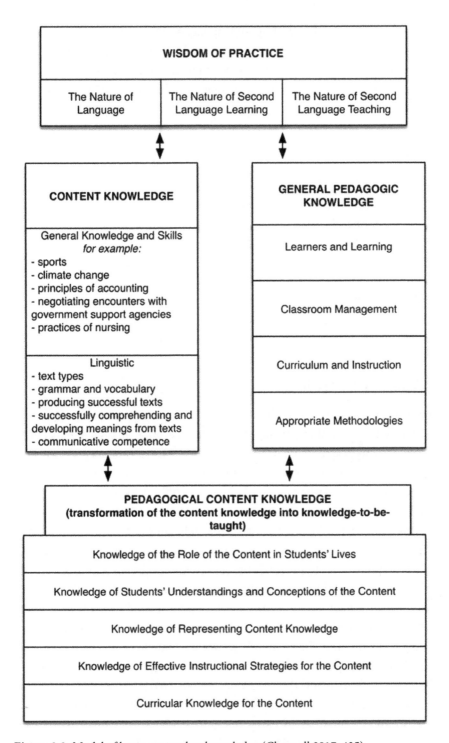

Figure 2.2 Model of language teacher knowledge (Chappell 2017: 435)

contrast their own understandings of language and learning with the different theoretical orientations in the literature, such as structural linguistics and cognitive linguistics. All aspects of the unit are conceived of in terms of the model of teacher knowledge developed in Chappell (2017), depicted in Figure 2.2.

Texts

Required texts

1. Derewianka, B. (2011). *A new grammar companion for teachers.* Newtown: Primary English Teaching Association.
2. Cobuild. (2011). *Collins Cobuild English grammar* (3rd ed.). Harper Collins.

Recommended text

1. Humphrey, S.L., Droga, L. & Feez, S. (2012). *Grammar and meaning.* Newtown: Primary English Teaching Association.

Pedagogical approach

The pedagogical approach is based firmly on a social interactionist approach to learning and teaching (Chappell 2014). Learning in higher education contexts involves applying new knowledge in the form of concepts, theories, principles and the like, in collaboration with others, to everyday practical activity that students were previously unable to fully carry out independently. Teaching involves being keenly aware of where each student is at and providing the right kind of support at the right times, in a variety of forms, wherever possible. Importantly, instructors on teacher education courses have the opportunity to model desirable teaching techniques and strategies. The notion of scaffolding, defined by Wood, Bruner and Ross (1976: 89) as 'the means whereby an adult or expert helps somebody who is less adult or less expert' achieve a task outcome, reflects one of the main pedagogic strategies in the unit. In many of the weekly seminars, the instructor will introduce new linguistic concepts by deconstructing texts, conduct a whole-class text analysis using the classroom audiovisual technologies and then assign small groups to conduct similar tasks. Student-teachers are provided with additional analyses to carry out independently out of class via the online learning environment, where they can also use the asynchronous discussion forums to share and discuss their work with their peers. Finally, student-teachers will demonstrate how well they can do similar analyses independently through the assessment tasks.

Given the novelty of SFL and genre pedagogy for many of the student-teachers, explicit reference to its relevance for second language learning and teaching is crucial. For example, once student-teachers are familiar with the concept of register as being those aspects of a context of situation that shape and are shaped by our language choices, it is important to demonstrate an application to ELT in a relevant and meaningful manner. This may be through explaining how understanding the context helps language students with their listening comprehension. While introducing a recorded dialogue in the language classroom, the teacher should aim to have the students understand what the social purpose (genre) of the conversation is, what is happening and being talked about (field), who is taking part and what the nature of their relationship is (tenor), and what channel of communication is being used (mode). A short small group brainstorming session can engage student-teachers in coming up with a variety of strategies to introduce the context to their students in their own classrooms.

Feedback from student-teachers suggests this approach is appreciated for its potential to positively influence their learning, as the following written comments demonstrate:

> As far as I can recall, you are also the only lecturer I have come across thus far who has convincingly modelled what has been taught – from the way we were assessed to the way you seem to value and welcome everybody's contribution in class. (TEDSCode APPL92112S115390)

> Using a student-centred approach with enough number of pair/group tasks/ activities to consolidate the concepts. (TEDSCode APPL92015S162739)

The syllabus

Decisions about selection of content for the unit are driven by the need to make SFL, SFG and genre pedagogy accessible for student-teachers from a range of cultural, educational and linguistic backgrounds. Theory and practice are woven together to present a pedagogically relevant and practical linguistics for second language teaching and learning. At the same time, given that a high percentage of student-teachers are from language backgrounds other than English, learning tasks are included that develop not only their knowledge of the English language but also their proficiency in speaking, listening, reading and writing.

Learning outcomes

To enable student-teachers to:

1. articulate their personal theories of language and language learning;
2. build the foundation knowledge of linguistics required for language teaching;
3. develop knowledge of the relationships between language, text and context;
4. recognize and differentiate a range of text types and their features;
5. develop knowledge of the units of grammar of English and the relationship between grammar and vocabulary;
6. plan strategies to present grammar and engage learners in understanding its communicative significance;
7. recognize and understand the differences between spoken and written language;
8. develop knowledge of the discourse features of English;
9. develop knowledge of the phonology and graphology of English.

Weekly topics

1. Introduction: Different views of language
2. Language in context
3. Register
4. Genre, text Types and text structure
5. Functions of language, levels of language
6. Language for expressing ideas
7. Language for connecting ideas
8. Language for interacting with others
9. Language for creating cohesive texts
10. Spoken and written English
11. Phonology and teaching pronunciation
12. Graphology and the mechanics of writing
13. Review

Learning and teaching activities for context of culture and context of situation

The syllabus is *top-down* in the sense that it starts at the higher stratum of the model, context of culture and context of situation, then works its way down to the expression level. Student-teachers are reminded of the practical implications right from the start. For example, after an initial mini lecture in the first week on different perspectives on language, involving cognitive, behavioural, anthropological and social semiotic perspectives, student-teachers are shown video recordings of a teacher introducing a text to students by introducing the social purpose, the text type and a summary of the field, tenor and mode of the text. In this way, theoretical aspects of SFL are introduced alongside practical classroom applications of the theory.

Moreover, early on, a variety of procedures are modelled for introducing the social context of a text to language students. In Topic 2, *Language in Context*, student-teachers are provided with a heuristic that they will use throughout the course. Given the widespread use of ELT course books in many contexts, the spoken, written and multimodal texts presented in these coursebooks are used in seminars to fulfil several aims, including inculcating teaching practices that relate language and text to its context of use; demonstrating the shortcomings of inauthentic written and spoken texts; developing analytical tools to efficiently evaluate texts for how authentic-like they are; and procedures for supporting language students in understanding appropriate and effective language choices according to the context of situation. One variation of this simple heuristics, adapted for spoken texts, is:

1. What is the purpose of this conversation? (Identifying genre)
2. What kind of casual conversation is this? Where is it taking place? (Identifying text and/or social activity type)
3. What things and activities are they talking about? (Describing field of discourse)
4. How would you describe the speakers' relationship? (Describing tenor of discourse)
5. Is this spoken language, written language, on the phone, by email, face to face? (Describing mode of discourse)

To develop a critical analytic approach to text analysis, several activities are aimed at developing student-teachers self-awareness of how they use their tacit knowledge of lexicogrammar and genres to predict and/or make choices from the language system. For example, in Topic 4, *Genre, Text Types and Text Structure*, student-teachers work in small groups to analyse the social purpose, field, tenor and mode of short excerpts taken from longer texts, such as:

> Will fifties be alright?
> Sold! they fit a treat. fanks babe. Wot u up 2 lata? Jx
> Rinse your mouth out and we'll wait for that to take effect.

Small group and whole-class discussions focus on the linguistic evidence that supports the student-teachers' descriptions of social purpose, field, tenor and mode, as well as knowledge about the activity that the text could be associated with. Student-teachers are then asked to develop their own short excerpts of texts from social activities from their own sociocultural contexts that may be interesting to people from other cultures. This underscores the importance for student-teachers to be explicit about cultural assumptions and possible cross-cultural misunderstandings that may occur due to cultural and linguistic differences.

Learning and teaching activities for the lexicogrammar of field, tenor and mode

The term 'language features' is used throughout the unit to refer to the linguistic features associated with a particular text that is associated with a context of situation within a broader cultural context. This is where the lexicogrammar of SFG is introduced.

Topic 5 introduces the clause as the basic unit of meaning in the English language. Student-teachers first self-assess their ability to identify clauses in a text containing mainly single-clause sentences and a couple of multi-clause sentences. The session then moves on to a number of collaborative learning tasks that develop student-teachers' understandings of the central elements that make up a clause, and then they revisit the self-assessment task. The concept of rank scale and rank shift is introduced. First, the concept of text as a semantic unit that is realized by sentences and clauses is revisited to underscore the relation between context, text and lexicogrammar. Next, the rank scale is introduced and student-teachers undertake some text analyses to identify morphemes, words, groups, clauses and clause complexes. Finally, texts are introduced where some simple rank shifting has occurred. This highlights the importance of looking at language both from its form and the function it is performing in a text.

Topics 6 and 7, concerned with ideational meanings, introduce the language features of field: processes, participants and circumstances. This is achieved in Topic 6 by using a variety of activities involving transitivity analysis (analysis of clauses for the processes that are unfolding, the participants who are involved, and the circumstances involved in the process, as in Halliday & Matthiessen 2014). In Topic 7 the attention turns to multi-clause sentences and how experiential meanings are combined logically in texts.

Topic 8 introduces the language features associated with interpersonal meanings, realized through the grammar of interaction – the systems of mood and modality (appraisal is not covered in any detail in the unit due to the constraints of time). A variety of written, visual and audiovisual texts is used to demonstrate how, when we speak, we take on different roles to achieve a variety of reactions from our speech partners (Halliday & Matthiessen 2014). When we write, we make choices from the mood system, by way of enacting speech functions, to interact with our readers. Further, by making choices from the system of modality, we can modify the level of delicacy in 'the region of uncertainty that lies between "yes" and "no"' (Halliday & Matthiessen 2014: 176). Course book dialogues are revisited to critically evaluate the language choices that the course book authors have used, both for their lack of authenticity and how an awareness of speech roles and speech functions can unveil hidden discrimination by, for example, gender.

Topic 9, *Language for Creating Cohesive Texts*, focuses mainly on textual cohesion and coherence, focusing largely on written genres, for example, reporting, explaining and arguing, that would normally be used in academic English courses. This is linked to Topic 10: *Written and Spoken English*, which includes a session on giving feedback to students on their writing. A model for carrying this out is introduced through modelling a feedback session for the class and focusing on all aspects of the language features of mode, as well as field and tenor. The students then analyse texts written by ELLs and discuss in small groups what kinds of feedback they would provide. This is assessed in a final summative assessment task, described earlier.

Learning and teaching activities for the expression level

Topic 11, *Phonology and teaching pronunciation*, starts off by tuning student-teachers in to the difference between speech sound and all other sound in our environment, using sound files from Halliday and Greaves's (2008) *Intonation in the Grammar of English*. This introductory task is aimed at having student-teachers think critically about the link between sound and meaning and also to view sound as the medium of transmission for human speech. After covering segmental and suprasegmental aspects of speech, the seminar moves into workshop mode, where student-teachers look through published course material for opportunities to integrate pronunciation into language lessons. Jazz Chants (Graham 2003) are introduced as effective ways to tune language learners into the rhythm of the English language.

Topic 12, *Graphology and the mechanics of writing*, is divided into two sections. First, orthography is introduced through a variety of language-learning tasks that both familiarize student-teachers with technical orthographic aspects, for example, punctuation conventions, as well as modelling a range of language-learning tasks to use in their classes. The second section links back to the previous topic, focusing on graphophonic awareness; that is, an awareness of how the sounds of English are represented graphically as letters and combinations of letters. This section allows for a focus on the relationship between an ELL's developing phonological system and their control over the macro skills of speaking, listening, reading and writing.

Wrapping up

The concluding topic in this unit is both a review of previous topics and an introduction to a planning procedure that serves to integrate the macro skills into a lesson or unit of work, as well as to demonstrate how the model of language can be applied to a range of language events. In a final activity, student-teachers are shown examples of *language event sequences* (Burns, Joyce, & Gollins 1996), and then in small groups they prepare their own which they present to the class. An example is presented in Figure 2.3.

Assessment tasks

All assessment is through completion of tasks that involve the analysis of texts. These tasks are formative in nature, being designed to engage and support student-teachers in the learning process, while at the same time, assessing achievement and providing feedback for further achievement in subsequent tasks. Assessment is standards based, whereby the tasks are mapped against course and unit learning outcomes. Each task has a marking guide that provides student-teachers and teaching staff with a rubric for assessing students' work against the predetermined performance criteria.

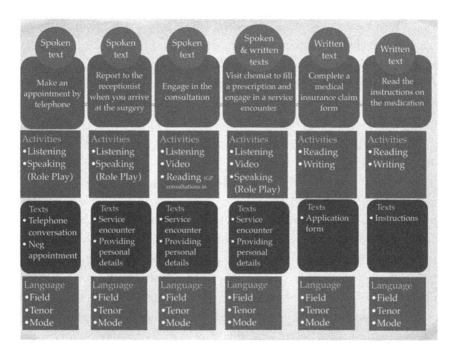

Spoken text	Spoken text	Spoken text	Spoken & written texts	Written text	Written text
Make an appointment by telephone	Report to the receptionist when you arrive at the surgery	Engage in the consultation	Visit chemist to fill a prescription and engage in a service encounter	Complete a medical insurance claim form	Read the instructions on the medication
Activities •Listening •Speaking (Role Play)	Activities •Listening •Speaking (Role Play)	Activities •Listening • Video • Reading (GP consultations in	Activities •Listening • Video •Speaking (Role Play)	Activities •Reading •Writing	Activities •Reading •Writing
Texts • Telephone conversation • Neg appointment	Texts • Service encounter • Providing personal details	Texts • Service encounter • Providing personal details	Texts • Service encounter • Providing personal details	Texts • Application form	Texts • Instructions
Language •Field •Tenor •Mode	Language •Field •Tenor •Mode	Language •Field •Tenor •Mode	Language •Field •Tenor •Mode	Language •Field •Tenor •Mode	Language •Field •Tenor •Mode

Figure 2.3 Unit of work planning using language event sequences (adapted from Burns et al. 1996)

The first assessment task is aimed at raising student-teachers' awareness of the range of text types they encounter on a daily basis. It requires them to keep a language diary over the period of one week and select six varied language events to analyse. The analysis is based on the newly introduced concepts of the social purpose for using language: language for expressing experience (field), language for interacting with others (tenor) and language for creating cohesive texts (mode). Analyses are presented in tabular form.

The second task is a more elaborate analysis of social purpose, genre and text type, and the grammatical features used in texts to realize experiential and interpersonal meanings. As textual meanings have yet to be covered, these are reserved for the final assessment task. A spoken text and a written text are chosen for all student-teachers to analyse. This task requires the student-teachers to use the grammatical constituents of field (processes, participants and circumstances) and tenor (mood block and speech functions, and modality) in their analyses.

The final task involves analysing an English language student's written text, using the entire systemic model presented throughout the unit, in order to identify where the student has good control over the language features important for this text type, and diagnosing where the student needs work, suggesting interventions that will support the student gaining greater control of the genre and text type. This is a summative assessment task requiring student-teachers to apply the understandings gained throughout the unit to an ELT context.

Reorientation

In this chapter, I have argued that a functional model of language provides an effective pedagogic grammar for language teacher education. It explicitly relates the functional language system to the cultural and social contexts in which it is used. It offers a systemic description of how language use varies from one context to the other by considering the differences in ideational content, interpersonal relations between speakers/writers/readers and the mode of communication. The pedagogical implications for this are that student-teachers can be apprenticed into an approach to language teaching where the social purpose of an interaction, the topic that is being talked about, the relationship between the interlocutors and the channel of communication all shape the spoken or written (or multimodal) text that unfolds during the interaction. These texts are clustered into a range of spoken and written genres that can form the point of departure for planning integrated skills lessons focused on meaningful communication. Through explicit focus on these texts, language features at the levels of discourse semantics, lexicogrammar and phonology/graphology can form the basis of language lessons. During the course of the unit, student-teachers not only learn about linguistics for language teaching they learn this through the English language, and for international students, they develop their language proficiency at the same time.

Questions for change

1. How does your language teacher wisdom of practice align with the views of language and language learning presented in this chapter? To start, write down your own views of what language is, and how you think it is learnt, and then compare this with the views in this chapter.

2. Are genre and functional grammar a part of the curriculum in your particular ELT context? If not, what opportunities exist for introducing genre and functional grammar into the curriculum?
3. How effective do you think the syllabus described in this chapter would be for your student-teachers? What adjustments would you make?
4. What might a taxonomy of genres and text types look like for your ELT context?

3

Reflections on English Grammar Instruction in EFL/ESL Educational Settings

Liliana Anglada

Introduction

The word 'grammar' often evokes the notions of structure, pattern, sequencing and rules. These notions have guided the teaching of grammar for centuries. Grammar instruction has a long-standing tradition in educational contexts where language is the focus of attention. Among the various approaches to grammar instruction in settings where English is taught as a second language or as an FL, at least two deserve attention because they compete in terms of foci and claims of effectiveness. A number of labels have been used to describe these two models: traditional, structural or formal, on the one hand, and functional or communicative, on the other. These models can be broadly characterized as (1) the form-focused approach and (2) the meaning-focused approach.

The form-focused approach, which was widely followed in the past and is still currently implemented at different levels of schooling, advocates showing students how to put words together to form phrases and sentences of varying degrees of complexity in the target language so that they will be able to build their own sentences successfully. This approach, often referred to in the literature as *traditional* or *formal* (e.g. Bloor & Bloor 2013; Nazari & Allahyar 2012; Thompson 2014), also seeks to prepare students to produce structures similar to those featured in textbooks or those provided by instructors. In many cases where this approach is used in IELTE programmes, it is expected that student-teachers will become capable of explaining the compositional meaning of those structures. The claim goes that student-teachers need to be prepared to provide informed answers to their future students. Within the confines of this approach, little attention is paid to the conditions that characterize the context of the situation in which sentences are produced. The sociocultural milieu, the interactants' shared knowledge and the particular communicative purpose that often call for one type of linguistic construction over others do not constitute a central concern. Although in their teaching activities instructors might point out the features of the circumstances that usually provide the setting for and give rise to specific oral and written stretches of discourse, the context of language production is often neglected. In general terms, this approach tends to disregard meaning-based concerns, thus privileging the internalization and automatic application of rules. As a result, students seldom see the relevance of contextual features to the construction of messages.

A more recent development in the conceptualization of grammar highlights the meaning-function dimension inherent in the choice and arrangement of words in an utterance. This emphasis emerged as a consequence of the important role ascribed to purpose and context in the use of language and has undoubtedly transpired in the teaching of grammar at all levels of language education. Even though it may not necessarily be as widely spread as the grammar teaching paradigm described first, the functional-communicative paradigm has made its way into many educational institutions and is steadily gaining ground. This teaching approach is based on the assumption that when human beings use language, they do so for a purpose and in a given situational context. Consequently, written and spoken messages alike convey particular meanings depending on the interactants' communicative goals and the situational and cultural contexts they share (Halliday & Hasan 1976; Halliday & Matthiessen 2014; Rose & Martin 2012).

Relying on teacher educators' experiences in using the two approaches briefly described above, this chapter will address some intricacies and challenges involved in the task of raising students' awareness of the relationship between two main dimensions: the formal or linguistic dimension, on the one hand, and the functional-pragmatic-communicative dimension, on the other. The first section will centre on actions and procedures that adhere to the tenets of the traditional approach and which are still being used in IELTE institutions. In the second section, the focus will shift to more innovative practices geared at striking a balance between meaning and form. In what follows, the first approach will be designated as the *traditional or formal approach/model* and the second one will be referred to as the *systemic functional approach/model*.

A formal model

Even though many curriculum designers and teacher educators believe that form-focused grammar teaching is probably not the best way to teach grammar, it can also be argued that when it comes to teaching the grammar of an FL there are some situations that might call for an emphasis on forms and structures. The main claim is that the task of learning the grammar of the target language is such that memorization of patterns and the internalization of rules are necessary and even unavoidable. Learning an FL requires not only understanding but also producing combinations of words and phrases that comply with the set of systematic constraints that characterize the language in question. This production is only possible if there is a considerable amount of practice involved. These beliefs might not be universal, but I dare say that very few English language educators would argue that this type of learning and the type of training it requires are incompatible with an approach that emphasizes meaning over form. As has been pointed out in the literature, especially in the case of adult learners, not only do they need to be explicitly taught what sequences of words convey what meanings and what rules must be followed for their utterances to be understood, but they also need to memorize a series of patterns so that they can develop a sufficient level of dexterity to handle them naturally and – if possible – automatically (Scheffler 2009).

In Argentina, at universities and tertiary institutions that offer IELTE programmes, English grammar is usually taught alongside other courses like English Phonology and English Language. English grammar courses are primarily taught as content courses that cover theoretical information and offer practical knowledge about language use and about the structures available to convey basic meanings. These are core courses meant to provide student-teachers with the necessary tools to both learn the language system and acquire the knowledge that will inform their future pedagogical practices. In the last thirty years or so, there have been some general tendencies in the selection of topics and the teaching methodologies included in the grammar syllabi of these IELTE institutions, both at the private and state levels. In degree programmes that extend over a period of four years of study, those courses are generally offered over the first two or three years. First- and second-year grammar courses centre on the teaching of simple language units like verbs, nouns, adjectives, adverbs, adverbials, prepositions and pronouns and longer or more complex structures such as verb complementation and all types of clauses. It is expected that these tools will help students to both acquire the basics of the target language and develop a good and fluent command of the spoken and the written language in about two years.

The predominant teaching methodology in these initial courses is implemented via the application of inductive or deductive strategies and sometimes through the combination of both. In inductive procedures, examples of linguistic units and structures are analysed in order to guide students to draw inferences – that is, arrive at conclusions concerning generalities – and also to detect idiosyncrasies. In deductive strategies, on the other hand, general rules are presented and discussed first and later instances of language that show those rules at work are identified and analysed. These two ways of introducing concepts and their corresponding linguistic manifestations in language samples are typically followed by numerous mechanical exercises and only a few meaning-focused oral and written activities; overall most tasks are meant to make student-teachers' production of lexical items in grammatically acceptable sentences more automatic. This automaticity and a pervasive focus on forms have been the targets of criticism by proponents of the systemic functional approach on two main grounds: lack of authenticity and an undue emphasis on correctness.

A formal model in action

I will now illustrate the types of class activities that focus on the teaching of form and syntactic structures that are typical of the traditional approach to grammar instruction. I will do so by taking the topic of *subordination* as one example. When teaching subordination following a deductive approach, IELTE teacher educators will most likely first provide a definition of the formal relationship that exists between a main clause and a dependent clause. For the introduction of the topic, they might rely on the explanations provided in a well-known and widely used textbook in IELTE institutions, for example, *Longman Student Grammar of Spoken and Written English*, and say something like, 'In the case of subordination, one clause (a dependent clause) is embedded as part of another clause (its main clause)' (Biber, Conrad & Leech 2002: 224).[1] They might write this information down on the board or use a couple of PowerPoint slides as visual aids for the students. These teacher educators will possibly contrast this information with that concerning other types of clauses that the students should have covered earlier in the course. A contrast might be drawn, for example, with coordinate clauses or non-finite clauses, depending on what the class already knows. After providing this basic description, teacher educators will proceed to show a number of examples where the concepts presented become apparent in stretches of discourse, something that the authors mentioned above also do in their book. These instances will generally consist of clauses created by the teacher or extracted from the textbooks. In other cases, instructors might work with free online concordancers[2] and provide authentic examples to their students. Finally, as an out-of-class activity, teacher educators will usually direct the students to read about the topic in a textbook and do a number of identification and production exercises. The former usually consists in having student-teachers pick out dependent clauses in authentic texts. The student-teachers will be asked to underline or highlight dependent clauses, for example. Production activities, on the other hand, can be more or less guided depending on the student-teachers' abilities, and will consist, for instance, in having them transform two independent clauses into one, where one of the given clauses will remain the main clause and the other will become the subordinate one in the new clause complex. Alternatively, in a much less guided fashion the students will practise by creating their own main and subordinate clauses to talk or write about various topics.

When using an inductive methodology, on the other hand, a teacher educator will first provide a list of sentences that are made up of a main (or matrix) clause which, in turn, contains one or more dependent clauses of different types. Via a number of prompts and questions, the teacher educator will help the students to *discover* the hierarchical relationships between the clauses. The list mentioned above might consist of sentences like the following, which have been extracted from a longer list in Biber, Conrad and Leech (2002b, p. 57):

1. If a merger between Coopers and Deloitte is successful, it will become the largest firm in the country.
3. While he was gone, a nurse poked her head through the doorway.
4. Billy didn't even know whether he was alive.
   ...
9. After I asked her out she told me that she prefers just my friendship.

Some of the questions or prompts that teacher educators can formulate about the sentences above, in order to elicit student-teachers' responses and to check their understanding of the topic, might include the following:

1. For each sentence on the list provided, if there are two or three clearly identifiable ideas, indicate where each idea begins and ends.

2. Identify the main idea in each sentence by underlining the section that contains it.
3. If you can find secondary ideas in the sentence that you are analysing, place them between parentheses.
4. If it is possible to separate one string of words conveying one single idea from the rest of the sentence, once you have identified that portion of the sentence, check whether it can be understood independently from the rest. In what cases is this possible? In what cases is it not?

This set is only a sample of possible questions meant to guide the student-teachers' exploration of main and subordinate clauses. Some teacher educators might use only a couple of these prompts, decide to reformulate them or rely on others altogether.

The procedures just described might be considered at best simplistic and mechanistic; yet more important than that, they can be characterized as not addressing meanings or functions that arise from situated discourse. In spite of the negative characterization, this course of action in teaching grammar seems to have been effective because many people who have graduated from IELTE programmes have become successful teachers themselves, many others have been able to further their studies, and a few others have completed a master's and/or PhD degree in English-speaking countries.

Some teacher educators might frown upon the teaching of grammar in the ways illustrated above on the grounds that those strategies, whether conducted in a deductive or inductive fashion, seem to emphasize form over meaning and, as a consequence, perpetuate a prescriptive view of language. Although the emphasis is placed upon rules concerning how words can and cannot be strung together into sentences, this way of teaching grammar cannot be objected to as *prescriptivist*, as it is actually based on describing what happens when clauses are combined. What might be considered prescriptivist, however, is the actions that are implemented later, once the topic has been introduced, in order to evaluate the student-teachers' ability to identify and combine clauses. When teacher educators need to assess student-teachers' work, they are forced to become prescriptive; there do not seem to be many other options.

A systemic functional model

Not all grammar teaching is carried out following the steps described in the previous section. During the last twenty to thirty years, Halliday's insights into the dialogical nature of the relationship between texts and the situational context in which the former are produced have exerted a considerable impact on linguistics as a whole and on educational linguistics in particular. There has been an increasing awareness of the importance of the interplay between those two facets of communication and a consequent shift from conceiving grammar as an autonomous system, an independent module of language disconnected from and unaffected by societal practices, towards a conception of grammar as a system of choices that has developed the way it has to attend to the communicational needs of a society. These changing views have transpired in the IELTE teacher-training schools in many countries of the world, and Argentina has been no exception. Nowadays, at least one of the grammar courses that student-teachers need to take as part of their study programme in most IELTE institutions in Argentina is often – if not always – a course with a clear emphasis on the choices of linguistic resources that speakers and writers have at their disposal when they need to communicate something. In an undergraduate grammar course of that sort, student-teachers are made aware of the fact that those linguistic choices are made in response to the demands imposed by a given situational context and particular communicative purposes. Besides undergraduate courses, more advanced and intensive courses of a similar nature are taught as part of graduate programmes in some universities.[3]

The main goals of undergraduate and graduate courses with a focus on systemic functional grammar revolve around making the student-teachers aware of the creative potential of language by having them read and analyse texts as instances of language in use. The selected texts usually constitute samples of both oral and written discourse and are often representative of various genres, for example, descriptions, reports, recounts, historical accounts, explanations and discussions among others (Martin & Rose 2008). The text analysis that student-teachers engage in is usually based on identifying the text producer's purpose in creating a given text and accounting for the text producer's linguistic choices. These choices logically respond to a communicative goal and are determined by the circumstances of production. The teaching-learning process consists of implementing tasks meant to have student-teachers find linguistic resources that establish meaning relationships that go beyond the boundaries of a clause complex, that is, relationships between portions of the text across clause complexes. In so doing, students should be able to detect how those meaning relationships hold the text together.

Besides working with authentic texts in order to uncover the intricacies of their woven meanings, the student-teachers develop content knowledge by reading and studying what scholars have explained about the lexicogrammatical resources of the English language and about how their appropriate deployment contributes to the effectiveness of texts. Students-teachers are required to read a selection of bibliographic materials before class to be prepared for class discussion and to acquire the disciplinary knowledge that will be evaluated later during exams. Some of the reading materials come from works by authors who have made Halliday's systemic functional model accessible to an audience of student-teachers (e.g. Bloor & Bloor 2013; Eggins 2004; Thompson 2014).

The previous paragraphs were meant as an introduction. The rest of this section will address one of the two closely related abilities that need to be developed when teaching various topics. I am referring to the reading and writing skills. The next section, '*A systemic functional model in action*', will suggest some class activities that can be used to teach a defining property of texts and a central topic to this approach: cohesion.

Methodologically, reading for the sake of understanding constitutes a preliminary stage in discovering how meanings are made and how linguistic resources encoding those meanings have been put together to form a unified whole. The other important ability, which necessarily derives from reading, is producing written texts. Writing, which will not be addressed in this article, is undeniably an ability that needs to be developed because it is through writing that teacher educators can measure not only student-teachers' knowledge about text cohesion but also their mastery in the use of cohesive ties. As far as reading is concerned, tasks geared at thorough comprehension and the identification of key textual signals are often implemented in class. With these purposes in mind, texts are selected from a vast array of materials, some of them published in paper and some of them online. Complete texts and text excerpts might come from newspapers and magazines, novels, short stories and so on; some might be transcripts of recorded conversations – what people have said on the radio or television; and still others can be advertisements, brochures, flyers and pamphlets that circulate unrestrictedly, that is, without copyright protection. I would like to illustrate some reading comprehension and identification tasks that students engage in when the topic under consideration is text cohesion. The activities will be delineated on the basis of a newspaper article in the subsection *A systemic-functional model in action*, after this general introduction to the model.

As mentioned earlier, both deductive and inductive strategies can be used when teaching grammar following the traditional approach. Likewise, making student-teachers aware of the lexicogrammatical choices available in the English language that are often deployed in cohesive texts can take place inductively or deductively. A combination of the two strategies and, at times, alternating between the two might offer the most appropriate option. The latter, a sort of bi-directional approach, will probably help teacher educators gauge their students' understanding of the content more accurately and judge the development of the attendant skills more easily.

As far as deductive strategies are concerned, one possible beginning is to have the student-teachers read about cohesion and about how texts achieve texture (i.e. unity). A good source of information is found in chapter 5 in *The Functional Analysis of English*, in particular sections 5.1 and 5.4.1 through 5.4.4 (Bloor & Bloor 2013). This reading material is usually assigned from one class to the next so that, in the second class, the teacher educator can begin by asking key questions to assess the student-teachers' familiarity with the concepts relating to text cohesion that they have read about on their own at home. In this particular case, the key notions are reference, substitution, ellipsis, lexical cohesion and conjunctive relations. After having checked for the understanding of these topics, the teacher educator can have the student-teachers read the text chosen for analysis. This activity can be done individually or in groups. Once the student-teachers have read the text, they will be asked to identify instances of the cohesive resources under consideration; as another option, the teacher educator might point out some of the cohesive ties in the text first and then prompt the student-teachers to describe them applying the information they have become aware of in their previous home-assigned reading. These activities are intended to ensure that the class shares the necessary knowledge about the topic.

Alternatively, the work with the text can be exploratory and the introduction of the disciplinary knowledge can be done inductively. In a scenario where inductive procedures are implemented, the class might begin by reading the chosen text collectively. After completing the reading task, the student-teachers can engage in the process of discovery with the teacher educator's guidance. The role of the latter will be to orient the former in locating linguistic resources that establish reference, linguistic expressions that indicate substitution of some sort, linguistic items that are missing (i.e. cases of ellipsis) and instances of conjunction; the teacher educator will help the student-teachers to visualize the links between those linguistic elements and the corresponding pieces of information in the surrounding text. The conclusions and generalizations about how the relationships are established, where and how the information can be retrieved, and how the many parts of the text coalesce – in other words, how the text forms a cohesive whole – will come after this initial process of discovery.

A systemic functional model in action

The text chosen to illustrate how the notion of cohesion can be presented and explored in class is an excerpt from the OpEd article 'Chicago's Violence and Its Leadership Deficit',[4] featured in the online edition of the *Wall Street Journal*, on 8 August 2018. In this text, author Gary MacDougal voices his opinion about the violence that prevails in Chicago and places part of the responsibility in the hands of the city's mayor. The activities proposed are meant to have students examine how various resources are deployed to produce a cohesive text.

By having the student-teachers identify a number of cohesive devices that hold the fabric of the text together, the teacher educator can help them see how the text has been structured and how the lexicogrammatical choices play a fundamental role in the construction of the text. After the student-teachers have read about cohesion as part of their home assignment (see previous section), some of the prompts and questions that can be used to guide their exploration of the OpEd article are the following:

1. According to the information you have read for today about cohesion and cohesive links, would you say that the article that you have read is a cohesive text? How can you tell?

2. If you believe that this is a cohesive text, do the following activities to be able to support your position:

   (a) Find two different examples of reference and be ready to explain how and why those instances are cases of reference.

   (b) Are there cases of noun, verb or clause substitution? If you find any, list them and be ready to describe them.

   (c) Find one case of ellipsis and explain what information has been left out and where in the text it can be retrieved.

   (d) Find two different cases of double cohesive links and explain how the relationship between those linguistic choices and sections of the text is established in each case.

   (e) Find two instances of lexical cohesion other than repetition (e.g. synonymy, hyponymy or meronymy) and be ready to describe why the chosen instances can be considered cohesive.

   (f) Although the use of conjunction does not play a significant role in creating cohesion in this article, there are a few instances that can be analysed. Identify two tokens of the conjunction *but*, one that plays a cohesive function and one that does not. In the first case, point out the ideas being linked and the meaning relationship established between them; in the second, explain why *but* is not cohesive.

Answering the prompts above will help the students-teachers to visualize the article's texture. At the same time, the analysis that they engage in will contribute to their thorough comprehension of the text's content. Students should be able to see how different parts of the text are tied together and how the interwoven threads of discourse converge to present the main reasons for Chicago's violence epidemic and the author's opinion on how to deal with the chaotic situation described.

Sample answers cannot be provided for all of the questions listed above. As an illustration of possible answers, however, questions (a), (d) and (f) will be dealt with. As for question (a), student-teachers can show how the demonstrative pronoun *this* and the personal pronoun *they* in the second paragraph, respectively, point to the number of people murdered in Chicago and to young men in the Windy City; both pieces of information were mentioned earlier in the text. These two instances of cohesion are cases of anaphoric reference, one demonstrative and the other personal or pronominal.

As far as question (d) is concerned, among the cases of double cohesive ties, that is a combination of a determiner (grammatical element) and a noun (a lexical element), the following two can serve as examples: 'the problem' (in the third paragraph) and 'this distrust' (in the last but one paragraph). The first is a double cohesive link because it points back to 'the violence in Chicago' via the definite article *the* and a general word *problem* (a hypernym), which can subsume a number of meanings but in this case summarizes the points made about violence in the first two paragraphs. The second, 'this distrust', is also a double cohesive tie since it refers back, via the combination of a demonstrative adjective and a synonym, to the lack of trust of the Chicago residents in the police department discussed in the previous paragraph.

Finally, the conjunction *but* plays a cohesive role in paragraph number six when it establishes a concessive relationship between the ideas developed in two clause complexes: that the distribution of the existing funds needs to be reassessed in order to restore peace in the city and the difficulty of having both local and federal agencies work together towards that aim. The conjunction *but* does not play a cohesive function, however, when it joins two clauses in the same clause complex, for example, in the last paragraph of the article: 'This is a good idea but it has been poorly implemented.' Although the meaning conveyed is also concession, in this case *but* establishes a relation within the same clause complex and not across clause complexes, which makes it non-cohesive.

Other texts related to this OpEd article are the letters to the editor sent by subscribers in response to the original article. These letters[5] can be exploited in a similar fashion with a different set of questions prompting other types of activities. One of those activities might consist in having the student-teachers explain cases of reference, substitution, ellipsis, lexical cohesion and conjunctive cohesion that have been first identified and pointed out to them by the teacher-educator. The letters to the editor can also be used as models for the students to write their own individual responses to the author of the opinion article; in this case, the student-teachers will be expected to build cohesive texts by using the linguistic resources they have become aware of during their text analysis. In both cases, their written pieces can be assessed to determine the student-teachers' knowledge about the topic and their mastery in the use of the target lexicogrammatical resources.

Even though the focus of this section has been on the notion of cohesion, thus foregrounding textual meanings, the OpEd article can be exploited in other ways as well. For instance, in order to explore interpersonal meanings the student-teachers might be asked to look into the author's choices in mood structure and modality. By doing so, they should be able to understand how those choices contribute to establishing a relationship between the writer and the reader and, at the same time, how they reveal the writer's judgements concerning (moral) obligation and evidence for knowledge. Furthermore, with the purpose of studying ideational meanings (i.e. experiential and logical meanings), some paragraphs or individual clauses can be selected for the student-teachers to identify the types of processes, participants and circumstances featured in them.

Final remarks

Although the discussion in the previous sections derives from experiences and situations encountered at a local level, I hope some of the examples given and some of the suggestions offered can be applied in other IELTE contexts. The obvious differences between educational systems and the varied local realities should not invalidate some of the concerns and reflections put forth in this chapter. It is expected that teacher educators in countries that are distant geographically and culturally from Argentina will still derive some ideas for consideration concerning current grammar teaching practices.

The underlying aim in describing the two widely known approaches to grammar teaching was to highlight one stratum of language that has been traditionally neglected. This stratum comprises the meaning choices that speakers and writers make when using language. Authentic texts can be exploited so that students might discover the rationale behind those semantic choices by looking into aspects of cohesion, lexical selections, mood and modality and the organization of information. Only one text was chosen here as an example, but many others featured in newspapers, magazines, advertisements and the World Wide Web can be fruitfully used for similar purposes.

Two Argentine publications are worth considering for IELTE because they offer a number of practical activities and theory-informed suggestions about how to implement the approach I have barely sketched in the last section. These publications are the following: *Working with Texts in the EFL Classroom* (Boccia et al. 2013) and *English Grammar: Basic Notions on Systemic-Functional Grammar* (Gaido, Oliva, Calvo, & Ríus 2016). Both publications are grounded in and advocate the tenets of SFL. These books, which are the result of years of experience working with the systemic functional model, were produced by teacher educators working in two state universities in Argentina and are being used as sources of information and guided practice in their respective institutions.

I would like to bring this chapter to a close by making reference to Halliday's conceptualization of grammar as 'the central processing unit of language, the powerhouse where meanings are created' (Halliday & Matthiessen 2014: 22). Among the various definitions of grammar advanced by scholars throughout the centuries, Halliday's metaphor seems to capture the twofold essence of this component of language, which is also a field of knowledge in its own right. The two facets in question are *form* (or linguistic expression) and *meaning* (or functional purpose). In Halliday's metaphor, at least two main correspondences between the source concept of a *powerhouse* and the target concept of *grammar* can be identified. On the one hand, in a powerhouse there are a number of machines, appliances, levers, control switches, screens and so on that allow for the production of energy. These tools and machines, in turn, allow for the creation of many useful objects and artefacts. On the other hand, powerhouses still need the supervision of a human brain; they cannot run autonomously all the time. In other words, human agency is needed to operate them.

The first scenario brings to mind the domain of grammar as an aspect of language that provides the mechanisms and tools necessary to manufacture texts. The second scenario evokes the text producer, a speaker or writer who is in control and plays a central role in running the powerhouse, that is using the lexicogrammatical resources in such a way as to produce effective texts, texts that attain the intended communicative purposes.

This analogy between a powerhouse and grammar could probably be extended further, but the main point I would like to make, however, is a simple one: grammar instructors in IELTE need to be aware of these two aspects of grammar in order not to reduce its teaching solely to the modelling of forms. Grammar instructors can and probably should allow their students to rely on memory work, to engage in transformation exercises and, to some extent, to do some mechanical activities – as more traditional approaches will recommend. However, they cannot forget that grammar is much more than the perfunctory and automatic action of stringing words together so that they will be integrated in complete, well-formed sentences. Grammar, or the capacity to use the powerhouse of grammar, involves more than that; it involves considering a number of variables. These variables derive not only from the dimension of forms but also, and more importantly, from the situational context. And the situational context encompasses – among other elements – what the message is about, who it is being addressed to and how it is organized so that the intended goal can be attained.

Questions for change

1. Michael Halliday's view of grammar mentioned at the end of this chapter, as 'the central processing unit of language, the powerhouse where meanings are created', seems to give grammar a prominent place in language-related matters. How central should the role assigned to the teaching of grammar be in IELTE programmes in your particular context?

2. What model does the IELTE programme you belong to, or were trained in, adhere to? The formal or the systemic functional one? Or a combination of both? Which one do you favour in your teaching practices and why?

3. How can current practices at the IELTE institution where you work be modified or adapted so as to incorporate the notion of situational context in the teaching of grammar?

4. What follow-up activities other than those mentioned in the chapter can be designed to reinforce the notions concerning cohesion?

5. In your ELT context, how effective can the use of authentic texts be for the teaching of a grammar point other than cohesion?

Notes

1   The view of embedding referred to here is quite different from the one proposed by Halliday's systemic functional model, which is the alternative approach to teaching grammar described later in this chapter. In the formal or traditional approach, embedding is a sort of synonym for all types of subordination. In Halliday's view, however, a distinction must be drawn between embedding and hypotaxis (both of which have traditionally been subsumed under subordination). For a concise description of the distinction between embedding and hypotaxis, the reader is directed to Thompson (2014, pp. 24–6 and 188–93) and for an in-depth account, the reader might want to consult Halliday and Matthiessen (2014, pp. 436–42, 451–60 and 490–503).

2   A list of commonly used online concordancers can be found at: https://corpus.byu.edu/corpora.asp

3   One example of these graduate programmes is the master's programme in TEFL offered at the Faculty of Languages, Universidad Nacional de Córdoba. This study programme includes Text Grammar, a sixty-hour core course that allows master's students to accumulate three credits towards their degree and which offers an overview of the emergence of the systemic functional model of language; covers basic notions such as system, text, choices, context of situation and context of culture; and focuses on the study of meaning from three different angles: the ideational (i.e. experiential and logical), interpersonal and textual metafunctions of language. Other key topics covered in the course are texture and cohesive resources, discourse genres, generic structure and genres' realization patterns.

4   This OpEd article can be found at: https://www.wsj.com/articles/chicagos-violence-and-its-leadership-deficit-1533767969.

5   These letters can be found at: https://www.wsj.com/articles/chicagos-violenc-e-shows-leadership-failure-1534436325.

4

Teaching Pedagogical Grammar in English Language Teacher Education

Bahiyyih Hardacre and Marguerite Ann Snow

Introduction

The master's in TESOL programme at California State University at Los Angeles is a two-year programme that prepares teachers-in-training for a wide variety of professional careers in the United States and abroad. Our graduates typically aim at teaching: ESL in the United States, EFL in non-English-speaking countries, ELLs in K-12 schools in the United States, adult second language learners at adult schools, ESL for multilingual writers at community colleges, Intensive English Programs (IEPs) and university extension programmes. Courses offered in the MA programme emphasize language-learning theories and teaching methodologies, including a course in pedagogical grammar. It is our experience teaching the latter that this chapter is concerned with.

This chapter focuses on the challenging task of teaching pedagogical grammar in an ELTE programme. One of the ongoing dilemmas in how to teach the course revolves around the content itself. Many of our teachers-in-training are native speakers of English who tend to lack an explicit background in and the metalanguage of English grammar, and this course must therefore assist them to develop the content knowledge of English grammar. On the other hand, part of our student body is comprised of international teachers-in-training, who typically have a solid grammar background and would therefore benefit more from a methods course in which the *teaching* of grammar, that is, the pedagogical aspect, is the focus.

Our solution has been to do both – to teach the course as its name implies: pedagogical grammar. This means that the goal of the pedagogical grammar course offered by our programme is twofold: to provide an overview of all major topics of grammar, that is, areas that are typically covered in ESL/EFL textbooks that are aligned with the CEFR standards' A1 to C2 levels (see the Common European Framework of Reference for Languages 2001), as well as strategies and best practices regarding the teaching of grammar. We have adopted the three-dimensional Form-Meaning-Use framework (Celce-Murcia & Larsen-Freeman 2016; Larsen-Freeman 2014) to discuss not only the grammatical forms but also the various meanings and uses associated with these forms. This Form-Meaning-Use system of grammar analysis is integrated with approaches to teaching and materials development, a component of this course that helps prepare our teachers-in-training to teach grammar well and create and adapt materials suitable for their future teaching assignments. When the course was offered under a ten-week quarter system, having a dual focus was very difficult. However, we now teach the course on the semester system, which has given us additional time to attempt more successfully this two-pronged approach.

This chapter aims at describing the pedagogical practices that our programme has adopted in order to teach grammar in a graduate-level teacher education programme which welcomes both international and local teachers-in-training; we must emphasize, however, that this is not a report of our own pedagogical research on how to best teach pedagogical grammar. The first part of this chapter elaborates on how our goals guided the design of a graduate-level course as a systems-oriented approach to English grammar. The second part provides examples of how our teachers-in-training can become more efficient and autonomous educators by (1) balancing the use of descriptive versus prescriptive grammar instruction; (2) focusing not only on form but also on meaning and use; (3) increasing their familiarity with linguistic corpora to generate meaningful and authentic materials emphasizing high-frequency grammatical forms; (4) learning how to provide level-appropriate and content-specific feedback on ESL/EFL learners' work; and (5) developing grammar activities in line with current teaching approaches like content-based and task-based instruction (Nunan 2017; Snow & Brinton 2017). Samples of our teachers-in-training's work are included to illustrate how course assignments are matched to the course's student learning outcomes.

Pedagogical framework

Descriptive and prescriptive grammar

In order to prepare our teachers-in-training to present all pertinent information about a grammatical feature when they teach, it is crucial that we cover not only the prescriptive rules but also the often unstated but very important descriptive rules.

Some grammar textbooks (e.g. Azar & Hagen 2016; Murphy 2015) focus only on what is considered *correct* in contemporary English such as the rules prescribed by scholars and grammarians. These are the rules of prescriptive grammar, and although many of which can be as old as modern English, they may not reflect how native speakers actually talk. Nevertheless, they are very helpful when it comes to using formal register in writing as one typically needs to abide by prescriptive grammar rules, such as when taking standardized English proficiency exams or writing academic papers.

Descriptive grammar, on the other hand, can be a moving target because spoken English subscribes to regional dialects and shared knowledge of pragmatics. It can be highly malleable and susceptible to influences from the media. Certain nuances in differences of grammar usage can be specific to generation or region. For example, there is considerable variation in the use of pronouns in regional dialects in the United States and the United Kingdom even though standard English has a strict distinction between the subject and object pronoun pairs I/me, he/him, she/her, we/us and they/them. Another example of prescriptive versus descriptive form is the contraction of *am not*: *ain't* (as a variation of *amn't*). It is believed to have originated in the eighteenth century, and since then has evolved to replace *isn't* and *aren't* in some variations of informal speech. Other features like *better than I* or *better than me* have long challenged grammarians and teachers. Formal prescriptive rules say that one must use the subject pronoun after *than*. This rule is appropriate when writing formal or academic letters or documents, but the descriptive rule dictates that in informal conversation, one should use *better than me* to avoid sounding awkward or even pretentious.

Teachers-in-training can be encouraged to explore grammar-in-use by using a guided discovery, or inductive approach teaching technique, in which they look for examples of variations in use in authentic, real-world spoken English texts. These examples can be compared to prescriptive rules in order to decide when they are to use them, and how they are to teach them.

Form, meaning and use

While grammar books have historically defined grammar as 'the description of the word-forms and sentence elements of a given language' (Lance 1977: 43), it can also be conceptualized with reference to linguistic and pedagogical frameworks (e.g. generative-transformational, structural or traditional grammar). For example, second language educators have defined grammar as 'a set of structural rules, patterns, norms, or conventions that govern the construction of well-formed and meaningful utterances with respect to specific language use contexts' (Purpura 2013: 2). This definition highlights the belief that context has a major role in the study of grammar.

Textbooks and other teaching materials must present grammar in context and not in isolated sentences in practice exercises involving rote repetition, manipulation and grammatical transformations. Unless practice activities provide opportunities for ESL/EFL learners to explore grammatical structures in context, they will not have access to the systematic relationships that exist between form, meaning and use (Nunan 1998).

In addition, ESL/EFL educators need to help language learners see that effective and authentic communication involves achieving harmony between functional interpretation and formal appropriacy (Halliday 1985). This can be achieved by creating classroom tasks that explore the relationship between grammatical items and the discourse contexts in which they occur. In authentic communication beyond the classroom, grammar and context are often so closely related that appropriate grammatical choices can only be made with reference to the context and purpose of the communication. In addition, as Celce-Murcia and Olshtain (2000) point out, only a handful of grammatical rules are free from discourse constraints. This is one of the reasons why it is often difficult to answer language learners' questions about grammatical appropriacy; in many instances, the answer is that it depends on the attitude or orientation that the speaker wants to take towards the events he or she wishes to report.

Purpura (2012) describes language knowledge as the interaction between grammatical knowledge and pragmatic knowledge. Grammatical knowledge is defined in terms of a range of linguistic forms and semantic meanings that occur at the sub-sentential, sentential and discourse levels. In Purpura's conceptualization, the form-meaning associations can be used as resources to understand the literal and intended meaning of utterances in L2 use situations as well as their pragmatic meanings, where context plays a major role. Thus, discussions of pedagogical grammar must bear in mind the contextual environment of a language item. Teachers-in-training must become aware of the fact that form cannot be taught in isolation from its meaning(s) and its use(s).

Using linguistic corpora

There is a consensus in the field of second language education that languages are best learnt through meaningful use and by engaging with authentic and interesting materials. Teachers-in-training, therefore, must learn to tap into collections of such resources in order to create instructional activities for their students to practice their language skills. One of such resources is linguistic corpora. They provide a vast source of language presentation and practice materials on any grammatical form (Conrad 2000; Frodesen & Wald 2016). If teachers-in-training learn to input search parameters to obtain instances of phrasal combinations, they can generate not only authentic materials for language teaching but also information about the number of similar tokens available in the dataset along with grammatical and usage constraints. Teachers can generate lists of authentic sentences (and also paragraphs) that use a specific language item or phrase which can be used in the classroom to present contextualized use of grammatical forms.

The following are the examples of linguistic corpora that we typically use on our programme:

1. The Corpus of Contemporary American English (COCA)
2. The Michigan Corpus of Academic Spoken English (MICASE)
3. The Santa Barbara Corpus of American Spoken English (SBCASE)
4. The Open American National Corpus (OANC)
5. The British National Corpus (BNC)

Teachers-in-training receive an initial in-class tutorial on how to utilize COCA and MICASE, and they are encouraged to search for other corpora that might better fit their needs and interests (e.g. formal vs. informal register, oral transcripts vs. written documents, academic publications, news, lectures, American, British, or other linguistic variations). This first tutorial entails an in-class demonstration of how to search for collocations and grammatical patterns.

A second tutorial is conducted in the following class in either a computer lab or our regular classroom if all teachers-in-training bring their own laptop computers so that each one of them can try to use a corpus with the instructor's assistance. This in-class session creates an opportunity for teachers-in-training to become familiar with the corpus they have chosen to work with. The teacher educator monitors the teachers-in-training's progress and helps them troubleshoot technical issues, and suggests ways to narrow down their scope, select parameters, count tokens, search for collocations and export and save their results.

The ultimate goal of these tutorials is to ensure that teachers-in-training will be able to work independently to conduct corpus-based research in order to describe grammar usage and to create their own ESL/EFL grammar teaching materials. In this particular class, they are expected to produce a grammar usage final paper, in which they discuss the descriptive and prescriptive rules of a grammatical aspect of their choosing, present and discuss all particular usage information based on data retrieved from a corpus, discuss pedagogical implications of their findings and suggest a few presentation and practice grammar activities that focus on form, meaning and use of the grammatical point.

One example of a teacher-in-training's paper made use of the Santa Barbara Corpus of American English (SBCASE) and the British National Corpus (BNC). This graduate student investigated the usage distribution of the relative pronouns *who* and *whom*. She found only one use of *whom* in the SBCASE corpus, as opposed to the seventy-nine tokens that she found in the BNC (Table 4.1), showing a possible dialectal distinction in the use of this pronoun.

Table 4.1 Number of Tokens of the Relative Pronoun *Whom* in a British and in an American Corpus

First Language	Tokens	Frequency (per million words)
British English	79	26.43
North American English	1	77.83

Interested in the distribution of tokens of the relative pronoun *whom* across discourse types, that is, written or spoken, she found that the vast majority of results of the use of *whom* were found in the written form (Table 4.2).

Table 4.2 Distribution of Tokens of the Relative Pronoun *Whom* Across Spoken and Written Texts

Types of Discourse	Tokens	Frequency (per million words)
Spoken	271	26.03
Written	12,287	139.78

The teacher-in-training was also interested in the age group distribution of users of the pronoun *whom* in written and spoken discourse. When she looked at the distribution of tokens by age in published materials only, she found that most examples were used by people over the age of 25 (Table 4.3). A similar tendency in age distribution was found for data sorted for spoken discourse (Table 4.4).

Table 4.3 Number of Tokens of the Relative Pronoun *Whom* in Written Texts Sorted by Age

Age	Tokens	Frequency (per million words)
0–24	97	161.09
25+	3,564	166.93

Table 4.4 Number of Tokens of the Relative Pronoun *Whom* in Spoken Texts Sorted by Age

Age	Tokens	Frequency (per million words)
0–24	1	1.02
25+	66	13.27

The teacher-in-training also found that the majority of the cases when *whom* was used, it followed a preposition, as in the example:

We accept responsibility not only for the acts and omissions of our own employees and agents but also for those of our suppliers *with whom* we contract to provide a holiday or reasonable standard. (excerpt from Cosmos Funbreaks by Coach to France, British National Corpus)

The teacher-in-training then created a lesson plan to teach about not only the form and the meaning of these relative pronouns but also the nuanced differences in the usage of *who* and *whom*. One example of a practice activity to help students think about the context and age of the speakers before deciding which relative pronoun is more likely to be used is given in Figure 4.1.

Pensioners' and Trades Union Association Meeting:
A: Mary indicated at the last executive meeting that she wants to retire from CHC and she would like Pauline to take her place, have you a nominee from here?
B: So _____ (who/whom) do we write to, to change Secretary. Secretary of _____ (who/whom). So we write to the Secretary of CHC.
A: Okay.

Literature: *The Reform of a Rake*: A play adapted from the novel by Samuel Richardson. Morgan, Fidelis and Giles Havergal. UK: Amber Lane Press, 1987, pp. 5-77, 1853.

PAMELA: I am divided, torn from my parents, forced hither with an impious black design to have my innocence and youth become the sacrifice of brutal violence. MR. WILLIAMS: There is an artless fervour in your grief that might awake compassion even in the cruel authors of your woe.

PAMELA: I perceive there is an open honest tender feeling in your eyes at the unfolding of my sorrows. Is there some way to be found out for my escape, without danger to yourself? Is there no gentleman or lady of virtue in this neighbourhood to _____ (who/whom) I may fly only till I can find a way to get to my poor father and mother?

News Tabloid: The Daily Mirror. London: Mirror Group Newspapers, 1992, p. 9942.
Our recent series commemorating the life of comedy king Frankie Howerd brought a flood of readers' letters. Most were from fans telling their happy memories of the comedian, _____ (who/whom) died in April. Many were ex-Servicemen _____ (who/whom) Frankie toured the world to entertain. But one man's story stood out. It isa tale of simple kindness which Frankie Howerd offered to a lonely teenage boy during one short summer. A kindness the boy never forgot.

Figure 4.1 Corpora-based activities

The information that this teacher-in-training learnt from using two different linguistic corpora clearly helped her find patterns that frame the use the relative pronouns *who* and *whom*. Because *who* is often used in lieu of *whom*, this information can be used to help ESL students understand when the form *whom* is required, and when it is not. Additionally, the texts available through linguistic corpora provided easily obtainable authentic materials for ESL presentation and practice activities focusing on form, meaning, and use.

Basic principles of feedback

An important part of a pedagogical grammar class in a teaching preparation graduate-level programme is to provide teachers-in-training with enough practice on giving written and oral feedback on language learners' oral and written production. Feedback is crucial for the development and consolidation of knowledge in a second or foreign language (Hyland & Hyland 2006a). The areas that merit a deeper discussion in our class are the best time to provide feedback, the amount of feedback that yields the highest uptake and the form of feedback.

The first step towards learning to give feedback is to become more aware of the right time to do it. It is important to consider the purpose of a practice activity to decide when it is the best time to provide feedback. For example, an ESL classroom activity can be designed to promote opportunities for ESL learners to practice using correct language, as opposed to activities that are intended to help learners develop fluency. In the case of the former, feedback should be more immediate, prompting students to produce the correct form as they provide their answers; however, if an activity is meant to help students develop fluency, it would be best to not interrupt them while they are engaged in the task; in this case, teachers can offer whole-class feedback on select language issues at the end of the activity.

Another major issue related to the art of giving appropriate feedback is learning to only provide the right amount and at the appropriate level. Teachers-in-training must learn to think about how much feedback their students might be able to process at a time. ESL/EFL teachers should not correct every single mistake that their students make; on the contrary, they should focus on areas that relate to the objective of the activity and that are appropriate to the students' proficiency level. In other words, ESL/EFL teachers must be careful to not overcorrect or correct mistakes that pertain to grammatical aspects that their students have not yet learnt.

The third dimension of feedback that our pedagogical grammar class covers is the many forms and techniques to provide feedback. Among others, these include providing oral versus written feedback, supplying the correction versus circling or highlighting the mistakes and letting students come up with the corrections or revisions themselves, using software and online resources (Ene & Upton 2018). Teachers-in-training learn to use feedback techniques like recast, explicit correction, clarification request, metalinguistic clues, elicitation, or repetition (Swain 1997) and use of gestures, hinting, echoing, and reformulation (Bohlke 2014). Also related to the form of feedback is to provide encouragement and praise to acknowledge areas that students have improved, solely focusing on areas that they need to improve.

A final consideration pertaining to the effects of giving and receiving feedback relates to who should be providing the feedback. Although most ESL/EFL learners prefer to receive feedback directly from their language instructor (Eom, Wen, & Ashill 2006), they can be shown that peer feedback can be very helpful (Li, Liu, & Steckelberg 2010), as their peers might have a better understanding or insight of what might be causing certain usage mistakes of grammatical forms (e.g. incomplete understanding, negative transfer, overgeneralization); for this reason, they have an advantageous perspective and can prove to be a valuable resource during classroom practice activities. Peer feedback activities can be used in grammar practice exercises to give students opportunities to rehearse their responses before being summoned by the teacher to perform in front of the whole class.

Grammar activities in content-based and task-based learning

Content-Based Instruction (CBI) and Task-Based Learning (TBL) offer excellent opportunities to integrate the teaching of language skills into engaging and meaningful activities (Snow & Brinton 2017). They offer a particularly good opportunity to teach grammar as the content or task can provide a contextualized setting for the targeted grammar structure. In this section, five examples of contextualized grammar activities are presented based on CBI and TBL.[1]

The first example was designed for ESL students enrolled in an adjunct class where they were concurrently enrolled in a university subject-matter class, psychology and upper intermediate ESL. To review article usage with count and mass nouns, the instructors took examples from the students' *Introduction to Psychology* textbook to review basic rules of article usage and then give the students practice with unedited passages from the psychology textbook. Articles are a difficult grammar structure for many students learning ESL/EFL and are especially difficult for the students enrolled in the ESL adjunct class who are primarily from Asian language backgrounds. Further many of the students had never been exposed to the systematicity of article usage particularly beyond the sentence level. The content passages provided an authentic context for discussing articles according to the meaning and use components of the Celce-Murcia and Larsen-Freeman framework, particularly in the later parts of the paragraphs as students discerned the definite article pattern dominate as most of all of the nouns became 'known'. It also reinforces the notion that some grammar structures such as articles are best taught with a discourse focus, in this case with a multi-paragraph context provided (shortened due to space limitations). In the activity, the students reviewed the diagram (Table 4.5) which presents the use patterns of the indefinite and definite articles with count and mass nouns.

Table 4.5 Schema for Article Usage

Count				Mass	
Singular		Plural			
a/an	the	the	Ø	the	Ø

They were then provided with the activity in Figure 4.2 for which they had to apply the schema represented in Table 4.5.

Instructions: The passage below is taken from your psychology text. Using the schema in Table 4.5, and applying the rules we learned for article usage, decide which form of the article to use in the blanks *below: a/an, the* or Ø. When you are finished, check your answers on pages 57-58 of your psychology textbook.

Superstitious Pigeons

Example: Ø pigeons have been used extensively in Ø operant conditioning studies.

(1) __pigeon can be put into (2)__ Skinner box and taught to peck at(3)__ small disk or key. In order to receive (4)__reward of (5)__ grain.In this procedure, (6)__ pigeon works for its by reward by pecking at (7)__ key in(8)__ box; (9)__ reward is not given unless (10)__pigeon pecks at (11)__key.

Skinner wondered what (12)__ pigeons would do if they were reinforced with (13)__ grain no matter what they did. Several pigeons were put into (14)__Skinner boxes and rewarded every fifteen seconds with (15)__ tidbit of (16)__grain; (17)__delivery of (18)__ grain wasnot dependent upon what any bird was doing. In effect, these birds were put on (19)__welfare; they did not have to work in order to be fed. After some time had passed, Skinner looked into(20)__ boxes to see what (21)__ birds were doing. He found that each bird was performing some highly patterned act. One bird was turning counterclockwise around(22)__ cage, making two or three turns between each feeding; another was repeatedly thrusting its head into (23)__ far upper corners of (24)__cage; a third was rocking with (25)__ pendulum motion; another bird developed (26)__ kind of (27)__ rhythmic dance. Skinner described (28)__behavior as superstitious.

Figure 4.2 Passages from *Introduction to Psychology* with articles deleted

The second example comes from a Business English course designed for marketing professionals who were intermediate EFL users. The focus of the lesson was the present perfect tense and the context was introductions. The teacher-in-training first reviewed the elements of the present perfect and then the students analysed a model a letter of application to the Marketing Department of Grover International, noting the usages of both simple past and present perfect to talk about oneself and one's experience. Afterwards, students completed a graphic organizer in which they listed some phrases they could use in an introduction, listing 'What I Do', and 'My Past Experience'. Next, students created notes they would use to introduce themselves to their classmates and practised introducing themselves with a partner. They then went around the room introducing themselves and used the checklist presented below to listen carefully to the both the content and tense usage of their classmates. The example incorporates the form, meaning and use components:

Instructions: First introduce yourself to a classmate, then use the checklist (Table 4.6) to pay attention to the language used by the speaker to introduce himself/herself to you.

Table 4.6 Checklist for Introductions

	Yes	No
Did the speaker use suitable language for polite greetings?		
Did the speaker use the simple past tense?		
Did the speaker use the present perfect tense in the introduction?		
Did the speaker tell you about jobs in the past?		

The third example comes from a sheltered[2] high-school history class composed of all intermediate ELLs who needed to learn academic language skills in order to succeed in mainstream classes. The teacher-in-training, a credentialed history teacher in California who is enrolled in the TESOL MA programme, sought to integrate history content and language skills in all her lessons, and to ensure that students met both the history content and English language arts standards. In this lesson, students were studying the Great Depression and Dust Bowl Migrants, a time in US history when man-made erosion accompanied by a drought caused people to leave their destroyed farms and migrate to unaffected states. In a previous lesson, the teacher introduced the topic of the Great Depression and students read parts of the textbook chapter. In this lesson, her content objective was for the ELLs to learn about the human toll of the Dust Bowl. Her language objective was for the students to use reporting verbs to support their opinions and conclusions. She started with a listening activity. Students listened to the song 'Brother can you Spare a Dime?' and identified key words in a bubble graphic organizer. Students then looked at the model sentence below and completed sentence starters using *the reporting verb + that + noun clause structure* and incorporating the key terms from the song. Next students did a gallery walk around the classroom, viewing photographs from the American photographer, Dorothea Lange, depicting scenes from the Dust Bowl era. Student selected their favourite photograph and analysed the details (Table 4.7). They then used the details to write sentences using *show/suggest + that* to make assertions about the photographs, as modelled in the chart below. The activity allows the students a variety of reporting verbs and all three components of the framework.

Table 4.7 Graphic Organizer for Gallery Walk

Detail #1_____ Detail #2_____ Detail #3_____	Detail #1 suggests/shows that_____. Detail #2 _____ that _____. Detail #3 _____that_____.
The details in the photograph suggest that _____.	We assert that _____.

The fourth example is a contextualized grammar activity that is part of a thematic unit based on the novel *The Lion, The Witch, and The Wardrobe* (Lewis 1950) designed for high-school students studying EFL in France. The teacher provided the students with graphic organizers and practice pre-reading, during reading and post-reading activities to prepare the students to read parts of the novel at home. The grammar activity focused on teaching compound sentences using the FANBOYS mnemonic to help students learn to correctly use the coordinating conjunctions: *for, and, nor, but, or, yet* and *so*. Student analysed the following explanations and examples taken from the novel (Table 4.8):

Table 4.8 Chart for FANBOYS Mnemonic with Explanations and Examples*

F for (car)	Used to express a cause/effect relationship	Peter and Susan did not believe Lucy for they thought she was crazy.
A and (et)	Used to list two or more statements that are equal	Narnia is a magical world and it is located in a wardrobe.
N nor (ni … ni)	Used to negate the second independent clause. Can be used with neither or not	Edmund did not try to stop eating Turkish delight, nor did he want to.

*The chart has been shortened due to space limitations.

After analysing the chart (Table 4.8), students read through example sentences, deciding if they were simple or compound sentences and why. They then found more examples of compound sentences and identified the different FANBOYS conjunctions, discussing the form, meaning and use of the conjunctions.

The fifth example is drawn from a one-week thematic unit, *Emergencies and Safety Preparation*, designed for adult ESL/EFL students. Among the many activities in the unit, students read a three-page text,[3] learn the vocabulary for common injuries, preform a role-play related to an emergency, practice the targeted vocabulary in a jazz chant and use a map to identify common household hazards. In the article, students find and underline infinitives and models. In the excerpt in Figure 4.3, students use the article and map to give safety tips with infinitives and models. This grammar activity attends to all component of the Form-Meaning-Use framework since infinitives and modals provide challenges to all three components (the exercise has been shortened due to space constraints).

Instructions to students: Using the article and map, write 10 safety tips using infinitives or modals. Two sentence frames are given:

1. *To prevent* poisoning, _____ .

2. Children *should* avoid_____ .

3. _____ .

Figure 4.3 Worksheet for giving safety tips

The five examples were devised by teacher educators and student-teachers to present selected grammatical structures based on the Form-Meaning-Use framework. All examples presented the grammar explanation and activities in an authentic context related to a theme, piece of literature or content area. Moreover, while only the grammar activities were illustrated in this chapter, the lessons also included reading, writing, listening and speaking activities so that the ESL/EFL students for whom the material were designed had opportunities for integrated language instruction in interesting and meaningful contexts.

Conclusion

Teaching a graduate-level pedagogical grammar class can definitely be a challenge as treating the form, meaning and use of all major grammatical topics as well as making sure there is enough discussion of good pedagogical practices, and implementation of useful teaching tools can prove to be a lot to cover in only one semester. However, it is important to provide teachers-in-training with the resources they will need in their future careers. In this chapter, we have shown how to incorporate learning about grammar through the use of the Form-Meaning-Use framework; how to use linguistic corpora as a source of information not only about the usage of grammatical language but also of authentic and contextualized teaching materials; and how to use content-based and task-based approaches to create engaging and meaningful activities for targeted grammar structures. The ideas presented in this chapter apply equally to teacher educators in ESL and EFL settings where providing a pedagogical grammar course that is both theoretically sound and practical for teachers-in-training is a perennial challenge.

Questions for change

1. How do you think that the Form-Meaning-Use framework can be applied in your teaching context? What are its benefits in terms of grammar teaching?
2. Have you attempted to use corpora to teach grammar in your own ESL/EFL classes? If yes, which corpus have you used? What worked? What did not work as well? If not, why haven't you used corpora? What do you think are the challenges?
3. What other teaching approaches besides CBI and TBL do you think can be used to create authentic, contextualized opportunities to teach grammar?
4. The examples cited in this chapter were developed for use with intermediate to advanced ESL/EFL students as CBI is typically implemented when students have a basic foundation in English. Do you think it is feasible to teach grammar to beginning or low intermediate students in a CBI or TBL class? Why or why not?

Notes

1 The example given in the 'Using Linguistic Corpora' section was used with permission from the MA TESOL programme student, Kelly Kent-Stoll. In the CBI section, the first example was designed by Brinton and Snow (2017) to demonstrate contextualized grammar strategies in CBI to teachers-in-training (used with

permission of the University of Michigan Press). The other examples are excerpted from student projects assigned in the MA TESOL programme; they are used with permission from Anya Frammolino (second example); Ana Herrera (third example), Megan Bowe and Susanna Semerdzhyan (fourth example); and Jennifer Kagawa (fifth example).

2 Typically, sheltered courses are made up of non-native speakers at the intermediate proficiency level. Instructors, who are generally content specialists, use a variety of instructional strategies such as those used by the history teacher to make the content accessible and to integrate the teaching of language and content skills. See Echevarría, Vogt and Short (2017).

3 www.homesafetycouncil.org

5

Multiple Languages in a TESOL Course

T. Leo Schmitt

Introduction

The New School's MA TESOL programme is a thirty-credit curriculum that prepares students to be able to teach English as a second/foreign/new language to adults in a wide variety of circumstances. It promotes a socially conscious approach to teaching with an emphasis on issues of social justice in the classroom. Students are encouraged to not only become familiar with various paradigms and teaching methodologies but also to build and expand their own approaches to teaching based on their own strengths and beliefs, their institutional expectations, and in particular their needs. Such flexibility in the many potential educational contexts is a hallmark of New School MA TESOL graduates. Students can complete the degree entirely online, entirely on site in New York City, or in a combination of online and onsite courses. Students come from around the world and from a diverse mix of personal and professional backgrounds.

The linguistic analysis courses form a core part of the New School's MA TESOL programme. The two linguistic analysis courses (Language Analysis for Teachers: Phonology, Lexis, and Syntax and Language Analysis for Teachers: Grammar and Discourse) are required of all graduates and aim to provide students with a fundamental understanding of the basic linguistic building blocks of language, including phonology, morphology, syntax and discourse. These courses support the other courses in the programme that address pedagogy by giving students the conceptual framework, as well as the metalanguage, necessary to understand how language is formed and how it can be analysed and examined. While an entire review of all of the idiosyncrasies of English would be beyond the scope of a two-semester sequence, students should gain the tools necessary to be able to approach any linguistic question intelligently, analytically and critically. They should also gain the ability to explain these features to learners when and if appropriate.

Students are expected to be able to engage in practical analysis to explore the various components of language and to consider the ramifications for teaching these elements to learners at different levels and from different backgrounds, with strong encouragement to make connections with their own previous language learning (and language teaching, if applicable) experiences. The core text is Scott Thornbury's (2017) *About language*, which includes practical exercises in linguistic analysis. Thornbury's (2006) *A-Z of ELT* is also used as a supplementary text. Scott Thornbury is the course creator, though individual instructors tailor elements as appropriate.

This chapter explores one element of personalization I made as instructor to these two courses. Students are also given a variety of academic articles discussing some of the finer points covered in class as exemplars of some of the depth which practical pedagogical analysis can go. They are encouraged to engage in their own research on the various subfields and produce a project on one such subfield as part of their coursework. In this chapter, I will outline the theoretical underpinnings of my teaching beliefs, provide some examples of the exercises I work with my students and their reactions to them and then explain why I believe these help support the learning objectives of our programme.

Theoretical framework

In teaching these classes to my students, I am influenced by multiple theoretical backgrounds that help to form my approaches. On an overarching level, this is because I have found that complex dynamic systems theory (CDST), (e.g. Larsen-Freeman & Cameron 2008) can be a very powerful model to show the multiple factors that can affect any given system and that these factors can engage in reciprocal causality (e.g. Larsen-Freeman 2018) as each factor can influence and be influenced by others. In my own reflections, I have found that the many different theories and learning experiences to which I have been fortunate enough to have been exposed have impacted various aspects of my thinking. The intellectual development of my own ideas is in constant flux as I continue to engage with different theories and review data presented by my peers. I hope to model and encourage such openness with my students.

Whether language is driven by a biologically imperative universal grammar whereby we are all genetically predisposed to develop language (e.g. Chomsky

1988) or it is more a matter of 'self-organization' (e.g. Wedel 2011: 130), or any other form of systematic growth, it does seem clear that there are many commonalities across most, if not all, human languages. These commonalities, as well as the differences, mean that when analysing language in general or analysing a particular language, we can hope to make fruitful comparisons.

While formal linguistics plays a central role in my linguistic analysis course, as a teacher trainer, I try to remain fully aware of the socially situated nature of language (e.g. Thorne & Smith 2011) and the role of language as a social practice (e.g. Fairclough 2013). Because language is clearly situated within human interaction and our social behaviour, it is responsive to the socially constructed views that each society develops.

In the English-speaking world, these views of the world are particularly relevant. The New School was founded in part as a stance against abuse of power and to stand for innovative ways to promote social justice. To continue this tradition of advocating for a more just world, our programme encourages our students to consider the ramifications of classroom practice in both the global and localized contexts. Our programme supports a practical outreach component that allows students to gain practical experience while working with marginalized groups. Class discussions often directly address the social, economic and political implications of any given pedagogical choice.

English occupies a position unlike any other language. Phillipson (1992) has forcefully argued that other languages occupy positions both culturally and structurally weaker than English, leading to a level of linguistic dominance which has few, if any, historical precedents. This leads to some uncomfortable questions about the role of teachers in perpetuating a dominance that has ramifications far beyond the classroom. As Phillipson (2009: 337) puts it, 'Linguistic imperialism now interlocks with the neoliberal economy, finance, the military, culture, and education.' Despite – or perhaps because of – this dominant position, however, a quiet revolution (Johnson 2000) is underway as teachers and teacher-training programmes pay attention to the needs of their learners. The growing plethora of different contexts and different speakers makes conformity and uniformity ever more unattainable. The so-called 'inner circle' speakers (Kachru 1985) are now a distinct minority as English becomes more and more globalized, yet the status of preferred varieties of English continue to constitute the most valued elements of linguistic capital, associated as they are with economic and cultural capital (Bourdieu 1991). If we want promote universal human values and give voice to the marginalized as bell hooks (1994) advocates, then we need to understand those languages and cultures of our learners, just as Dewey (1933) advocated so long ago. Thus, while a central part of the language analysis class is precisely to analyse, evaluate and become familiar with formal mainstream English, a socially just approach requires that these questions be situated in the broader social and political context in which mainstream English exists.

This eclecticism may alarm some linguistic and theoretical purists and seems to alarm those whose understanding of linguistics is limited to folk linguistics ('Folk linguistics', as in Jackendoff 2003, is the term used to express the beliefs, typically unfounded, lay people have about language). Yet, I have found it effective when working with such a diverse group of students. I always endeavour to ensure my eclecticism remains a principled one (e.g. Cushing-Leubner & Bigelow 2014) whereby I may calibrate my use or focus of one element or another, depending on the immediate needs of the class.

Overall, this chapter emphasizes the importance of teacher language awareness (TLA) as described by Andrews (2003). It focuses on 'knowledge about language (subject-matter knowledge)' over 'knowledge of language (language proficiency)' (Andrews 2003: 85) in this case simply because the latter is typically a given in US graduate programme. It further pays close attention to Andrews's (2003) other two defining characteristics of TLA, growth in metacognitive awareness of how language works and a sensitivity to the learner's perspective.

Working with the context

A significant part of my pedagogy therefore is to intentionally incorporate other languages in the analysis of English that is required for teachers of ESL. This may strike some, particularly those who work in a multilingual cultural context, as obvious and jejune. However, for others it may seem needlessly complicated and a detraction from the focus of the course.

I am fortunate to work in an environment where there is considerable linguistic diversity. While a majority of the students speak English as their first language, a significant part of the student body speak another language as their first language or are true bilinguals. Among the native speakers of English, there is also considerable diversity, with many varieties of English such as South Asian Englishes, African American Vernacular English, Southern English and New York City English among others. Students' facility with other languages similarly varies from essentially monolingual English speakers to proficient speakers of multiple languages. With which particular languages my students will have familiarity with varies enormously each semester; though as we are in

New York City, Spanish has always been represented and is typically the default second language for illustrative purposes. The diversity of the languages that my students may bring to the class requires me to tailor the languages used accordingly (more reciprocal causality), but this flexibility also underscores the emergent nature of the flow of the classroom. The languages and varieties I use reflect not just my students' prior knowledge but also my own. I have been fortunate enough to have been exposed to many languages, though the disadvantage of being a native speaker of English has made it harder to become truly proficient in any of them. I have also been exposed to many varieties of English. I use my personal explorations of other languages and dialects to help enrich and diversify the classroom.

Sample exercises to engage with other languages

One example is my use of a YouTube video (Xhosakhaya 2009) to explore the use of click phonemes in Xhosa. In this video, students are introduced to the 'supposedly difficult' (Xhosakhaya 2009) click phonemes. This video is shown as part of the module on phonemes after a discussion about the challenges English learners have in differentiating and producing English phonemes. Examples are given of Spanish speakers having trouble with the /b/ and /v/ distinction, or Arabic speakers having trouble with the difference between /p/ and /b/. By challenging the students to differentiate and produce highly unfamiliar phonemes ([kǀ'], [kǁ'], and [k!']), students gain a level of depth in understanding how challenging phonemes can be when learnt as adults. Students are asked to practise the click sounds and then try to produce and identify them in communicating with each other. I highlight that this exercise is highly decontextualized, allowing them to focus solely on the phoneme, whereas in communicative speech, there would be other demands on their attention.

Another example is one where I will use a variety of texts to explore the concept of discourse. These may include a stop sign in Farsi, a Chinese menu, and sign in Portuguese. In each case, I try to find signs in languages that are not immediately familiar to the students. In the first example (Figure 5.1), some students may be familiar with the Arabic alphabet, but that does not help if they do not know Farsi. However, despite having no familiarity with this language, and likely no understanding of the phonetic components, they are quickly able to decipher the entire meaning of this sign due to the increasingly universal signal of a red hexagon.

Figure 5.1 Stop sign in Farsi (/ist/). Taken from https://www.dreamstime.com/stock-photo-stop-road-sign-persian-farsi-language-photo-taken-iran-image72161834

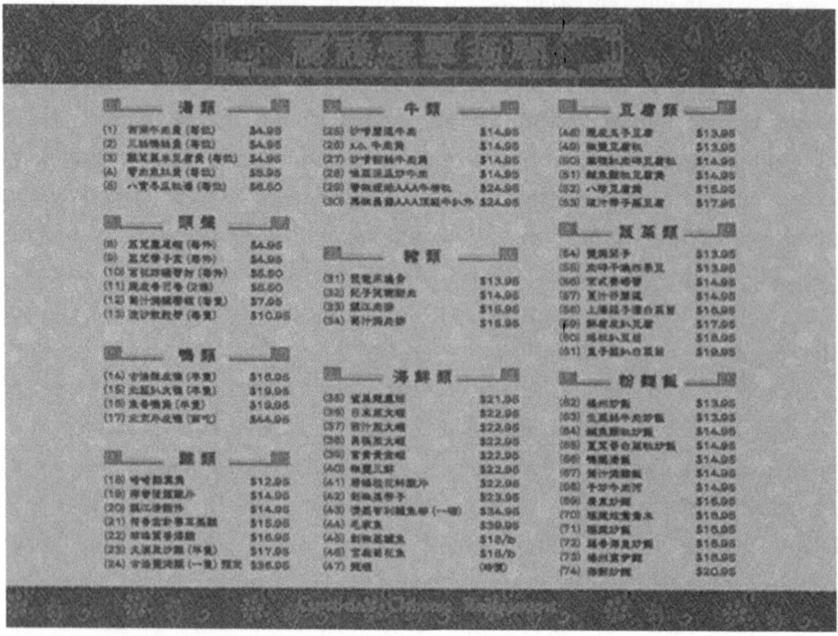

Figure 5.2 Chinese language menu. Taken from http://www.gr8tables.com/cynthias-restaurant-vaughan/gallery/

In Figure 5.2, the students see a longer text, again in an unfamiliar script. I usually cover the tell-tale English language notation at the bottom of the image. However, again and even with no knowledge of Chinese or its script, learners are usually able to identify this as a restaurant menu. Many are able to correctly predict that the sections correspond to beef dishes, seafood dishes and so on. In these first two examples, students lack even a shared orthography that might help them identify cognates or other linguistic similarities with languages they know. Yet they are able to deduce a fair amount of information in both cases.

In the third example, Figure 5.3, the students are brought to the more familiar Roman alphabet. I use this when I do not have students proficient in Portuguese, substituting it with one in another Romance language if necessary. Typically, over half of my class will be familiar with at least one Romance language, usually Spanish or French, though even those who only know English can succeed with this exercise. I then challenge them to make sense of the text using their understanding of English and any other language.

The style of the street sign is not particularly familiar to North Americans, so this creates a minor barrier. However, the word *Avenida*, along with other cognates, may be recognizable for many even without a smattering of Spanish.

Figure 5.3 Portuguese language street sign. Taken from https://en.wikipedia.org/ wiki/List_of_places_named_after_Vladimir_Lenin#/media/File:Avenidalenin.jpg

Students then work through the rest of the text, including the very accessible dates, and are inevitably able to make sense of the text.

In addition to these and other exercises, I encourage students to share their insights into their languages based on the linguistic concepts that we cover in class. For example, in morphology when we discuss the categories of lexical, functional, derivational, and inflectional morphemes and explore examples in English, I challenge them to come up with several examples of each in their first, second, or third language and to share their justification for this categorization with their classmates. Similarly, when we explore phonemes, I may challenge them to find phonemes that exist in their language or dialect but not in mainstream English, or to find examples of allophones.

These and similar exercises are hardly an innovation and many have been adapted from experiences I have had in both the classroom and the real world. They do, however, play multiple important roles in my teaching practice that I think bear sharing. I have identified six main reasons for this use of other languages in exploring mainstream English that I endeavour to keep at the forefront of my mind while teaching. These six reasons, elaborated below, are as follows:

1. Students enjoy engaging with other languages.
2. Students can better empathize with their learners.
3. Students who are non-native speakers can be empowered.
4. Students can become more aware of the sociopolitical implications of ESL in the world.
5. Students can better explore the concept of translanguaging.
6. Students can engage in contrastive linguistics to deepen their understanding of the English language.

Benefits of using other languages in the classroom

The first reason is that I have found my students respond well to the use of other languages. They generally find my exercises both engaging and relevant. Student comments such as 'I really enjoyed the inclusion of other languages in this class', 'Personally, it was interesting to have examples from other languages in terms of learning a concept' and 'I found the use of languages other than English in this class very useful, not to mention interesting' highlight the motivational element for some learners, particularly those with an intrinsic interest in language. I believe part of this is because the exercises generally maintain the same foundational pattern (e.g. phonemes or homophones), but shift the lens from a familiar English language to one less familiar. The intellectual challenge of making connections between prior knowledge and introduced concepts is one that my graduate students, who as current or future ESL teachers generally have some level of intrinsic interest in language, find invigorating and engaging. Students are inevitably on task and stretching to see connections between mainstream English and other varieties and other languages. These connections should, in turn, lead to deeper understanding of the concepts.

Additionally, I try to make these exercises as relevant to teaching ESL as possible. Thus, while exploring the signs in various languages described above, I make reference to potential pedagogical applications in the ESL class and how this can raise learners' awareness of key elements of language. For example, in looking at the Farsi stop sign or Chinese menu, we can explore a more top-down approach to reading, where the broader picture is of particular help, whereas the Portuguese sign engages in more bottom-up analysis of individual words. We can then discuss how these skills can be presented to learners in different contexts to help them apply different reading skills. Similarly, when looking at clicks, we can discuss how effective it is to compare them together as opposed to apart as well as the value of using vowels together with the target consonants. In all of these explorations of pedagogical applications, a key component is the dialogic nature of the discussion. All students are expected to participate and to link the concepts to their own experiences, beliefs and contexts. These connections to prior knowledge and personal stances are important for them to develop new and effective approaches to teaching that work in their particular situations.

In this vein, a second advantage is that the process of having to engage in making sense of unfamiliar texts or engaging with new linguistic elements, as in the example of the clicks above, should lead to increased empathy with their learners. This highlights Andrews's (2003) point about TLA including an understanding of the learner's perspective. I explicitly point this out, for example, when students complain about the challenge of producing and differentiating clicks. In the students' words: 'First is our experiment with making the three "clicking" phonemes from Xhosa. Struggling to make the right sound based only on a demonstration and a suggestion of where to put my tongue truly made me sympathize with our learners who have to do the same with unfamiliar English phonemes.' and 'I loved the YouTube video about the Xhosa, click language "See, it's easy" Is that what it feels like for our students?' This is particularly relevant for monolinguals who may not have progressed beyond basic high-school Spanish and who have seldom, if ever, been in a position where their language deficit led to significant real-life consequences. While we hope that all teachers can experience a level of empathy for the challenges their students face, that is not always the case and even when it is, it bears reinforcing. The students, being students, were able to empathize with these challenges and hopefully will carry these experiences into the classes they themselves teach. The following are the examples of their realization: 'What may seem common sense to say a native-speaker of English is not so common-sensical to a non-native speaker'; 'The use of different languages in class, made me recognize that learning new words, sentences, sounds, and texts take time and effort'; 'Also, not being able to produce the target language can increase anxiety levels in students' and 'Overall, I think using other languages in the classroom is one of the best ways to help native-speaker TESOL students understand what their learners will go through as L2 English speakers.' These all speak to their understanding that learners are frequently disempowered (e.g. Larsen-Freeman 2018) and anxious. Standing in the teacher's spot is clearly different from sitting in the student's chair, but we should aim not to forget what that was like.

Indeed, some students are painfully aware of these challenges because they have already faced them. As noted above, many of my students speak ESL, and others' first variety was not mainstream English. For a variety of reasons, these students may not always feel as included and valued in formal American educational contexts as their peers. So, a third reason is that by valuing other languages and varieties and encouraging their presence in the class, I hope to offer these students an opportunity to become experts and to feel a stronger sense of belonging. When students are able to contribute meaningfully by sharing their home language (or dialect), they become more valued in the class and increase the shared sense of community and respect. Students were less likely to comment on this aspect when asked to consider the value of a second language in the classroom. I believe this is partly because of the overwhelming expectation that English should dominate a TESOL class in an American institution and that the concept that other languages may have a right to a seat at the proverbial table is poorly established. One student did comment: 'As someone who grew up speaking another language alongside English, I found references from other languages to be quite refreshing in the classroom', indicating the level of comfort may have been improved. In the words of bell hooks (1994: 174), 'We may disrupt that cultural imperialism that suggests one is worthy of being heard only if one speaks in Standard English.'

It is further hoped that an additional benefit is that international students may build friendships with domestic students. See, for example, Gareis, Merkin and Goldman (2011) for a discussion of the challenges faced by international students in making American friends. Anecdotal evidence did seem to support the idea that international students made solid friends in this class.

A fourth reason builds on this. The very fact that our MA TESOL programme prepares teachers to teach English and not, for example, Malay speaks to the outsized role English plays in the world today. English continues to be the dominant language on multiple levels, yet as Phillipson (2016: 13) puts it, 'This should not and need not occur at the expense of creativity in the mother tongue, or through downgrading national languages that are important for ensuring an informed general public.' I hope that by offering avenues for other languages and varieties to be heard even in a class that focuses on the analysis of mainstream English, we can resist the trend towards monolingual dominance and go some way towards protecting linguistic diversity in the world. The demand for mainstream English is unlikely to diminish in the foreseeable future and its dominant position similarly seems assured. However, with teachers who are able to understand the value, diversity and beauty of other languages, we may yet be able to promote a stronger sense of social justice tied with respect to people's home languages and dialects in our spreading of mainstream English. Students seemed to take this on board, with comments such as 'One of the most important things I learned in this class is that I have an English-language-centric lens and that I need to be aware of that as a teacher and try as much as I can to adjust and hopefully remove that language filter', 'its [sic] another strategy to give another perspective of other languages and a more objective view of the English language – as one of the languages of many' and 'The TESOL community itself has a multicultural and multilingual identity. I felt that the use of other languages in the classroom created a more inclusive environment'. These comments indicate that our students have a growing realization that while English remains a highly sought-after language, this need not and should not be to the detriment of other languages.

A connected fifth reason why using other languages in the classroom improves the learning experience is that it supports more practical application of the concept of translingualism. 'Translingualism' is an umbrella term, which includes two key concepts (Canagarajah 2011: 6), 'communication transcends individual languages' and 'communication transcends words and involves diverse semiotic resources and ecological affordances', and can be connected to perhaps the more common term 'translanguaging'. Translanguaging, in essence, accepts that the inflexible ideology of linguistic purity is problematic to say the least. Garcia, Ibarra Johnson and Seltzer (2017) talk about the application of this translanguaging in the classroom and the two points that they make about the value of translanguaging in the classroom particularly resonate.

First, they argue that translanguaging improves the flexibility of the teacher, allowing additional resources to improve student engagement with and retention of the target language/structure/concept. This flexibility is crucial for our students; without a rigid and dogmatic approach to language instruction, the New School seeks to build independently minded students who are able to apply the best approaches in the field to their particular context. As our graduates go on to work in extremely varied contexts with students from many different language groups, educational backgrounds, learning motivations, socio-economic statuses, and a plethora of other variables, flexibility is the key to their teaching preparation. We discuss translanguaging in depth and consider its value and application in different situations. As De la Fuente and Goldenburg (2018) argue, a principled use of another language, typically the L1, in the FL classroom has multiple benefits. It is this principled use in particular that is highlighted by exploring its use in the MA TESOL class. The class can critique my and their use of other languages and discuss what it adds or does not add in a particular situation and consider its transferability to other situations, including ESL teaching. This opportunity to explore translingual practice is another positive reason for using other languages in the course.

The second point of note made by Garcia, Ibarra Johnson and Seltzer (2017) is that such use promotes a more democratic space and enriches the classroom by making connections to students' home languages. Again, this reinforces the previous point about the value of creating a more just, egalitarian, and respectful linguistic landscape.

In addition to all of the reasons for using other languages in analysing mainstream English mentioned above, a final point of which I make considerable use is the value of contrastive linguistics in developing students' knowledge of language as a meaning-making system. Students may struggle understanding the concept of phonemes, for example, but when they see that /ban/ and /van/ signal two completely different concepts in English, but not in Spanish, while /pʰai/ and /pai/ are essentially indistinguishable in English, but signal two very different words in Thai, the concept becomes more manageable. In the words of one student, 'I really learned so much about TESOL by learning about how other languages work.' Particular areas could be better understood, as illustrated by the comment 'I especially enjoyed the inclusion of other languages during the suprasegmental discussions. Contrasting English tone, rhythm and intonation to other languages' suprasegmentals certainly helped me to understand these features/concepts better.' They are thus able to develop Andrews's (2003) second characteristic of TLA, an increased metacognitive understanding of language as a system. The value of the ability to engage in this contrastive exercise is heightened by the students using languages and varieties that are familiar to them. Students who can compare two languages with which they are familiar and can now better understand those differences because they understand the conceptual framework are better prepared to share that knowledge with their students.

An additional benefit is that all students are encouraged to share their insights with the rest of the class, giving these teachers-in-training helpful insights into languages with which they may not have been familiar. For example, when discussing phonemic inventories, a speaker of Arabic may help prepare her classmates for teaching Arab students by highlighting the lack of the phonemes /p/ or /v/ in Arabic. As one student put it, 'I found the use of other languages helpful in understanding contrastive phonology of specific languages. E.g. (l/r v/b f/p in Japanese/Korean, b/p in Arabic) This can be very helpful in the classroom especially when the lesson is on pronunciation.' This type of contrast can help students understand possible home language reasons for their own students' errors. By encouraging other students to share their own linguistic expertise to help their classmates, the third reason mentioned above is also reinforced.

Conclusion

The overarching premise of using other languages in the linguistic analysis courses, then, is to support the central goal, the demystification of the English language, and this is achieved through multiple avenues. Mainstream English is dethroned as a truly unique and uniquely situated language and placed in its larger temporal, geographic, political, economic and social context. While it remains the central focus of the study, by juxtaposing mainstream English next to different varieties of English and other abstand languages, students can more readily recognize the position of the language that they will teach. They are able to see, through contrasting with other languages, how it is similar to other languages as well as how it relates to other recognizably English dialects. This can then lead them to build their own understanding of language in general, formulating and revising hypotheses about broader or even universal characteristics of human language. Such an understanding can lead them to better examine their teaching philosophy and how they can help their own learners make vital connections to build their communicative competence. At the same time, they are better able to see the areas where mainstream English in fact differs from other languages and even dialects of English. This can help prepare them for likely challenges that their learners may face through unsuccessful attempts at transfer and consider how they might best present the target language in an accessible way in their particular teaching context – one that can help their learners make meaningful connections.

But perhaps more importantly, the inclusion of other languages reinforces a crucial sense that mainstream English is not a preordained and inevitable language that will subsume all others in its path. It highlights the idea that other languages and other dialects not only can have a presence in the dialogue but that that very presence can enhance both mainstream English and the languages that interact with it. Despite the continuing push for monolingualism in political circles (e.g. Rico 2018), the cognitive benefits of multilingualism are clear (e.g. Diamond 2010). In addition to the personal benefits that we gain by learning a second (or a third) language, we should consider the social justice implications of promoting multiple languages rather than simply championing mainstream English. The inequalities produced by virtue of one's native or non-native speaker status may be mitigated by promoting the social, cultural and linguistic capital that varieties other than mainstream English carry.

Such a role for other languages in a MA TESOL class leads to questions about their role in ESL classes. Many of my students over the years have worked at institutions where there is an implicit or explicit ban on languages other than English. In some cases, we would share policies that could culminate in their learners being expelled from the programme for using anything other than mainstream English. By putting other languages and varieties in our language analysis classes, we can confront many of the myths upon which these policies are based and better prepare our students to advocate for a more socially just and more pedagogically sound approach to teaching ESL.

Questions for change

1. Consider your own use of an FL in the classroom. How is it positioned vis-à-vis mainstream English? Are there ways that you could introduce familiar and unfamiliar languages to your students to improve their understanding of how language and language learning work?

2. Consider your own use of non-mainstream English in the classroom. How is it presented? What status does it have? How is it contrasted with mainstream English? How can we challenge students to re-evaluate their personal ideologies towards non-mainstream forms?

3. Consider the core goal of teaching English as foreign/second language. To what extent do you consider the social, political and economic implications of continuing the expanding dominance of English in the world today? How does that affect the position of your students and their learners? Are there ways that you can advance a more socially just world while balancing the current demands of the social and political realities?

6

Knowledge Shock for MA TESOL Students in a World Englishes Module

Yi Zhang and Rining Wei

Introduction

The notions of WE, EIL and ELF have been frequently addressed and explored in ELT and curriculum development among many countries. Although the tendency of recognizing the *inner circle* norms of English varieties, such as those of the United States and the United Kingdom, is still prevalent in terms of English learners' learning goals (Jenkins 2009; Kachru 1986), scholars have suggested various concerns regarding this approach towards English pedagogy and application. In contrast, it has been proposed that a critical conceptualization of English learning/teaching and language ideology should be adopted to reflect the plural reality of Englishes around the globe.

Bearing a critical and plural conceptualization of Englishes, various inquiries have been conducted in order to understand the attitudes and ideologies of English learners in terms of English teaching and use in the *expanding circle* (Kachru 1986) and EFL (e.g. Jenkins, Cogo & Dewey 2011; Seidlhofer 2009). It has been pointed out that the investigation of English education in a multilingual and globalized world should not neglect the cultural and economic imbalance of language learners' accessibility, and that a monolithic view on the English norm prescribed by the so-called native speakers continues to be questioned (García & Wei 2014; Kubota 2012). Unfortunately, despite various efforts in the theoretical and empirical research of WE and EIL, the applications of such research in terms of language programmes, curriculum development and applied linguistics/TESOL courses remain relatively scarce. In addition, many of the existing programmes that address the plural reality of Englishes in the expanding circle (e.g. D'Angelo 2012; Hino 2012) have not yet included China, the world's most populous country where the number of English users/learners of Chinese nationality already exceeded 390 million in 2000 (Wei & Su 2012).

This chapter provides an overview of an applied-linguistics module specifically focused on English as a global/international language offered by the Department of English at a research-led Chinese–UK joint university. We will first briefly describe the main approaches towards English as a plural concept, then showcase the context of the target module and finally present five MA TESOL student-teachers' reflections on their evolving understanding of English after learning the key themes of the module. In this way, we are in hope of demonstrating a workable design of an ELTE curriculum that advocates English language learning through a pluralistic paradigm, which comprises the key notions of WE, EIL and ELF in China.

A pluralistic paradigm

The notion of considering English as a plural concept has generated different schools of thoughts and research interests in applied linguistics, ELTE and English curriculum reforms. Researchers are mainly focused on the debate revolving the ownership of English, legitimacy of varieties of Englishes beyond the inner circle and potential pedagogical implications that reflect the plural reality of English in a globalized world (e.g. Blommaert 2010; Canagarajah 2011).

World Englishes and English as an international language

With the development of globalization and digital communication, the notions of WE and EIL have gradually gained scholarly attention in applied linguistics. The main foci of WE research have revolved around the distinctions of language use in terms of phonology, lexicons, syntax, discourse and pragmatics by speakers from the inner circle (e.g. the United Kingdom and the United States), the outer circle (e.g. Singapore and India) and the expanding circle (e.g. Japan and China) (Canagarajah 2013). This strand of research is largely influenced by the increasing population of English users of other varieties who seek for their voice to be recognized beyond the inner circle norm (Wang 2016). Moreover, the vibrant reality of intercultural communication demands people of different professions to be able to communicate with English speakers of different English varieties. In this way, the core of English communication becomes intelligibility, and the emphasis on linguistic forms has shifted towards users' communicative competence. This trend of conceptualizing English as plural has inspired practices and research in ELTE. With the continuing development of globalization and migration, practitioners of English education have raised critical questions regarding the conventional view on English with some varieties being the norm and its legitimacy in English teaching (Martínez Agudo 2017). However, the notion of WE may inflict the concern that the involved English varieties are divided in a narrow manner only according to different nations. In an increasingly more multicultural world of communities, users of English may encounter and acquire English varieties through different contact zones and activities (both online and offline), and the notion of WE cannot fully reflect the complex linguistic and/or semiotic repertoires of these English users. On the other hand, EIL emphasizes the language communities beyond the notion of nations. However, EIL also shares a similar limitation with WE in the sense that it reflects the English varieties through the 'enumerative strategy of counting languages' (Pennycook 2010: 82) and treats English varieties as discrete systems.

English as a lingua franca

Similar to WE and EIL, ELF proposes a paradigm of English communication that does not rely on the inner circle norms. Instead, ELF mainly focuses on how speakers of different L1 backgrounds communicate with each other via negotiation of meaning and effective communication strategies (Canagarajah 2007). In ELF communication, the often emphasized features of English learning and use, such as phonological, lexical and syntactic features from the inner circle norms, are downplayed for effective communication. Rather, it is the communication strategies, such as asking for repetitions, clarification questions, wait time and so forth that become the vital concerns for ELF users. ELF as a reconceptualization of English norms for effective communication among users of different L1s provides space for users of the outer and expanding circles. It is an empowering concept that promotes the voice of English users of other varieties and contributes to the reconstruction of the English language in an increasingly globalized world. On the other hand, scholars have also critiqued ELF as the notion that seems to push English users of other varieties away from the core of 'native' speakers despite its claim of being neutral (Canagarajah 2013; Kubota 2012). In this way, users of ELF are somewhat 'marked' and kept peripheral from the inner circle and ownership of the language, which are only compensated by effective communicative strategies.

Native versus non-native dichotomy

While new concepts, such as WE, EIL and ELF gradually gain their foothold in English communication, the discussion of native/non-native dichotomy still exists in English language learning, teaching and use within various cultural contexts. The idea of achieving native-like proficiency as the goal of second language acquisition (SLA) has been widely pursued by learners and L2 users of English (Jenkins 2007).

Critiques of the native versus non-native dichotomy, however, suggest that the ownership of English should be reconsidered due to the sheer number of English users from the outer and expanding circles, and various phonological and lexicogrammatical features of English from the so-called non-native speakers have been gradually accepted. English speakers from the outer and expanding circles now compose the largest body of English language users, and their literacy creativity and successful re-adaptations of English in various communicative activities and contexts have been acknowledged as a sign of effective communication (Canagarajah 2009; Pennycook 2010). Some researchers in the field of sociolinguistics also point out that our linguistic repertoires are often imbalanced, and we are in an ongoing development of language proficiency in different nationally defined language categories (e.g. English or French) and various specific aspects of language use (e.g. academic writing or medical languages) (e.g. Blommaert 2010). Another pitfall of (non) nativeness is that this notion fundamentally distinguishes users who learnt English at a later stage from those who acquired English as their L1. In this sense, the notion of inner circle normalized English becomes a 'birth right' that cannot be attained by L2 English users who are forever barred from the core group of English users (i.e. English users of the inner circles). Therefore, competent L2 speakers of English will still be considered as incompetent, which may lead to the devalued ideology towards speakers of ESL.

With the above notions on reconsidering English communication against the inner circle norms, some universities and programmes have started to reshape curricula in ELTE. By introducing the concepts of WE, EIL and ELF, students and novice teachers of ELTE are able to reconstruct their understanding of English ownership and the importance of communicative competence and strategies (Clayton & Drummond 2018). Unfortunately, it appears that China as the country with the largest population of English learners/users has witnessed few attempts by programmes or universities to offer courses or training related to the new paradigm. However, the MA TESOL programme that the authors teach has made such an attempt.

The context

We attempt to equip our MA TESOL students with essential knowledge about the English language derived from the pluralistic paradigm by means of requesting them to audit one undergraduate module entitled *English as a Global Language* (see the next section for more details). This focal module is offered as a level-1 course (equivalent to the first-year module in the UK) by the Department of English at Xi'an Jiaotong-Liverpool University (XJTLU). XJTLU was established in 2006 as a Sino-British university located in Suzhou, Jiangsu Province, China, through the collaboration between Xi'an Jiaotong University and the University of Liverpool. XJTLU, aspiring to be a research-led international university, has become the largest among the current ten 'Sino-foreign' universities in China, attracting over 4,600 students from over 30 countries for their undergraduate or postgraduate studies in the 2018–19 academic year alone. The university aims at cultivating capable global citizens and adopts English as the main teaching medium in its language policy.

In the Department of English, while most of the students in traditional Chinese universities study modules with heavy emphasis on English skills (e.g. spoken English, English writing and so forth), the department in XJTLU provides various courses in relation to applied linguistics, translation and literature. In the field of applied linguistics, the department offers both compulsory and elective modules in SLA, sociolinguistics, DA and many other linguistics-related modules. In addition, the department offers two postgraduate programmes in MA TESOL and Mass Media Translation. Against the academic background described above, modules that reflect the latest conceptualizations of various aspects in applied linguistics are offered to students in both undergraduate and postgraduate programmes. Our focal module is a typical one in the undergraduate curriculum.

The focal module

The focal module, ENG 115 *English as a Global Language*, was developed as an elective course for both undergraduate students in the Department of English and postgraduate students from the MA TESOL programme. The module lasts for fourteen weeks with weekly two-hour lectures and one-hour tutorials. The key learning objectives of the module are:

1. to introduce students to a wide range of phenomena related to English as a global language at both global and local levels,

2. to introduce students to some key conceptual and theoretical resources useful for understanding these phenomena,
3. to enable students to apply their knowledge and understanding gained in this module to critically assess some major historical, cultural, and/or sociolinguistic issues arising from published papers in the field (e.g. those published in *English Today*).

The learning objectives described in the module specification are clearly designed to reflect the ongoing discussions on the global status of Englishes and their applications, as well as the related linguistic, sociocultural ideologies in various contexts. The lecture topics of the module include the historical development of English as a global language, the native-speaker controversy, major differences in different English varieties, issues of identity and acceptability of WE, English in global business and media and hands-on analyses of empirical cases related to these topics.

Throughout the module, the students report their understanding and reflections of issues on English as a global language via one group project, a presentation, and an essay, each composing 15 per cent, 15 per cent and 70 per cent of the entire assessment marking. In the following section, we will describe our data collection process through the focal module and present the testimonies from five MA TESOL students' perceptions of English as a global and international language with a plural reality.

Our study

Following an exploratory and qualitative approach, we conducted semi-structured interviews with five MA TESOL student-teachers. The interview questions were designed to understand their developing perceptions of *nativeness* in English and other varieties of Englishes. Each interview, conducted in English, lasted approximately thirty minutes. Sample interview questions included the following:

1. What was your understanding of native English or native English speakers before taking the module?
2. What is your current understanding of native English or native English speakers?
3. What surprised you the most during your learning experience in this module?

4. In addition to what you have shared, what other new things/ideas have you learnt in this module?

The student-teachers were selected through convenient sampling. Tiffany was the only Year 2 MA TESOL student at the time of the study. In her Year 1 of the TESOL programme, Tiffany completed modules on SLA and English teaching methodologies, among others. She was particularly interested in sociolinguistics topics related to the learning, teaching and social interactions of English in various contexts. After auditing the focal module, Tiffany indicated that her understanding of English had changed dramatically.

The other MA TESOL student-teachers, Tix, Sherry, Nancy and Eric, were in their first semester of the programme when auditing the focal module. They decided to audit the module because they had a passionate interest in sociolinguistics issues in teaching and/or were simply eager to learn more. Both Tiffany and Eric (the only male student-teacher) had several years of English teaching experience, whereas the other student-teachers were fresh graduates from English-related (Tix and Nancy) and non-English (Sherry) majors.

All the interviews were recorded and transcribed verbatim. The interview data was then coded for identifying the emerging themes guided by the objectives of the study. This process involved getting familiar with the data by multiple rounds of reading, underlining and annotating the transcript.

MA TESOL student-teachers' perceptions

Through the above-reported process of inductive data reduction for capturing the general themes in the interviews, we identified four common themes pertaining to student-teachers' evolving understanding of English. In the following subsections, we present excerpts that illustrate those common themes.

Students' previous monolithic perceptions of English

The interviewed student-teachers held a relatively traditional view on the English language and its users in the past. For Tiffany, before taking the target module, she regarded the native speakers of English as people from specific countries of the inner circle:

> Actually as I knew in the past, a native speaker or a native English speaker in my mind refers to those who live in England or America or something like this ... yeah just these two countries.

In the above example, Tiffany suggests that she used to believe native speakers of English only come from the United Kingdom and the United States, two key countries of the inner circle model according to Kachru's model (Kachru 1986). Although English is not the official language in the United States, Tiffany suggests that it is nevertheless the de facto official language of the country. Other lesser known inner circle countries, such as Australia and Canada, were not thought of by her. Tix offered a similar response:

> Before taking this module, I was thinking native English speaker refers to the English people. I mean specifically for the UK and US. The two countries. That's common when we think about native English speaker.

It is interesting that both interviewed student-teachers responded that the English varieties from the United Kingdom and the United States were considered the standard for English learning and usage in their past experience. Other varieties from the inner circle, however, were not explicitly mentioned by Tiffany or Tix but were mentioned by the others. However, the student-teachers unanimously indicated that before taking the focal module, they had held a rather monolithic understanding of English and standard English. The only criteria for their judgement of native English used to be attributed only to the national origin of the speakers. In Tix's response, she suggests that it is common for 'we', namely the Chinese learners of English, to think of native speakers as people from the United Kingdom and the United States. This should not come as a surprise, because for many people Standard British and American English have been the main acceptable varieties for English teaching in China (see He & Zhang 2010; Wang 2016).

Realizing the plurality of Englishes

Despite their previous impression of *native* English and English users, the interviewed student-teachers started to realize the plural reality of Englishes soon after taking the target module. They pointed out that other English varieties, especially those used in the outer and expanding circles, have also been adopted and utilized around the globe. For instance, Tix reported that her understanding of English had shifted from the RP style which has been considered a key feature of standard English in the UK, to Englishes with different varieties:

> Because I used to think that English is only one variety ... RP ... that's all we are looking for. But after I took this module, I changed my thinking ... there are different varieties of English.

Tiffany shared a similar idea regarding varieties of Englishes beyond the so-called Standard American and British English, and reported her realization of different communities of English and English users. In this case, she specifically mentioned the notions of the inner and expanding circles:

> Actually I know something about Expanding Circle countries or something like that ... I think those people who live in Inner Circle countries can be called 'native' English speakers. These are the countries where English can ... is regarded as the official language. I know something like Chinese English, Singapore English, or British English, American English that can be covered in this term 'Englishes' ... I think it's highly acceptable.

In this excerpt, Tiffany showed her understanding of English varieties beyond the inner circle norms, such as Chinese English and Singapore English. What is more interesting is that she presented the above English varieties in parallel with British and American English, suggesting an equal status.

Legitimatizing the plurality of Englishes

While it is vital for students to be aware of English varieties other than those of the inner circle, what is more important is to deconstruct their understanding of English ownership. In other words, how to inform TESOL students about the legitimacy and power of English varieties beyond the inner circle remains a challenging task for any WE-informed modules. This was not exception for the target module, which also included lectures and learning activities regarding English ownership for English users from various sociolinguistic contexts. As the students auditing the focal module, the interviewed student-teachers seemed to have learnt extensively regarding the legitimacy of the plurality of English and expounded their critical reflections on the ownership of English as a global language during the interviews. To Eric, the term 'Englishes' was a positive one, partly because 'we can appreciate different cultures' through different Englishes. He believed that China English could become a member in the WE family. Sherry also found the term 'Englishes' a positive one.

Both Tiffany and Tix questioned some of the traditional notions regarding the concept of nativeness and the ownership of English, and challenged the notion of nativeness. For example, Tix demonstrated her indifference of the existing dichotomy of nativeness versus non-nativeness of English in an increasingly globalized and interconnected world:

> Currently, actually I do not care so much about native/non-native thing, because I realize the native … how to define native? There are a lot of difficulty … I don't have specific concept for native.

Tix's response is interesting in the sense that she was vocal about her unwillingness to acknowledge the so-called native norm of English. Her suggestion that it is difficult to capture the idea of nativeness reflects the linguistic reality of today's English. Tix's point resonates with the current works in WE which question the use of the native/non-native dichotomy as it is a term in relation to the origin of birth that tends to neglect other sociocultural factors such as race and language accessibility (Canagarajah 2013; Kubota 2012). Moreover, the notion of *native* cannot account for the complexity of various current English-speaking communities where dynamic layers of communicative contexts and linguistic norms encounter and interact. Tix's response is in line with Tiffany's answer in which she raised the issue of language ownership:

> There are so many kinds of different English and so many different English varieties now in the whole world. … Maybe English cannot be regarded as the only language of so-called native speakers.

After the learning of English varieties in the globe from the target module, Tiffany has become aware of the existence of Englishes in various linguistic contexts, as well as the legitimacy of Englishes beyond the inner circle norm (i.e. so-called native speakers). In the above excerpt, Tiffany brings about the issue of English ownership, and she suggests that the notion of English that is to be owned and explained only by the native speakers of the inner circle should be challenged given the fact that other varieties of Englishes have established their roles in the world. In the following conversation, Tiffany continues to develop her argument on the plural nature of Englishes and English ownership:

> People like us who live in Expanding Circle countries can have a kind of ownership of English I think. So I think this 'Englishes' is acceptable. I think it's *reasonable*. (italics added by the authors)

In this final piece, Tiffany argues explicitly for the claiming of English ownership by users in the expanding circle. She further emphasizes her stance of owning the language by stating that it is not only 'acceptable' but also 'reasonable' to claim the ownership of English by users beyond the inner circle. These arguments, documented in the interview, would not have been developed without the learning experience of the WE module.

Reflective thinking on the English variety in China

As one of the countries in which people have been described as enthusiastic about English and English learning, China has witnessed waves of English learning and teaching reforms, and Chinese learners' attitude towards the so-called native English has been reported as desirable (He & Zhang 2010). The notions of *Chinglish*, *Chinese English* or *China English* are often ridiculed. Interestingly, in three interviewed student-teacher' responses, they mentioned the term 'Chinglish' and offered critical insights towards the legitimacy of the so-called non-standard English variety based on the concept of English as a global language.

For instance, Nancy admits that it was 'a bit shocking' to learn about the term 'Englishes' in the focal module, as she used to believe that *Chinglish* was something bad and only *native English* was proper English. When Tiffany was approached for the question 'what surprised you the most during your learning experience in this module', she specifically mentioned the notion of *China English* and other varieties of Englishes which resonate with the concept of Englishes being plural. She pointed out the notion of *Chinglish* as a derogatory term that implies the failed proficiency of English use by users from China and its diaspora:

> I think the most impressive term I learned from this module is called 'China English'. Actually I have never heard about China English before. I know Chinese English or 'Chinglish' – imperfect use of English. Our kind of English. Something like 'good good study, more more … day day up'.

Before taking the module, Tiffany, like many other English learners/users in China, held a monolithic view on English varieties other than the inner circle. The notion of *Chinglish* is a common exhibition of such an idea. In this way, the English variety denoted by *Chinglish* is often considered as non-standard, inefficient and powerless, which seems to be shared by other student-teachers (e.g. Nancy). However, Tiffany suggests that this type of English is starting to gain a foothold in WE, and has been recognized by other English users. She expounded that *China English* is a better term in order to capture the English variety originated in China and/or used by Chinese people than *Chinglish* which bears the inclination of inefficiency and inferiority.

Tix pushes the argument further and indicates that the often-mentioned *native speaker myth* is usually attributed to the English users of the outer and expanding circles. In the following excerpt, she explains how certain norms of English have been strengthened by Chinese learners:

> Actually I have read a paper about 'Chinglish', and I think maybe the most … . It is the Chinese people who are more … who will judge upon their accent and on their own variety. For other people, for example the native English speakers, they do not care that much about their accent of what we think – the Expanding Circle … . I think it's because they are [English users of the expanding circle] not confident about themselves.

The above statement by Tix exhibits her critical reflection on the potential causes of the situation in which speakers of the inner circle and their nativeness of English are desired by many English learners and users in China. According to her fieldwork in which she conducted interviews with both 'foreign speakers' and 'some Chinese people', she concluded that the pursuit of nativeness in English is related not only with building confidence but also with the desire of joining the *white* or *native*'s community:

> Chinese people cared so much about their accent just because they are not confident. They want to join the community … the white community or native's community. And for them, the standard English seems to be the label of well-educated or higher class.

Tix's response on how being native in English is related to the joining of the *white* and *native* community critically reflects the role of race in learning/teaching and research of WE. As suggested by Kubota (2012), the lingering issue of research about native versus non-native English language learning/teaching and use is the often-neglected discussion on the role of race in English communication. Tix, however, sharply points out the racial factor of pursuing the native English norm, which suggests that being native packs various societal factors rather than linguistic features such as accents, word choices and so forth.

Implications for ELTE

Implications for ELTE at other Chinese universities

Based on the testimonies from the student-teachers interviewed, it is reasonable to believe that the student-teachers auditing the focal module have, after the initial knowledge shock, developed an awareness of the pluralistic paradigm, reconceptualized the notion of English ownership and started contemplating the challenges of applying ideas (e.g. WE) from the pluralistic paradigm to their ELT in the future. Therefore, the focal module proves to be a useful and relevant element in the ELTE curriculum at XJTLU, China's largest Sino-foreign university. As XJTLU and its counterpart Sino-foreign universities share highly similar socio-culture backgrounds and ambitions for internationalization, the successful attempt of running the focal module can be replicated at XJTLU's counterparts.

The focal module, which incorporates elements from the pluralistic paradigm, offers implications for undergraduate and postgraduate ELTE programmes not only at Sino-foreign universities but also at Chinese universities aiming for internationalization. Similar to many other expanding circle countries, China puts immense emphasis on learning EFL, and the notion of standard English has prevailed in various educational settings (Wang 2016). Many stakeholders in ELTE have been so influenced by this notion that they seem very much attached to only one standard of English from the inner circle (e.g. American or British English). Not surprisingly, the modules run in ELTE programmes at traditional Chinese universities have exclusively focused upon the curriculum designs and pedagogies oriented towards training language (English) skills such as close reading and academic writing, and/or content knowledge and skills in literature analysis and translation. To internationalize these conventional programmes, one way is to offer a module similar to the focal module discussed in this chapter. In this way, students and novice teachers in ELTE programmes at Chinese universities with ambitions for internationalization will gain useful and applicable insights from the pluralistic perspective of English and ELT.

Implications for ELTE beyond China

The target module also presents pedagogical implications for ELTE beyond China. While some changes have been made to reflect the plurality of Englishes in English testing and learning/teaching materials (e.g. including listening materials of English speakers from areas beyond the United States and the United Kingdom, such as New Zealand and Australia, for further complication of English varieties), there is still a long way to go for Englishes of the expanding and outer circles to be recognized as legitimate varieties. One possibility is to provide exposure of more diverse English varieties to the involved stakeholders and English teaching practitioners through modules that reflect a pluralistic paradigm. After all, it is essential to first establish the awareness of the plural reality of Englishes for ELTE. The case presented at XJTLU offers a workable curriculum of English as plural and may be adopted by other programmes beyond China. Another direction can also be considered in terms of the design of English tests and materials. To address the plural reality and ownership of Englishes, the design of English tests and materials may include samples that reflect features of Englishes in outer and expanding circles (e.g. pronunciations, expressions, pragmatic usage). In ELTE, it would be beneficial to provide WE/EIL/ELF-informed literature, curricula, materials and activities for student-teachers as well as in-practice English teachers.

Conclusion

The module, ENG 115 *English as a Global Language*, provides a working example of WE/EIL/ELF course that is incorporated in the linguistic curriculum for undergraduate and postgraduate (MA TESOL) student-teachers in China and beyond. The module demonstrates a successful attempt in clearing the myths of *native speakers* and re-establishing language ownership of English. By introducing the global status of English and its increasingly acknowledged varieties, the module offers a deconstructive view of English in the contemporary world and promotes the non-native English-speaking TESOL student-teachers' voice as potential competent English users/teachers. Hopefully, similar modules can be adopted in more institutions of higher education not only in China but also in other contexts where English may have been taught and represented through a normative paradigm. With more curricula and courses designed around notions of WE, EIL and ELF, non-native speakers of English should gain increasing ownership and voice over English teaching and communication, as Tix suggested that 'the Expanding Circle … the countries or the people from the Expanding Circle will change or just … we should change the language itself'.

Questions for change

1. For all readers: What is your view now on standard English?
2. For ELTE programme planners/designers: To what extent does your programme focus upon the curriculum designs and pedagogies oriented towards training language (English) skills, and/or content knowledge and skills in literature analysis and translation? Are you willing to incorporate

elements of the pluralistic paradigm of English and ELT into your ELTE programme? If so, how?

3. For student-teachers in ELTE programmes: What can you do to counterbalance the hegemony of standard English in your future teaching practice within the pluralistic paradigm?

7

Teaching Pragmatics in an EFL Environment

Gerardo Esteban Heras

Introduction

English has been a mandatory subject in secondary schools since 1992 in Ecuador. Since then, two main reforms have been launched in order to improve the learning of English among public and semi-public schools. The first reform called Curriculum Reform Aimed at the Development of the Learning of English (CRADLE) was created in 1992 (British Council 2015). The second reform, the National Curriculum Guidelines, started in 2012, with an update in 2014. Nowadays, this document is the main manual for primary and secondary English teachers. It should also be noted that English has become a compulsory school subject from Grade 2 since 2016–17 (Ministerio de Educación 2014a,b).

The University of Cuenca (Ecuador) offers an IELTE programme called Lengua y Literatura Inglesa (English Language and Literature) in which EFL student-teachers study for nine semesters in order to obtain an English teaching diploma. The teacher educators of this programme try to focus mainly on a student-centred communicative approach to teaching (Nunan 2013). The following definition of this type of learning best describes what teacher educators aim at implementing in this programme:

> Student-centred instruction [SCI] is an instructional approach in which students influence the content, activities, materials, and pace of learning. This learning model places the student (learner) in the centre of the learning process. The instructor provides students with opportunities to learn independently and from one another and coaches them in the skills they need to do so effectively. The SCI approach includes such techniques as substituting active learning experiences for lectures, assigning open-ended problems and problems requiring critical or creative thinking that cannot be solved by following text examples, involving students in simulations and role plays, and using self-paced

and/or cooperative (team-based) learning. Properly implemented SCI can lead to increased motivation to learn, greater retention of knowledge, deeper understanding, and more positive attitudes towards the subject being taught. (Collins & O'Brien 2003: 338–9)

By making students the centre of the teaching and learning process, the faculty of this programme strive for effective teaching practices: presenting students' learning outcomes using cooperative learning (CohenMiller, Merrill, & Shamatov 2018), as well as modelling, giving students opportunities to respond and providing feedback (Harbour, Evanovich, Sweigart, & Hughes 2015). It should be noted, however, that effectiveness in teaching could be viewed in many different ways, depending on the context where the learning is taking place. What might be considered good teaching practices in one country could be viewed as even irresponsible traits in another (Richards 2010).

The present chapter aims to argue for the importance of incorporating pragmatics in the teaching and learning of English. In addition, I describe the experiences we have had at the ELTE programme regarding the teaching and learning of pragmatics. I discuss the strategies used in our programme as well as some of the recommendations given by experts in this field around the world in terms of how to teach pragmatics.

A pragmatics course in IELTE

Among the different courses that are taught at the University of Cuenca ELTE programme, there is one called Basic Pragmatics, which began to be taught in 2013. I have taught it for the last two years. The main purpose of this course is to raise awareness in students on the necessity of taking pragmatics into account in their journey of English language learning. This course is taught three hours a week for a total of about forty-eight hours during the whole semester. We use a textbook that covers the theoretical as well as the practical aspects of this area of linguistics. Students are assessed mainly on their awareness and pragmatic development (e.g. their response in a given speech act or imaginary situation), and their comprehension of and critical thinking about the most important concepts of the reading materials provided to students. Although the development of pragmatic ability helps student-teachers enhance their overall communicative competence (which includes other skills and subjects such as reading, listening, and writing), this course largely articulates with two other courses in this programme, Sociolinguistics and Conversation II. The reason is that sociolinguistics is closely related to some concepts covered in Basic Pragmatics, and in Conversation II, the students can apply their pragmatic comprehension of the language during oral interaction. The research on interlanguage pragmatics has focused mainly on oral communication (Ishihara & Cohen 2010). This subject contributes mainly to the following aspects of students' exit profile of this programme:

1. Understands and comprehends most of the language used in elaborate discourse, television programmes and film
2. Uses language in a fluid, spontaneous, flexible and effective manner

It may be agreed that in order for students to achieve these goals, they have to learn more than grammar, syntax, phonology and vocabulary; they have to also learn the pragmatics of the target language (English in this case). Learning a language is basically trying to develop as much as possible learners' ability to mean (Halliday 1993). But, what is pragmatics?

Ishihara and Cohen (2010) claim that researchers have become more concerned about the study of pragmatics in the last four decades or so due to its importance in the development of communicative competence. Other authors have shown the importance of pragmatics in language teaching and learning (Abrams 2014; Bardovi-Harlig 2013; Cohen 2016; Grice 1975; Hardin 2013; Kasper 1997; Kasper & Rose 2002; Kwai-peng 2016; Reyes 1994; Taguchi 2015).

Ishihara and Cohen (2010) warn us that having pragmatic ability in the field of applied linguistics goes beyond the general definition of this term, taking a practical approach to something. These authors claim that pragmatics in linguistics takes a deeper and more complex meaning, and it incorporates the four major communication skills, namely listening, speaking, reading, and writing, even though, as mentioned earlier, speaking has been the main focus of study in this branch of linguistics.

Pragmatic ability is demonstrated through the use of these communication skills in different situations people face. As listeners, we need to be able to understand the message, which might be communicated even without words. As readers, we must identify messages that sometimes are not clearly stated in the tone or style of the author. As speakers, we have to make our utterances clear taking into account the social status/distance of our listeners and that of our own. In addition, we should be able to communicate things sometimes without even uttering a word. In other words, taking many different factors into account, we have to be pragmatically appropriate when speaking. As writers, we need to communicate what we want to convey, keeping our audience in mind at all times (Ishihara & Cohen 2010).

If we go back to the exit profile mentioned above, Yule's (1996) definition of pragmatics better explains why it is important for student-teachers to incorporate it in their own teaching and learning. The author says that

> pragmatics is concerned with the study of meaning as communicated by a speaker (or writer) and interpreted by a listener (or reader). It has, consequently, more to do with the analysis of what people mean by their utterances than what the words or phrases in those utterances might mean by themselves. Pragmatics is the study of speaker meaning.
>
> [...]
>
> Pragmatics is the study of contextual meaning. [...]
>
> Pragmatics is the study of how more gets communicated than is said. (Yule 1996: 3)

So, based on this definition, we can say that both speakers and listeners have to negotiate meaning. Most of the time, this is done subconsciously, especially among native speakers, but when we talk about teaching, it might be a good idea to explicitly teach some pragmatic rules. Nevertheless, people (can) learn the pragmatics of a language through different ways without realizing it is called that way.

There are many ways student-teachers can benefit from the studying of pragmatics. Let us analyse the next explanation provided by Paltridge (2012):

> *Pragmatics* is the study of meaning in relation to the context in which a person is speaking or writing. This includes social, situational and textual context. It also includes background knowledge context; that is, what people know about each other and about the world. Pragmatics assumes that when people communicate with each other they normally follow some kind of cooperative principle; that is, they have a shared understanding of how they should cooperate in their communications. The ways in which people do this, however, varies across cultures. What may be a culturally appropriate way of saying or doing something in one culture may not be the same in another culture. The study of this use of language across cultures is called *cross-cultural pragmatics*. (p. 38)

This definition is important for us because we feel our future English teachers need to be aware of the fact that culture plays a big role in communication. They have to be mindful of the fact that in order for effective communication to take place, other elements of communication such as context and background knowledge, which are not normally covered in textbooks (Ishihara & Cohen

2010), have to be taught in the classroom. It may not be evident for Ecuadorian English learners, especially the ones with a real low English level, that the ways we use to communicate with one another in Ecuadorian Spanish are not (always) the same as the ones used in other countries such as the United States, for example. The learning of pragmatics helps our student-teachers improve their communicative competence, which in turn should help their students' communicative competence.

Pragmatics can and should be taught in the classroom. Kasper (1997) showed us that, according to many studies carried out in different contexts for about ten years, this area of linguistics is indeed teachable. Following this call, 'early studies produced in the 1990s showed that most aspects of pragmatics are amenable to instruction, meaning that instruction is better than non-instruction for pragmatic development' (Taguchi 2011: 291, see also Kasper & Rose 1999; Rose 2005). In our IELTE programme, we discuss this with students, emphasizing that in the future, when they teach English, in most cases they will have to adapt the textbook given in order to teach a kind of language that is less artificial. Student-teachers become aware that most English programmes and textbooks do not offer research-informed instruction, and that language samples and communication formulas often come from writers' and editors' intuition and introspection (Ishihara & Cohen 2010).

Following the fact that many studies (e.g. Alcón-Soler 2012; Cohen 2017; Johnson & de Haan 2013; Narita 2012; Yates 2014) have demonstrated that pragmatics can and should be taught, we at the University of Cuenca ELT programme have attempted to do so by adhering as much as possible to what experts have advised in terms of methodology, techniques, and resources. There are not many resources available for teachers to teach pragmatics (Ishihara & Cohen 2010). Most of the research has focused on showing the state of affairs with regard to L2 learners' interlanguage pragmatic development, which is a good start, but more efforts should be made among teachers to incorporate it in their classroom. However, this situation seems to be improving as nowadays – 2018 – we have more scholars who are trying to use what research has found in order to create guidelines that could be used by teachers around the world who would like to include pragmatics in their practice (e.g. Alcón-Soler & Martínez-Flor 2008; Bardovi-Harlig & Mahan-Taylor 2003; Houck & Tatsuki 2011; Ishihara & Cohen 2010; Ishihara & Maeda 2010; Martínez-Flor & Alcón-Soler 2005; Taguchi 2009; Tatsuki & Houck 2010). This body of knowledge could be increased if teachers from around the world start to analyse the competence and performance of their students (taking context into account) in relation to that of native speakers of the target language and other FL learners of that language. Thus, they might create context-specific guidelines for the development of the pragmatic competence in their students.

Teaching pragmatics is not an easy task due to the fact that its rules are not clear cut. The pragmatic rules of one country might be completely opposite to those of another country. Even within one speech community, people have problems in communication due to lack of pragmatic ability. Another issue to discuss is the idea that textbook writers and editors do not make use of what research has found when they include examples of language data in the books. Therefore, we find many language examples in textbooks that seem unreal or not used by the majority of that speech community (Ishihara & Cohen 2010). In an attempt to try to contribute to students' development of their communicative competence, the subject matter is growing and even changing each semester.

How can pragmatics be taught?

In this section, I describe the aforementioned course, Basic Pragmatics, taught at the University of Cuenca. Therefore, I discuss the course programme and some of the activities that are carried out in it.

Syllabus

Faculty staff at the University of Cuenca have to follow the same syllabus structure in all departments. The syllabus includes a description of the course. The syllabus must contain a description of the subject and the manner(s) in which the course contributes to student-teachers' learning outcomes. It also describes the objectives of the course, among which we have to raise awareness in students on the necessity of learning pragmatics and to improve their communicative competence.

Teaching materials and activities

I focus on some of the theory of pragmatics (e.g. definition of key terms such as speech acts, politeness theory, implicature). Moreover, I try to raise student-teachers' awareness, usually done by watching educational videos in which the importance of pragmatics is discussed. For instance, I show them a video where both native and non-native speakers talk about some aspects of pragmatics, and then they also act out some scenes containing failure in communication due to lack of pragmatic competence on one of the participants (see more advantages of using video below). My students have to guess what the problem in each context is (see Appendix A for a sample activity). This seems to help students further develop their own pragmatic ability.

By developing their pragmatic skill, their ability to better communicate in the target language improves. Better communication includes following some rules when interacting with others (Paltridge 2012). In class, we talk about how communication takes place. We might touch on the subject of lying, for instance and we might say that it is not a good idea to lie to other people, even though we all know there are occasions where lying is better than telling the truth. Be that as it may, this idea of always telling people the truth (maxim of quality) was emphasized by Grice (1975) as part of the four maxims of the cooperative principle (already mentioned above in Paltridge's definition of pragmatics). The other three maxims refer to always using the exact number of words in order to make ourselves understood, not more and not less (maxim of quantity). This presents a challenge to EFL students, especially when examining language data performed by native or high-proficiency speakers because boundaries and notions of what is exact blur. Next we have the maxim of relation, which basically says that our interventions have to be relevant to the topic. The fourth maxim (in no particular order) tells us that people should avoid ambiguity; they have to be clear when they involve in interaction (maxim of manner) (Grice 1975). As part of the theory that we discuss in class, we include the cooperative principle.

Another activity that students like is identifying hidden messages in people's utterances. We do this by reading authentic language samples or watching videos. Some of the language samples are obtained online, or whenever I have the opportunity, I ask a native speaker or high-proficiency speaker of English to record a conversation in that language. Then, I transcribe it or have someone do it for me (Appendix B), and then I might ask my students to read it and tell me if they find something they do not understand. We also try to find pragmatic features such as the use of the filler *like*, which was very common in the case of Appendix B. As for the videos, most of them are movie or series clips and the activities revolve around identifying pragmatic features. We try to focus on language aspects that are not usually taught in textbooks or in conventional classrooms. Among the features explored, we have identifying some grammar mistakes in people's utterances. For instance, native speakers tend to ask yes/no questions using an affirmative statement structure (You're still going out?) instead of following the rule. We talk about the fact that native speakers tend to break some grammar rules when they talk, especially in informal settings, and that it is the same in all languages; we talk about some examples of this when we talk in Spanish. Another feature we explore is the use of sarcasm in some movies or series. I explain to the students that these utterances are usually not to be taken seriously. For example, questions like 'What are you doing here?' might mean that the person asking is not pleased with the listener's presence.

These activities are an excellent opportunity to talk in class about the locutionary act (words uttered); the illocutionary act (the intention of the utterance); and the perlocutionary act (the effect of what people say has on their listener) (Austin 1962). Out of these three kinds of pragmatic meaning (Widdowson 2007), the illocutionary act seems to present more challenges to students. This might be due to the fact that people do not always say directly what they want to say. Let us take a look at the following exchange:

A: *Okay. It was nice talking to you. Let's get together sometime* (Hoping the hearer would understand that it is just part of the ritual of saying good-bye, in this case). If the learners are not aware of this, they might answer with

B: *That would be nice! When do you want to get together?* which, of course, could create an awkward situation to say the least.

By discussing these types of exchanges, student-teachers understand that it is part of the teacher's job to explain to students that in many cases, sentences such as 'We must get together sometime' are only part of a friendly/kind way of saying goodbye. Other examples of this type of formulaic language include 'How are you', which in most common situations is a way of greeting. The person (mostly native speakers or high-proficiency learners) who asks that question does not expect the listener to answer with more than a 'Fine, thanks' (Ishihara & Cohen 2010).

Another activity that helps student-teachers develop their pragmatic ability is the reading of research studies in this field. Hence, they discover what mistakes other EFL learners from different contexts make, which interestingly enough sometimes coincide with their own mistakes. Student-teachers also learn the main research instruments used within this branch of linguistics.

One of the most interesting activities that student-teachers have to work on is a project in which they have to use one of the research instruments (mostly the Discourse Completion Task or DCT) discussed during the course to carry out a short research project. This project includes obtaining answers from both English students and native English speakers. The fact that many native speakers of English live in the city of Cuenca makes this project feasible. The direct contact with this speech community gives students extra practice in developing their communication skills. The student-teachers have to present the results of this short project in class, and we discuss the main differences found in the answers provided by the participants. In addition, the student-teachers reflect on how they themselves perform the speech act that was used in the project. This helps them become aware of the things they need to improve. I am aware of the flaws that these kinds of research instruments may have, but still I think it is a good starting point. Sometimes, I have found totally opposite differences between the answers provided by native speakers and that of non-native speakers in our context.

Videos for teaching pragmatics

One of the resources that I use the most in class are videos. Through the use of videos student-teachers have the opportunity to not only listen to the exchanges but also look at the setting (context) which, as we know, plays an important role when trying to convey meaning. For example, when we are trying to raise awareness in students, we can show them a video containing the target pragmatic feature being discussed (Taguchi 2011).

Rose (2001) states that the use of videos in the classroom has been an important resource for many years and adds that films have been used especially for the teaching of listening and speaking. What is more, some scholars suggest, is the use of videos in the classroom to teach pragmatics. However, Rose (2001) admits that 'this use of film (...) appears to be far less established than its applications in the development of listening and speaking. The use of film for the purpose of pragmatics research is even less established' (p. 310). The use of video for teaching pragmatics has not been researched to a great extent, and Ecuador is not the exception. In Ecuador, even the notion of pragmatic competence is recently starting to be recognized (Burbano 2011; Heras 2014).

Furthermore, Ismaili (2013) presents evidence that using videos in the classroom could make students become more interested in the subject. Subjects such as reading could benefit from the use of movies to enhance the understanding of stories, for example. The most common benefits of using movies in the classroom include the participation of target language native speakers, the setting is usually a native speaking country, and the situations mostly reflect what happens or could happen in real life (Ismaili 2013).

There has to be preparation before using videos to teach pragmatics. For instance, it is a good idea for the teacher to pick a scene in which some pragmatic feature is being played. Besides the other activities planned, the instructor has to be prepared to answer students' questions about the pragmatic feature they are discussing. I have used a clip from the movie *Rush Hour* (Birnbaum et al. 1998) in which one of the actors Chris Tucker, Carter in the movie (who is African American), takes his Chinese friend, Jackie Chan, Lee in the movie, to a bar packed with African Americans. Carter says to his friends at the bar something like, 'What's up my niggas?' And then Lee, after seeing that, goes up to Carter's friends and says the same thing, at which point they start beating up Lee. Quickly, Carter helps Lee as he explains to him that 'nigga' could only be used in a friendly way among African Americans. Before Carter's explanation takes place, I usually stop the video and ask my students why Lee was being hit. Interestingly enough, sometimes even advanced learners of English do not know the answer.

Who can teach pragmatics?

It might be a good idea for teacher educators to have a high level of pragmatic competence in order to incorporate this feature of language in the classroom (Cohen 2016). However challenging the teaching of pragmatics may be, I have tried to do it mainly by reading books and articles, watching videos, and the experience gathered through the teaching of this course at the University of Cuenca. This is, in part, due to the fact that in our context teacher education programmes do not even mention pragmatics in most cases, even though the communicative approach has been one of the central themes of recent seminars/workshops. Also, even in countries such as the United States, teacher development events that focus on pragmatics take on a rather theoretical approach, assuming that by learning the theory, teachers will incorporate the practical aspects of it in the classroom (Ishihara & Cohen 2010). As can be expected, there is no standard approach to teaching pragmatic competence. For instance, some scholars such as Chalak (2015) have discovered that the combination of explicit and implicit instruction is better than the use of either modes alone. Nevertheless, it seems as though explicitly teaching it brings more benefits because in most cases students cannot learn by osmosis (Cohen 2008).

Since there are limited professional development opportunities for teachers and teacher educators who want to embark in the teaching of pragmatics, Ishihara and Cohen (2010) propose a set of traits that educators must have/learn if they want to include this part of linguistics in their practice. Table 7.1

Table 7.1 Teachers' Knowledge to Teach Pragmatics

Selected components of teacher knowledge for teaching L2 in general	Components of teacher knowledge specifically required for teaching of L2 pragmatics
Subject-matter knowledge	Knowledge of pragmatic variation.
	Knowledge of a range of pragmatic norms in the target language.
	Knowledge of meta-pragmatics information (e.g. how to discuss pragmatics).
Pedagogical content knowledge	Knowledge of how to teach L2 pragmatics.
	Knowledge of how to assess L2 pragmatic ability.
Knowledge of the learners and local, curricular and educational contexts	Knowledge of learners' identities, cultures, proficiency and other characteristics.
	Knowledge of the pragmatics-focused curriculum.
	Knowledge of the role of L2 pragmatics in the educational contexts.

describes the authors' view (based on previous attempts of other scholars) in terms of teacher knowledge in relation to the teaching of pragmatics.

Conclusion

The teaching and learning of pragmatics in this ELTE programme is a work in progress. Since 2013, when the course called Basic Pragmatics began to be taught, I have noticed that at least student-teachers have gotten curious about it. For instance, they have begun to question if the language samples used in certain English textbooks reflect what happens in reality. Some student-teachers have started to use what they learnt when analysing authentic language samples. Others have made more questions in terms of how to teach pragmatics to certain age groups. Moreover, I have noticed that some student-teachers (about ten so far) have embarked on a research project based on pragmatics in order to fulfil a requirement for them to graduate. It could be said that this course has helped to raise awareness in student-teachers on the fact that good communication involves a lot more than just the linguistic part. Nonetheless, there is still a lot to be done in terms of teaching and researching pragmatics. Research in the area of pragmatic development in EFL in Ecuador is not even in its infancy; it has not been born yet.

Questions for change

1. Is pragmatics taught in your context?
2. Do you think pragmatics should be taught?
3. What are some approaches/techniques/resources you have used to teach pragmatic competence?
4. Has pragmatics been researched in your area?
5. How does pragmatics contribute to acquiring communicative competence?
6. How do you evaluate student's pragmatic competence?

Appendix A: Sample of in-class activity

UNIVERSITY OF CUENCA
ENGLISH LANGUAGE AND LITERATURE
Basic Pragmatics

In-class activities

Work on your own: Do the following activities related to the video 'Pragmatic Failure in Intercultural Communication'.

1. Read the title and guess what the video might be about.

   _____

   _____

   _____

2. Circle the phrases you hear during the first part of the video. There are three correct answers.

   A. English is a versatile language.
   B. The world's economy.
   C. To be able to speak English.
   D. Learning English from a grammar book is not enough.

3. What is the problem in each case?
   First case:

   A. The student is not dressed well.
   B. The student is too demanding.
   C. The student interrupts the teacher when he is working.
   D. The teacher doesn't understand the student.

Second case:

By saying 'of course', the learner makes the native speaker sound:

A. Lazy

B. Stupid

C. Too direct

D. Enthusiastic

Third case:

A. The native speaker only offers the drink once.

B. They don't get along with each other very well.

C. The learner is sick.

D. The learner doesn't understand what the native speaker says.

Fourth case (fifth case in video):

A. The native speaker is impolite.

B. The learner likes the native speaker.

C. The learner doesn't understand English very well.

D. The learner doesn't know that 'nice to meet you' also means goodbye.

4. After you have watched the video, please answer the following questions.

According to the video, what are some of the subjects you should not talk about with native speakers of English unless you know them very well? Circle the correct answers.

A. How much you earn

B. How much you paid for something

C. Politics

D. How old you are

E. Global warming

F. If you are married

G. Invasions

5. Talk to your partner. What are some taboo subjects in Ecuador?

Appendix B: Sample of authentic language transcript.

'*You're in New York.*' Like, and then he was saying, like, how he would … he could come here potentially, like, two times a month. And I was like … telling him how that's just too much for me and … I dunno, it must've gotten into, like, my issues. And … I was like, '*You know I barely know … I still barely know you …*' And … I told him I'm like, '*You know, I already have doubts or, like, fears about relationships so if I'm gonna commit to somebody exclusively I'm gonna need to, like, make sure the person's worth doing that for.*' (Emphasis mine)

Discourse Analysis for Undergraduate Language Teachers

Leticia Araceli Salas Serrano and Blanca Adriana Téllez Méndez

Introduction

This chapter is organized in six sections. The first three sections allow readers to have a context of the situation starting from Mexico's location and its educational system in relation to ELT. The remaining sections describe how the DAC that serves as a basis of analysis for this chapter is organized and contextualized in an IELTE programme and, finally, present our main understandings from teaching this DAC.

Due to its geographical location, in the south border of the United States, there is a misleading idea that the level of English among the Mexican population is highly competitive. Campos and Hernández (2013) claim that only 2 per cent of the Mexican population has a good command of the language. However, learning the language of the neighbour country has become a goal for many Mexicans. The lack of official sources with trustable statistics establishes a huge gap of accurate conclusions. Therefore, it is possible to say that Mexico is far away from speaking ESL, yet it is taught as a FL in all levels of the public education system.

Initially, the national system of education at its initial stage tried to establish access to education to everyone in the country, based on a national idealism of providing education free of religious ideology and control. Currently, the educational system in Mexico is divided in the following stages: (1) the basic level (pre-school, elementary and junior high or secondary school); (2) the intermediate level (high school), which prepares students for their entrance to college and where they can get a bachelor degree in an average of four years; and (3) graduated studies, which include, masters, doctorates and specializations. Of these educational levels, only the basic level has been mandatory for decades.

English had been included as a mandatory subject only in secondary- and high-school levels; however, educational authorities have made an effort to implement the teaching of this language in earlier stages. Programmes such as PNIEB (National English Programme in Basic Education, for its initials in Spanish) or PRONI (English National programme) have emerged as preventive and remedial programmes for teaching English in all Mexico. Therefore, English is now taught, in general, at the basic level of Mexican education in all the country. To attend to the needs of this scenario, a huge number of English teachers are required.

Thus, a significant number of IELTE programmes have appeared in the country in order to supply the need of English teachers in Mexico. Most of the programmes are offered by public universities; however, some private institutions have also opened their own programmes to prepare English language teachers. One of the first institutions which has offered this kind of programme, since 1984, is the BUAP, (Huerta 2005) located in the central state of Puebla.

The institution

The BUAP or Meritorious Autonomous University of Puebla had its roots in 1578 on the ecclesiastic institution founded by Jesuits and a very long path of transformations until 1956 when the College of the State became an autonomous university. It was in 1987 that the state gave it the title of Benemérita (Meritorious) due to its rich history. This institution is mainly focused on offering bachelor and graduated programmes but it also offers high-school programmes.

The School of Languages (Facultad de Lenguas in Spanish) is the educational unit in charge of offering language courses to all students at the institution. In addition to the language centre, the School of Languages also offers an IELTE programme at the level of a BA and a masters' programme in TESOL.

The programme

The IELTE programme is based on three main elements: English language learning, teaching skills and language knowledge. The total number of subjects student-teachers need to take is thirty-nine courses divided in the three knowledge areas mentioned before. Students can also take some optional courses to complement the programme, such as teaching children, English for specific purposes, literature, or psycholinguistics, just to mention some.

The programme of the major in English teaching was modified in 2009 after the implementation of the Modelo Universitario Minerva (MUM), the educational model to follow at the BUAP. This educational model has a socioconstructivism approach based on sociocultural humanism. At present, the Teaching English bachelor programme at BUAP is one of the biggest programmes on teaching English in the whole country. It is within this frame that the School of Languages establishes as its general objective to integrally educate English teachers that would positively respond to the educational and social needs of Mexico and in special of Puebla.

Some of the traits LEI teacher-students should acquire are:

1. to be an integrally educated person: a critical and creative individual,
2. to have attitudes and values that match those of the MUM,
3. to be aware of their membership to a specific social and cultural environment,
4. to be able and willing to solve problems and innovate as well as to go for change.

Besides the general characteristics of graduates and according to the programme, they must develop some professional competences such as:

1. integrate theories and methodologies of language teaching-learning process for the development of their teaching practice in diverse contexts, situations and communicative needs;
2. design and assess appropriate classes for the diverse situations that they will face in the classroom;
3. apply their knowledge and research abilities to identify and solve problems in the areas of English teaching and learning;
4. recognize and critically and creatively argue about situations that happen in their social and professional environment in order to make decisions and solve problems, aided by the use of different ICTs.

The general characteristics and the professional competences of IELTE graduates emphasize the practical use of the theoretical knowledge that students receive during their time at the university. However, the understanding and analysis of language as one of the core activities of their teaching practice has not been emphasized enough, as they will become teachers of the English language. When they graduate, they hold a very basic command of language structures and its uses, so they might be missing the richness of the language as a system.

The course

Linguistics has been defined as the scientific study of the language. Mahboob (2017: 14) has stated that 'the key role of English language teachers is to teach language', not a language. Therefore, from the very beginning of the creation of the syllabus for the IELTE programme, there has been a linguistic area as one of the main components. According to Bathia, Flowerdew and Jones (2007: 1), DA took a more relevant role in the linguistics field in the 1970s when it emerged as the exploration of a group of linguistic and non-linguistic systems. The epistemological stance that has led this IELTE programme adaptation and its further implementation has been the constructivist approach following the requirements from the institution; as this approach allows students to create their own knowledge from the experiences provided during the course. Additionally, due to the nature of DA, an interpretive approach that allows students to critically think has also been established as the source of knowledge where to base the actions that originated this chapter.

DA has been defined as the study of how people use language in different contexts. DA explores the way the structures of written and spoken language are woven to serve textual and social purposes. English language teachers and student-teachers may have some misconceptions about the target language, following Nunan (2004, p. 1) who stated that language learners 'might misuse lexical items due to its similarity to their first language (L1) or because of the context in which they learned the words', student-teachers might not be aware of the linguistic, social and cultural knowledge that learning another language implies. Therefore, the study of DA can provide the knowledge required to analyse language, but it can also raise student-teachers' awareness on the appropriate linguistic use by exploring the construction and making of discourse, being this the reason why the DAC has been considered critical in the student-teachers' preparation. There seems to be no single definition of DA; however, the term has been used to mean the study of language in relation to social practice (Potter 2004). Including DA as part of the base knowledge teacher-students should acquire may provide students with the elements to deepen in the structural, semantic and functional aspects of the language.

Preparing English teachers, who work with language, to analyse language, has become relevant and necessary; therefore, the DAC has been included as one of subjects in the linguistics branch in this IELTE programme. Being language the raw material with which English teachers work, it is important for them to know the way language is constructed, understood and used for appropriate communication in order to strengthen their awareness as language users and future English teachers. One of the core characteristics of the DAC is its cross-disciplinary scope, which allows pre-service English teachers to apply different competencies at exploring how language is used in varied and real communication contexts. Besides, it allows pre-service English teachers to make connections on how DA provides them with tools to have a better understanding on previous classes such academic writing, research seminars, among others and opens the door to new possible approaches to the study of language and to teaching now with a deeper understanding on how the language works and how it can be taught.

DAC is offered right before student-teachers start their teaching practice and the writing of their research thesis required for graduation. Then, the DAC might serve them, on the one hand, as a bridge to connect the knowledge acquired between theoretical subjects such as syntax and pragmatics and the practical use of the linguistic knowledge to start teaching. On the other hand, the DAC might also raise student-teachers' awareness on the internal and external structures of the language in order to start doing research at the level of genre analysis, which helps them become critical users of the language by utilizing DA tools. However, the importance of this chapter lies in claiming that DA in IELTE programmes can provide student-teachers with the theoretical and practical skills (competencies) for identifying, analysing and doing social action using the language they will teach when becoming practising English teachers in and outside the classroom.

DAC aims to take student-teachers in a journey along the different views that linguists have taken on DA since it became a recognized branch of linguistics. However, the emphasis of the course is to expose students, future English teachers, to social approaches for doing DA such as CDA, SFL and multimodality. Traditionally, English teachers have not been empowered to analyse the construction and use of the target language, instead, they have been asked to reproduce it. Therefore, a workshop format for the course allows student-teachers to experience doing DA on authentic texts that might make them aware of the social reality surrounding them as citizens and teachers.

As the original approach of the syllabus was traditional and the DAC was given as theoretical knowledge transmitted by the teacher, a task-based syllabus was designed to give the course an updating shift. TBL is, according to Nunan (2004: 1), 'based on content selection with an emphasis on learning to communicate through interaction where students could focus not only on the language but also on the learning process'. Diaz-Maggioli and Painter-Farrel (2016: 424) define TBL as an 'approach to language education in which topics of relevance to students are selected in order to give students opportunities to engage in meaning-focused communication'. More specifically, Ellis (2003: 16) has defined a pedagogical task as a 'workplan that requires learners to process language pragmatically'. In this way, the texts (authentic materials) for the course were selected in order to do DA using the different approaches seen during the course and to enhance communication and reflection from student-teachers by experiencing doing DA.

Therefore, the DAC states as its general objective:

> By the end of the course, the student will be able to unite the aspects of linguistics, culture and academic skills that conform the necessary knowledge to teach English. The integration of these areas of knowledge will facilitate the use of analysis instruments that will enhance the evaluation of Discourse Analysis proposals in the field of ELT. (IELTE/LEI programme 2009)

The specific objectives of the course are:

1. to identify the principal theories and models that explain the relationship between language and culture;
2. to identify and define key concepts on discourse and text;
3. to classify and describe the functions of the text;
4. to analyse and explain the meaning of texts in English and Spanish;
5. to organize the probable elements of texts that allow their classification as discursive genres;
6. to apply this knowledge to evaluate models and materials that facilitate learning and the development of communicative skills.

The course considered sixty-four hours of instruction in the classroom divided into two sessions of two hours each per week. Recognizing that new technologies play a main role in transforming teaching and learning, a class in Edmodo was opened. The platform also provided a virtual common space for communication and interaction between participants and facilitator as well as the place for submission of tasks and homework. The platform also allowed the provision and sharing of materials. The course lasted for sixteen weeks and a research project in DA was assigned as the final work. The evaluation of the course was based on four task submissions, participation in class and a final project. The provision of feedback was highlighted as part of the formative and summative evaluation.

Implementation and adaptation of the course

Considering what Halliday (1985, 1993), Fairclough (2003, 2010) and Van Dijk (2008) have contributed to the field of DA, Paltridge (2012) has claimed for DA to be considered in different dimensions: a textually oriented DA and a socially oriented DA. These two dimensions provide a holistic view when language is explored through DA. Given the previous perspectives, when planning before the beginning of the course by analysing the DA syllabus, we could realize that the programme did not allow the current social action orientation as part of DA suggested by the authors mentioned.

The mismatch between the existing DAC syllabus and the current demands of DA could be explained by the date when the last revision to the program was made, which took place in 2009. Evidently, the study of language and discourse has broadly changed since the latest modifications of the programme. Bhatia, Flowerdew and Jones (2007: 1) mention that social sciences have undergone through a *discursive turn* focusing their attention on the importance of language and the idea that language can be analysed at different levels and from different perspectives.

After the analytical views on DA from last century were regarded as not sufficient to understand how language actually functions, Halliday (1985, 1993) and Martin and Rose (2003) have highlighted the fact that language intertwines multiple layers of structure and functions so that proper communication can be achieved. These authors state that language functions can be analysed through three broad functions: (a) the interpersonal function by enacting social relations between speakers, (b) the ideational function by construing experience and (c) the textual function by presenting meaningful discourse in context. Therefore, language from this perspective is seen as a system of functions that work together to convey the intended meaning and which can be traced in texts by doing DA.

This idea has influenced the practice of DA in a relevant way. Moreover, the emergence of different social approaches on the analysis of language has addressed not only the study of discourse form but also the social and cultural functions of discourse use. More specifically on the practice of the analysis of language in a community, Kaplan-Weinger and Ullman (2015) claim that when analysing the way a community uses language, three levels can be identified and then patterns, practices and social projects emerge. In words of these authors, DA might be done in the following levels:

1. micro-level analysis, which considers the patterns of grammar or intonation or stress;
2. mid-level analysis, which looks at the content of what people say and do. This kind of analysis focuses on meaning;
3. macro-level analysis, which explores the social process that connect data with context.

A core concept to update the DA syllabus was the study of language from the perspective of social practice in which interactions and collaboration would allow teacher-students to make connections among different contexts, situations and the actual use of language from practical activities were. After having established the perspectives and models that would guide the adaptation of the course, six models of DA were chosen to be taught and experienced during the DAC. The course was then organized around the six models or perspectives on DA as Table 8.1 shows only for the purpose of this particular course taking into account a chronological and situational DA development.

Table 8.1 shows the way the course was organized. Each unit was designed for two weeks of classes (four classes). In the first two classes, the theory was seen and the two last classes were for doing the tasks, which is the workshop approach for the course as learners are encouraged to carry out DA tasks following the theory presented, some of the activities designed for the workshop are mentioned later in this chapter. As Table 8.1 shows, the main authors of each DA approach were included; however, the list might be adapted to a different course according to the level of proficiency of the students or their particular interests. Authentic readings, such as original scientific articles from the authors included in each approach, are uploaded to the Edmodo platform so that students could have access to them. During the workshop sessions, authentic texts were used for the analysis according to the perspective of each unit. Table 8.1 also shows the kind of texts and materials used for analysis in each one of the approaches; these texts might vary, too, according to the students' level of proficiency and interests.

Table 8.1 Six DA Approaches

Unit	Discourse Analysis Model	Authors	Materials
1	Ethnography of Communication	Gumperz and Hymes (1986)	Videos Images, pictures and photos
2	Genre Analysis	Bazerman (1994, 2004) Bathia (2004) Hyland (2008)	Scientific articles Theses in the area Short stories Biographies
3	Conversational Analysis	Drew (2005) Schegloff (2007)	Videos of interactions interviews Students' own recordings
4	Critical Discourse Analysis	Fairclough (2003, 2010) Van Dijk (1993, 1998)	Songs Tweets Ads Newspapers Biographies
5	Systemic Functional Linguistics	Halliday (1993) Halliday and Hassan (1985) Martin and Rose (2003) Ghio and Fernández (2005) Ignatieva (2011) Ignatieva and Rodríguez Vergara (2016)	Scientific articles Short stories Biographies Theses
6	Multimodality	Kristeva (1986) Kress and Van Leeuwen (1996, 2001)	Posters Commercials Videos Cartoons Images, pictures and photos

The workshop

A successful approach to teaching and doing DA should involve activities and exercises that address meaningful tasks – that is doing something with the data. In order to make the activities and exercises meaningful for the student-teachers, the course included a two-week period of practice that is referred in this chapter as the workshop, one of the elements that made the course significant and more updated. These tasks provided student-teachers with the knowledge and tools that led them to participate and immerse themselves in analysis processes in order to make them aware of the linguistic aspects of their base knowledge as language teachers. The tasks had the intention of integrating and matching the linguistic knowledge with the capacities they must exercise when they become practising English teachers. Among the capacities in which the DAC could empower student-teachers were the identification and the analysis of discourses in the classroom or in selecting teaching resources critically as Tomlinson (2013) claims.

The different approaches and activities encouraged the development of linguistic exploration, metacognitive and critical awareness, and skills, as well as the enhancement of social debate among student-teachers. The fact that ICT elements were integrated in the course facilitated and enriched teaching and learning by making the processes in the classroom more dynamic and attractive. At the same time, the workshop presented the student-teachers with a diversity of resources available for their own analysis and teaching in the future, stimulating their reasoning skills.

The particular objectives of the workshop were:

1. to provide learners with essential theoretical concepts and tools for the analysis of texts;
2. to consider the analysis of written, oral and semiotic texts as the basis for social action.

Therefore, a series of activities or tasks were designed to allow student-teachers to have the experience of doing DA first, in the classroom and then, on their own, for their final project. The following are the few examples of activities implemented during the workshop sessions of the course:

1. Political speeches were used to identify moves according to the genre theory. The students chose a speech, either the video or the podcast; made the transcription; and analysed the text. The student-teachers accomplished the task in teams and presented their results to the class.
2. Newspapers' headlines were used to do CDA, marked for Unit 3. Student-teachers worked in teams choosing a piece of news that was interesting for them and identified the techniques that the newspaper authors used to appeal to public attention.
3. Commercials and ads from different years and decades were used to do multimodal DA. In this way, student-teachers could identify the semiotic elements that represented the historical context of the material. They worked in teams for the analysis and then presented their results to the whole class.

The previous examples show the kind of tasks that were developed throughout the course. It must be mentioned that the student-teachers reported that they had enjoyed the process, and during the course, they showed initiative and willingness to participate, which is not the norm in the courses given in the IELTE programme. An important aspect that must be highlighted is that most of the materials were taken from the Internet and the student-teachers themselves selected them. The task-based modality of the workshop allowed the student-teachers to take hands-on DA approach.

At the same time, the exposure of student-teachers to authentic texts taken from real and current contexts improved their language skills. One of the usual complaints from the student-teachers is that they can understand standard or classroom English, but when they face the language used by native speakers, it is difficult for them to understand them due to the dialect in which the text is either written or spoken. Finally, these student-teachers said that after the DAC, they could understand authentic texts such as newspapers or scientific articles from the ELT field more easily.

Students' voices

The DAC being the last of the subjects that the student-teachers in the IELTE programme take in the area of linguistics, they are supposed to have accomplished an average proficiency of B1 according to the CEFR. In our experience, this level of proficiency allowed the class to be completely delivered in English, which becomes the target and the means of instruction in this IELTE programme, as Bale (2016) has proposed. Moreover, this level of proficiency also allowed student-teachers to handle the readings and audiovisual material in English. At the end of the course, the student-teachers were asked to reflect on what they had learnt during the course. Their words showed that most of them could realize of the relevance that DA has in the processes of learning and teaching EFL in Mexico.

Some of the comments they included in the last part of their final projects were as follows:

> Now, with the knowledge of these methods, I am able to notice not only what is said, but also beyond, making distinctions of opinions, comments and to know about what is implied in texts.
>
> The Discourse Analysis course was very useful for me because I learnt different things about how people use and understand language according to

their contexts, intentions and necessities. I also learnt how to analyze different kinds of texts and what type of elements should be taken into account to do a successful analysis such as verbs, nouns or adjectives.

I did not know the advantages we can get if we knew how to analyze texts. It can save us from uncomfortable situations or misunderstandings. Moreover, we can learn how to behave so as not to be misunderstood or to respect people when we have to take turns, for example.

From the final student-teachers' reflections, it was clear that awareness on DA was reached to some extent. These student-teachers could relate the theories of language acquisition and the study of linguistics to the practical and current use of language in different contexts. DA is about relating discourse, text and context, and the awareness that by analysing texts, student-teachers may understand how language shapes society and how society is shaped by language.

Conclusions

This chapter has presented the way the study of DA is approached at an IELTE programme in Mexico. Prior to the course, the programme was analysed and an updated perspective was taken as findings and advances have emerged in the area. The study of DA can provide student-teachers with deeper linguistic knowledge and methodological insights. This type of provision allows them to experience how DA is done from different dimensions and what it might imply in terms of social action and interaction in their personal and professional lives.

Student-teachers became aware of cultural and social bias and manifestations with the variety of texts used: newspapers, magazines, videos and podcasts, interviews, short stories and other authentic texts that lead students to perform meaningful DA. The results and comments obtained during and after the DAC course were encouraging since the student-teachers had the opportunity to explore and appreciate how the theoretical concepts studied could be transferred to their everyday life too.

Finally, this kind of approach to teaching DA might provide student-teachers with the means to expand their schematic and functional awareness on the target language as it may lead them to better understanding, participation and questioning the processes and assumptions involved in the interaction between people and texts. By identifying and exploring patterns in texts, student-teachers could internalize their knowledge on language; its actual use and how the linguistic choices of the users of a language can shape the discourse of a society with all its implications such as motivations, values and cultural messages.

Questions for change

Many countries around the world, especially in Latin America and beyond, are living critical situations regarding economy, violence or social issues. DA might provide specific tools to explore the phenomena from the perspective of language. Given the current situation of your country, answer the following questions in order to explore how language might influence current critical issues going on in different countries.

1. What role does language play in the construction of the reality you live in?
2. What kinds of texts have an impact on the ideology of your surroundings?
3. What kinds of texts are supported and reproduced by higher education institutions in your country?
4. What kinds of texts are supported and reproduced by the media in your country?
5. How would DA be helpful in identifying, exploring and analysing how language is used and reproduced by citizens in your country to perpetuate or overcome social situations in your country?

9

Breaking the Ice with Phonetics and Phonology

Bettiana A. Blázquez, Gonzalo E. Espinosa and Leopoldo O. Labastía

Introduction

Teaching pronunciation in language courses has traditionally followed two approaches: the intuitive-imitative approach and the analytic-linguistic approach. The former consists in reproducing the target language on the basis of a good model without any explicit instruction. The latter proposes reflection on pronunciation features through such tools as graphic representations like the phonetic alphabet, articulatory descriptions and contrastive information. It is meant to complement the former as analysis follows imitation. The role of pronunciation teaching has varied through time in the light of the development of different methods following either of these approaches. While the grammar-translation, reading-based and cognitive methods tended to deemphasize or even ignore the importance of pronunciation, the direct method, audiolingual method and naturalistic approaches paid more attention to pronunciation features. The communicative approach has brought renewed interest in pronunciation as an important tool for communication. In the light of this new perspective, work on pronunciation has started to combine different techniques which include not only imitation but also analysis to develop awareness (Celce-Murcia, Brinton, & Goodwin 2010).

In an attempt to combine these two approaches, in this chapter we focus on the teaching of the first module of phonetics and phonology at the ELTE programme at UNCO, Argentina. In the first section of this chapter, we offer an overview of the teaching of pronunciation in non-English-speaking countries and specifically in our country. In the next, we concentrate on the area of phonetics and phonology in the context of our institution, in which students are educated to become teachers. Finally, we describe the aims, principles, contents, activities and assessment of the first stage of teaching in this area. The chapter concludes with reflections on drawbacks and challenges of teaching pronunciation at an introductory level in ELTE that might serve as a springboard for other educators to reflect upon and pursue research into.

Teaching phonetics and phonology in Argentina

In ELTE programmes in non-English-speaking countries, the goal is to enable future teachers to reach a high level of intelligibility of the English language so that they can in turn help their future learners to communicate successfully. This notion involves both being understood by different speakers and understanding a variety of native and non-native speakers of English (Crystal 2012a; Taylor 1991). As Derwing and Munro (2015) point out, communication entails not only intelligibility, the extent to which listeners can understand the speaker's intended message and be understood by them, but also comprehensibility, the ease or difficulty a listener experiences in understanding an utterance.

Choosing a model of pronunciation is an essential requirement to provide learners with a reference system. The most common standard accents are General American and Southern British English, as they are well documented and described in great detail. In fact, these varieties have been researched by a large number of phoneticians and phonologists and have been applied to the design of numerous textbooks and dictionaries (Rogerson-Revell 2011). At present, the emphasis has shifted from aiming at a native-like pronunciation to communicating effectively in terms of the learners' goals. Authors like Jenkins (2000) and Walker (2010) have offered a new perspective on the role of English by suggesting that this language is spoken internationally by a far larger number of non-native speakers and, accordingly, the teaching goals and the chosen model should become more flexible.

In Argentina, a country where English is not spoken outside educational settings, ELTE and translator programmes in higher education have traditionally paid special attention to phonetics and phonology. With the aim that future teachers and translators should acquire an intelligible pronunciation, these programmes have specific modules for the development of both theoretical knowledge and practical skills of segmentals (i.e. vowels and consonants) and suprasegmentals (i.e. rhythm, stress and intonation). In the past, individual sounds were dealt with first, whereas suprasegmental features were addressed in more advanced stages in the programme. Undergraduate students were expected to improve their pronunciation to fit a standard model. Accordingly, having a good command of English pronunciation was, and still is, an important prerequisite to graduating.

Argentinian ELTE and translator institutions have traditionally favoured RP as a model (Cruttenden 2014). This accent was adopted by British speakers as the standard pronunciation of the ruling class and, for many years, it was the variety chosen by the BBC as a prestige accent. Social changes in the late twentieth century have led to stigmatization of this accent and the adoption of a broader standard known as General British (Carley, Mees, & Collins 2018; Lindsey 2017). In the wake of these changes, Argentinian English phonetics teachers in ELTE programmes are progressively adopting a more flexible attitude to matters of pronunciation. Core pronunciation features in proposals of ELF and EIL have also exerted influence on this shift in emphasis (Jenkins 2000; Seidlhofer 2011; Walker 2010).

Becoming a teacher of English at UNCO

In the ELTE programme at UNCO, Year 1 contains a macro module called *Introduction to the English Language*, which is divided into three modules: *language* (sixteen hours a week), *grammar* (two hours) and *diction* (two hours). This latter module is the focus of our chapter.

Students who join this programme at UNCO come from different locations in northern Patagonia. Before joining the programmes, some have reached a B2 level in terms of the CEFR. Others have barely reached a B1 or even a lower level of language proficiency. Some of these students have also attended English courses at secondary schools and private institutes, where phonetics and phonology is not generally explicitly taught, so they have no systematic knowledge of this aspect, and whatever degree of skill they have developed in this respect is intuitive. The policy at UNCO is that all students should be able to enrol in undergraduate programmes without an entrance examination, which means welcoming even those who do not have any knowledge of English. Teaching pronunciation skills to such large mixed-ability groups proves to be a daunting task, especially when many of the students are learning the basics of the language and pronunciation at the same time.

The pronunciation model we have chosen as a guideline is Southern British English. Our selection of this standard pronunciation is based on the fact that this accent is often found in the media, the Internet and in many textbooks for the teaching of English as a foreign or second language (L2). It is regarded as a neutral variety, which is recommended for learners of English as an L2 (Upton 2015). We consider that this reference model meets the requirements necessary for learners to be able to develop intelligible and comprehensible language. Even though we favour this particular variety, we are still flexible when accepting features of other types of accents in our student-teachers' oral production, like a rhotic pronunciation in words containing the letter *r*, typical of General American English and other varieties.

By the time they graduate, student-teachers are expected to have attained a high-proficiency level at perception and production. As listeners, they should be able to understand the main varieties of English. In relation to production, they should be accurate and fluent speakers in a wide variety of registers. The ultimate goal is that future teachers should not only be highly intelligible users but also have professional and declarative knowledge about the English language. In the light of this expected outcome, our five-year ELTE programme includes five phonetics and phonology modules. In a growing level of complexity, these modules are meant to cover all the aspects of English pronunciation, that is, segmentals, suprasegmentals and features of connected speech (Collins & Mees 2013). Even though each module focuses on some specific aspects of English pronunciation, previous contents are constantly recycled and further developed as student-teachers advance in the programme.

Breaking the ice with *diction*

This section attempts to describe the specific features of the diction module in terms of what is taught and the rationale underlying it. First, the aims and guiding principles of the module are outlined. Then the section focuses on the contents, bibliography and activities. Finally, assessment of student-teachers' pronunciation is described.

Aims

The diction module is aimed at helping future teachers to develop their communicative competence both as listeners and speakers. As listeners, they are expected to learn to perceive phonetic and phonological features in the English language in terms of their communicative potential. As speakers, they are supposed to learn how to produce some of these features, especially those which have a bearing on communication.

In order to develop communicative competence, the module seeks to foster intelligibility and comprehensibility in student-teachers. To become intelligible users of the language, future teachers are taught those features of their speech that could interfere with communication. They develop their ability to perceive features of pronunciation so as to lessen the amount of effort in understanding a message. Another aim in the module is to help student-teachers to develop self-monitoring and self-evaluating strategies. These strategies enable them to become aware of the accuracy and fluency of their production, noticing errors and learning from them, and assessing their progress (Oxford 2011, 2016).

The activities in diction are also designed to guide teachers-to-be on establishing connections between ordinary spelling and sounds. As there is not a one-to-one correspondence between letters and pronunciation, these connections are expected to help student-teachers to become familiar with English pronunciation in a systematic way, especially because Spanish, their mother tongue, exhibits a clearer match between letters and sounds. Representing pronunciation in graphic form by means of the International Phonetic Alphabet (IPA) is meant to raise awareness of different pronunciation features, which may be obscured in written form. Another main goal in teaching the IPA is to promote autonomy in mastering pronunciation. Student-teachers are thus encouraged to learn the conventions of the English pronunciation dictionary and use it effectively so that they can develop a proactive attitude towards finding out how words are pronounced by themselves, and not depend on the teacher or a native speaker.

All in all, the diction module attempts to contribute to the development of student-teachers' knowledge of and about the language and their skill in using it effectively. This dual perspective builds their confidence and competence as non-native speakers and future teachers, which is based not only on an effective use of the language but also on technical knowledge and expertise of how it works.

Guiding principles

Oral communication implies the development of both listening and speaking skills. Comprehension involves two types of processes: top-down and bottom-up. In the former, listeners resort to their knowledge of the world, speaker and context to make sense of the intended message. In the latter, they use their knowledge of discrete units of language (segments and syllables) to decode the message. In fact, listeners employ both types of approaches to utterance comprehension (Wilson 2008). In our diction module we follow an eclectic approach that combines both types of processing. We pay attention to segmentation of speech into tone units, rhythm and intonation; at the same time, we focus on individual vowels and consonants as well as syllable structure. Our perspective is never dissociated from context and pragmatic meaning as no teaching points are taught in isolation.

The module emphasizes perception over production. The purpose is to sensitize future teachers to contrastive categories and some allophonic variants. The idea is to develop student-teachers' awareness by explicitly drawing their attention to phonological form so as to lay the foundations for further work on segmentals and suprasegmentals as they advance in the programme. We encourage an inductive approach where teachers-to-be hypothesize about how language functions and discover underlying regularities.

Considering that both teachers and student-teachers are native speakers of Argentinean Spanish, we take into account the influence of our mother tongue on the target language. In the light of this, we reflect on student-teachers' difficulties, set priorities and take methodological decisions to deal with them. For example, the Spanish vowel system consists of five sounds, two high vowels (/i, u/), two mid vowels (/e, o/), and one low central vowel (/a/) (Hualde 2014), whereas English has twelve pure vowels. Consequently, our student-teachers need to expand their phonological categories. For instance, in the face of English /æ, ʌ, ɑː/, Spanish learners of English might process them as just one category as the Spanish vowel system includes just one open vowel, that is /a/ (Estebas-Vilaplana 2009). In this process, sound discrimination is an essential phase both intra- and interlinguistically. Accordingly, our activities are designed so as to enable future teachers to perceive and eventually produce new sound contrasts. Likewise, at a suprasegmental level, Spanish speakers of English are encouraged to notice rhythmic differences between the two languages. As Spanish tends to give equal weight to all syllables, whereas English tends to weaken unstressed syllables, it is important for L2 speakers to perceive this characteristic of English rhythm and later be able to reproduce it. In relation to syllable structure, Spanish exhibits a rather simple structure in comparison with English. Spanish typically allows for two elements in onset position and one element in coda position, while English clusters up to three consonants in onset position and four elements in the coda of the syllable. This difference entails another difficulty for our student-teachers, because they tend to simplify complex syllables to fit the Spanish syllabic template. Therefore, mispronouncing segments like /æ, ʌ, ɑː/, not weakening unstressed syllables or producing Spanish-like syllables might have a negative impact on intelligibility and comprehensibility.

As to the limited oral production we try to develop, another guiding principle in the diction module is that we attempt to set the groundwork for both accuracy and fluency. An accurate speaker is one who uses the language in a precise manner, without deviations from the features of the target language which interfere with intelligibility. Building fluency, at the same time, is necessary for speakers to convey their message efficiently by organizing their speech in linked meaningful chunks, including phonological features of connected speech, without excessive hesitation or slowness (Derwing 2017). We adopt a balanced view on accuracy and fluency because both sets of abilities are necessary for intelligibility and comprehensibility to take place.

Although we focus on phonetic and phonological form, we do not teach theory overtly in class. We only resort to some basic theoretical concepts that are reflected in practical activities, but phonetic and phonological theory is discussed in depth in the subsequent modules in the programme. In diction, student-teachers only get the necessary and sufficient knowledge about English pronunciation to guarantee awareness and promote acquisition. This knowledge encompasses articulatory aspects and rules governing the production of weak forms, plurals and past forms, among others.

Contents and bibliography

In the diction module, we pave the way for the work to be done in the next module in the programme, English Phonetics and Phonology 1. Student-teachers learn to recognize vowel and consonant contrasts, and some allophonic variants like aspiration in voiceless plosives. They work on the rules for the pronunciation of regular plurals, third person singular verbs in the simple present, and past and past participle forms. At a suprasegmental level, they become acquainted with segmentation of speech, rhythmic patterns, the nucleus in the tone unit and some basic intonation. They also learn to recognize strong and weak forms, and become familiar with the main rules governing their use, as well as features of connected speech such as linking *r* and liaison (i.e. the connection between word-final consonants and word-initial vowels). Rhythm forms the basis of the pronunciation teaching process, because it is the starting point in our module and all the other pronunciation features are derived from it.

Student-teachers progressively display their perception of segmentals and suprasegmentals through phonetic transcription with the aid of a pronunciation dictionary. We advise future teachers to consult the latest edition of the *Longman Pronunciation Dictionary* (Wells 2008). As far as production is concerned, student-teachers are encouraged to gradually incorporate the different features of English pronunciation, a process which will continue to take place in the following phonetics and phonology modules.

To cover the contents of diction, teachers-to-be use a booklet designed by the phonology team (Arana, Blázquez, Labastía, & Lagos 2017). This booklet contains both written and oral activities based on materials that the teachers have produced specifically for the module and that require the learners' active participation, as they are expected to complete a variety of exercises and infer pronunciation rules. Some texts are taken from language coursebooks so as to integrate diction with the language modules. Considering the potential of using authentic materials, as shown by Ghirardotto, Canavosio and Giménez (2013), the booklet progressively incorporates authentic texts from different sources (advertisements, news, shorts and scenes taken from films).

As self-study and practice, student-teachers are expected to resort to *Tree or Three? An elementary pronunciation course* (Baker 2006). In class, a useful teaching aid is a poster with the IPA symbols. This resource is intended to help future teachers to associate sound symbols with representative words they can remember.

Activities

Throughout the year, student-teachers engage in individual, pair, group and whole-class activities aimed at enhancing the learning experience. Considering that the work in class is limited to two hours a week, the diction module requires doing an array of home activities so as to consolidate the learning process.

Acquiring the English sound system implies dealing with new sounds for Spanish learners of English. These new sounds correspond to new manners and places of articulation. This is why student-teachers are first encouraged to perform proprioceptive activities so that they become aware of how the English sounds – as well as the Spanish ones – are produced. In these activities, future teachers are guided into feeling the position and movement of articulators in the production of vowels and consonants. The benefit of understanding how these sounds are produced in English and contrasting their production with Spanish sounds is twofold. In most cases student-teachers correct their pronunciation and become more accurate speakers and better listeners and, additionally, they acquire technical knowledge about the language, which they can later use in their teaching practice.

Following a communicative approach, both the presentation of new segmental and suprasegmental content and activities related to dictations and transcriptions are fully contextualized. First, student-teachers are expected to focus on meaning and speaker's purpose and attitude by means of comprehension questions, true-false tasks or whole-class discussions. These activities promote the activation of schemata and serve as scaffolding for language acquisition. This approach has proved to be successful as reported by Zabala (2015) in relation to phonemic dictation. Figure 9.1 shows typical meaning-oriented activities that lead onto the subsequent pronunciation phase. This set of five activities is based on a campaign clip by Greenpeace[1] (Greenpeace International 2018) which addresses the issue of deforestation and the extinction of species. The first two activities in Figure 9.1 invite student-teachers to draw inferences from the pictures. In the first activity, they predict the setting, purpose, participants and genre of the audiovisual material in a whole-class discussion. In the second, they anticipate content by deciding whether some statements are likely to be true or false, either individually or in pairs. In Activity 3, they watch the clip for the first time to confirm their hypotheses.

As one of the main goals in the first level of phonetics and phonology is to help student-teachers to become familiar with the IPA, there are two other main activities that are aimed at consolidating the perception – and eventually production – of English pronunciation. These activities encompass dictations and transcriptions, in which student-teachers put into practice the contents dealt with in class (Arana, Blázquez, Lagos, & Valls 2016) and display their skills at using the pronunciation dictionary. Key sounds are removed from the phonetic transcription and gaps are left in line with the cloze test format. In dictations, the corresponding blanks are completed by student-teachers when listening to the teacher or audio(visual) material, as shown in Activity 4 in Figure 9.2.

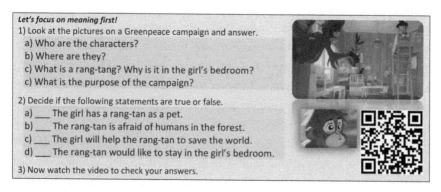

Figure 9.1 Meaning-oriented activities (Images and link courtesy of Greenpeace)

Now let's focus on pronunciation!

4) Watch the clip and complete the transcription, following the instructions in a), b) and c) below. The first line has been done for you.

a) First fill in the gaps with the following missing plosive consonants and long vowels.

b) Then add aspiration and liaison where necessary.

c) Finally, draw the circles to show the rhythmic pattern of the tone units.

There's a rang-tan in my bedroom and I don't know what to do.
/ðəz‿ə ˈræŋ-tæŋ‿ɪn maɪ ˈbedruːm / ən‿aɪ dəʊnt nəʊ wɒt tə duː /
/ • • ○ ○ • • ● ○ / • • ○ ○ ○ • ● /

She plays with all my teddies / and keeps borrowing my shoe.
/ʃi __leɪz wɪð __l maɪ ˈ__ediz / ən ___ps ˈ__ɒrəʊɪŋ maɪ ʃ__/
/.../

She destroys all of my house plants /and she keeps on shouting 'oo'.
/ʃi diˈs__rɔɪz __l əv maɪ haʊs __l__nts / ən ʃi ___ps ɒn ˈʃaʊtɪŋ __/
/...................................../...................................../

She throws away my chocolate /and she howls at my shampoo.
/ʃi θrəʊz əˈweɪ maɪ ˈtʃɒklət / ən ʃi haʊlz ət maɪ ʃæm'___/
/...................................../...................................../

Let's keep on practising at home!

5) Rehearse the following extract from the girl's reply. Imitate the speaker's sounds, rhythm and intonation. Record your own version and upload it on the Moodle platform.

/əʊ ˈræŋ-tæŋ‿ɪn maɪ ˈbedruːm /naʊ aɪ du: nəʊ wɒt tə du: /aɪl faɪt tə seɪv jɔ: həʊm / ən‿aɪl stɒp
/ ○ ○ ○ • • ● ○ / ○ • ● ○ ○ • ○ / • ○ • ○ • ● / • • ○
ju ˈfiːlɪŋ bluː/aɪl ʃeə jɔ: ˈstɔːri fɔːr‿ən waɪd/ səʊ ˈʌðəz kən faɪt tʰu: / əʊ ˈræŋ-tæŋ‿ɪn maɪ ˈbedruːm /
• ○ • ● / • ○ • ● / • ○ • ○ • ○/○ ○ ○ • • ● ○/
/aɪ swear‿ɒn ðə stɑːz / ðə ˈfjuːtʃəz nɒt jet ˈrɪtən / bət‿aɪl meɪk ʃɔ: / ɪt‿ɪz‿ˈəʊəz /
/ • ○ • • ● / • ○ • ○○ • • / • • ○ ● / • • ● •/

Figure 9.2 Pronunciation-oriented activities (Images courtesy of Greenpeace)

When it comes to transcriptions, they are asked to provide the correct sound symbols on the basis of the text in ordinary spelling. Throughout the module, these gapped dictations and transcriptions become continuously more complex in the sense that student-teachers start filling the gaps with some single sounds, but, eventually, they are faced with more and more gaps until they make use of the IPA in full simple phrases.

The pronunciation dictionary is a useful source for working with transcriptions and learning how to pronounce words. The underlying idea of using a pronunciation dictionary is to help student-teachers to become familiar with this significant tool not only for the rest of the teaching programme but also for their future careers as English teachers. In other words, after future teachers get their feet wet with the dictionary, autonomy in how to find out the pronunciation of words (in isolation and in context) is gradually exercised and gained.

Apart from the segmental level, dictations and transcriptions include the representation of the rhythmic aspects of pronunciation. On the basis of the perception of strong and weak syllables, student-teachers learn to identify and represent syllables by means of big and small circles. They first recognize the rhythmic patterns of individual simple words. Later, they are exposed to compound words and learn to perceive and represent primary stress and distinguish it from the secondary one. This step provides the foundation for the idea of the nucleus in the tone unit, as they are finally asked to perceive and represent the rhythm in whole phrases and segmentation in tone units.

The integration of rhythm and other pronunciation features is worked on throughout the module. Aspiration is a key feature, which helps to distinguish voiceless plosives from voiced plosives at both the perception and production levels, and is taught early in the module. Another important aspect which has a bearing on understanding connected speech is that of liaison, especially in decoding word boundaries. Activities 4 and 5 in Figure 9.2 show the association between strong syllables, strong forms and aspiration in voiceless plosives, on the one hand, and weak syllables, weak forms and lack of aspiration in these plosives, on the other. Also, recognition and production of word-final consonants in relation to initial vowels (i.e. liaison) are included in the activities. In Activity 4, the teacher plays the video with pauses after each tone unit and student-teachers are invited to fill in the gaps with the missing sounds. As they listen to the clip again, student-teachers add aspiration of voiceless plosives and liaison. Finally, as they listen to the campaign for the third time, they show rhythm.

Other important activities in the diction module are those meant to promote oral production. Student-teachers are asked to listen to and imitate a stretch of spoken language. After rehearsing at home, they record their own production and upload the sound file on the university Moodle platform for teachers to provide feedback about their performance. The first recordings are based on materials designed for pedagogical purposes, whereas at a later stage in the year future teachers work on authentic materials, such as Activity 5 in Figure 9.2. Another related activity involves creating original short films, in which student-teachers prepare a script of their own, rehearse it considering the features dealt with in class and finally videotape it. These films are jointly supervised by the tutors of the language and diction modules. To summarize, the ultimate goal of the different activities proposed in the diction module is to provide the bases for future non-native teachers of English to develop intelligibility and comprehensibility, as they gain confidence in the use of the language.

Assessment

In the diction module we assess both our students' learning process as well as the result of that process on the basis of their oral and written productions. Testing tools are assignments and term exams which consist of dictations, transcriptions and recordings both in class and at home. These reflect the different teaching points that have been discussed. Once the assignments have been corrected, we provide in-class feedback on common errors in their productions. As mentioned in Grasso (2017), we consider error analysis as an important resource to consolidate pronunciation learning. In fact, every assessment instance is a learning opportunity (Giménez & Aguirre Sotelo 2015). We employ different strategies such as discovering errors in sample oral and written productions, correcting them, applying rules and finding the correct pronunciation in the dictionary. Errors are considered a positive and inherent aspect of the learning process. This view contributes to the creation of a comfortable atmosphere which lowers anxiety and promotes self-confidence. We encourage peer correction as a way of raising awareness and incrementally developing self-monitoring and self-evaluating strategies. Student-teachers' spontaneous oral production is assessed in the language modules.

Final remarks

The diction module follows not only an intuitive-imitative approach to the acquisition of the target pronunciation but also an analytic-linguistic approach which provides scaffolding for the students' learning process and their future careers as teachers. At the same time, knowledge of pronunciation goes hand in hand with metalinguistic knowledge about phonetics and phonology, which contributes to the development of communicative competence in other areas such as grammar, semantics and pragmatics. We believe that this approach could be valid in any ELTE programme.

Despite the relative achievements of our teaching goals, there are some inherent problems which somehow we try to overcome and which could be of relevance in other educational settings. As described above, teaching the fundamentals of English pronunciation to large mixed-ability groups is a challenging task. To ensure that all student-teachers have access to explanations, at the beginning of the module we use Spanish and English and, progressively, lessons are taught only in English. Another difficulty that we cope with is student-teachers' affect. Learning a new sound system may be experienced as an intimidating task and very often learners are unwilling to participate as they are afraid of being judged. In the face of this, we try to create a non-threatening atmosphere where students' errors are seen as a chance to progress. Boosting their self-esteem through the employment of different types of learning strategies – such as encouraging risk-taking and self-monitoring – should be viewed as essential in all contexts.

In the diction module, we prioritize the acquisition of rhythm and the sound system, especially in terms of perception, considering the pronunciation features of our student-teachers' mother tongue. This criterion could be useful for those ELTE contexts in which future teachers' mother tongue shares similar features with Spanish, but might not be applicable to languages from other typological families.

As mentioned before, with such little exposure and practice, we do not expect student-teachers to have mastered all of the phonetic and phonological aspects dealt with in class by the end of the academic year. In fact, our student-teachers eventually succeed in recognizing and representing strong and weak syllables, all vowels and consonants, and features like liaison and aspiration. Yet, they are able to apply some of these features in their production with a reasonable degree of success. Focusing on perception could be an effective strategy when it comes to other ELTE contexts in similar conditions as regards students' initial proficiency and instruction time. All in all, by laying the foundations of English pronunciation in the diction module, we just chip the tip of the phonetic and phonological iceberg.

Questions for change

1. What is the relevance of vowel reduction and its connection to rhythm?
2. What are the effects of teaching segments first or suprasegmentals first?
3. How applicable is the Lingua Franca Core (Jenkins 2000; Walker 2010) in different ELTE contexts?
4. What pronunciation teaching techniques help to lower the affective filter?
5. How do factors such as motivation, personality traits, self-esteem and cultural identity affect the acquisition/learning of English pronunciation of student-teachers?
6. As regards the teaching of pronunciation, what are the (dis)advantages of non-native teachers of English as compared with native teachers of English?

Note

1   We would like to thank Greenpeace for allowing us to make use of this video clip. We are also grateful to our colleague Professor Valeria Arana for sharing this resource with us.

10

Developing Language, Academic and Professional Skills in a Teacher Education Course

Cristina Banfi

Introduction

Teachers of English require a high level of linguistic competence and metalinguistic awareness, cultural sensitivity, as well as a set of academic and professional skills pertinent to their work. Teacher preparation courses should also develop autonomy and reflection with a view to preparing future teachers for their development as independent teaching professionals.

Building on Banfi (2003), this chapter reviews the approach adopted within English Language IV, a capstone module of a teacher education course taught at several institutions in Buenos Aires, Argentina, over a twenty-year period. Within the general curricular guidelines provided for the course, the module has been designed to fulfil various objectives deemed pertinent for teachers-to-be. This chapter discusses the focus and rationale of the module. Student feedback was collected over the years and contributed to a number of changes and improvements. This chapter incorporates former student-teachers' feedback collected via an online survey administered in July 2018 on the following issues:

1. recollections of the module, for example differences from other modules, disconcertment experienced by students;
2. extent to which the aims the module reflected the needs of practising teachers;
3. perceptions regarding the kind of evaluation and feedback provision adopted.

The answers provided by students have been interspersed in the body of this chapter to illustrate student perceptions of the different aspects of the approach. Pseudonyms have been used throughout.

The context

English Language IV (henceforth ELIV) was taught by the author at first in 1998 and 1999 at the Universidad de Belgrano, a private university where students from the teacher's and translator's courses were integrated in the same class, and at the Instituto Nacional Superior del Profesorado Técnico of the Universidad Tecnológica Nacional, a state university where two groups of student-teachers were taught; and then, between 2009 and 2017, at the Instituto Superior de Profesorado, Dr Joaquín V. González, a state teacher education college, all in the City of Buenos Aires, Argentina. The student-teachers involved are post-secondary native speakers of Spanish who have extensively developed their English language skills. The entry-point of the programme involves a selective English language exam which can be considered B1–B2 level (although there is no formal alignment). Upon graduation, students can be said to have reached a C1–C2 level, although this is an estimate as no assessment is made using the CEFR or any other independent framework (e.g. ACTFL, Canadian Benchmarks). The certification obtained upon graduation enables individuals to take teaching positions within the Argentinian school system.

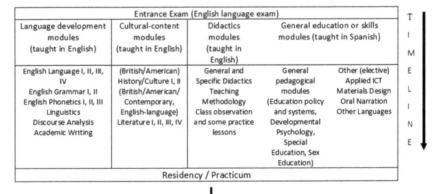

Entrance Exam (English language exam)					T
Language development modules (taught in English)	Cultural-content modules (taught in English)	Didactics modules (taught in English)	General education or skills modules (taught in Spanish)		I M
English Language I, II, III, IV English Grammar I, II English Phonetics I, II, III Linguistics Discourse Analysis Academic Writing	(British/American) History/Culture I, II (British/American/Contemporary, English-language) Literature I, II, III, IV	General and Specific Didactics Teaching Methodology Class observation and some practice lessons	General pedagogical modules (Education policy and systems, Developmental Psychology, Special Education, Sex Education)	Other (elective) Applied ICT Materials Design Oral Narration Other Languages	E L I N E
Residency / Practicum					

Qualified Teacher Status

Figure 10.1 Curricular structure of foreign/additional language teacher education programmes

Although certain variations and reforms have taken place over the years, the matrix on which these programmes are based is long standing (e.g. Banfi 2013; Blanco 1970) and follows the overall general structure presented in Figure 10.1.

The students taking ELIV are advanced learners in that they are seeking a greater level of competence in the language beyond the high level they have already achieved. According to Maley (2009: 3), these learners are self-motivated, independent and determined, and the tasks proposed for them have to be challenging in terms of self-investment and effort. These aspects have shaped the approach for the delivery of ELIV.

The module

Aims

ELIV is a yearly module of six 40-minute periods a week, that is a total of 192 periods or 128 hours. It is taken after the completion of three English language modules, which can have between 256 and 320 hours each. Given the resources devoted to it and its status as a capstone course, questions arise as to what the goals of the language modules should be, both in general and specific terms. It is widely assumed that teachers should know (enough) English to teach, that is to be able to use English in contexts and for purposes required in their profession. On the other hand, merely being a proficient speaker of general English, or a native speaker of the language, may not be sufficient (Medgyes 2017). In this sense ELIV aims fundamentally at integrating the contents covered and skills developed in previous modules providing the students with an opportunity to apply them to concrete tasks pertinent to a teacher's practice and requiring them to apply their language proficiency, use metalinguistic knowledge, and exercise professional and academic skills, while receiving feedback to improve their practical performance. The fact that students often have teaching experience is crucial to the approach as connections can be made throughout to students' real-life experience.

Students are expected to –

1. Develop writing and oracy skills of texts pertinent to teachers, for example essays, journal papers, textbooks, research reports, encyclopaedias and lectures. The skills are as follows:
   - selecting a topic and narrowing it down to a manageable scale;
   - organizing and supporting ideas with evidence;

- identifying, selecting and incorporating sources correctly;
- searching for and selecting appropriate visual aids and data to support points made;
- making adequate grammatical, lexical, punctuation choices considering register and topic; and
- developing awareness of linguistic variation (regional, social, (sub-) standard), stylistics and register, and making choices accordingly.

2. Develop pertinent attitudinal skills such as the following:
   - sticking to pre-agreed rules, for example time limit, presentation format and conventions (e.g. text types, conference submissions);
   - working collaboratively with peers.

3. exercise reflection, autonomy and creativity, for example:
   - reflecting on cultural traits of different communities making comparisons and identifying contrasts;
   - reflecting on the needs of students, on the characteristics of professional and academic development of teachers, on different teaching trends and realities;
   - developing the ability to monitor and self-correct and to provide feedback to peers;
   - developing autonomy as regards professional development.

4. Assess and design teaching materials.
5. Select the most appropriate technological and bibliographical resources needed to complete tasks.

Components

The key components of ELIV are the production of portfolios, non-fiction reading and analysis, debates, oral presentations, and essay writing. Each of these components has been discussed further in the chapter.

The production of portfolios within certain pre-set parameters include the following: (1) an individual portfolio on a lecturer-selected novel, (2) one group portfolio on a novel selected by the student-teachers and (3) one individual portfolio on a novel selected by the student-teachers. These portfolios are composed of ten out of thirteen possible portfolio components, that is author's biography, biographical card, novel review, reading group questions, abridgement of an extract, reading task, listening task (with student audio recording), loosely based teaching task, short story, further reading, culture capsules, supplementary material and language quotes.

Since the publication of my article on portfolios (Banfi 2003), a growing body of work that deals with the use of portfolios in language learning in different contexts has been published (e.g. Kömür & Çimen 2017; Martínez Lirola 2012) and to different ends such as promoting autonomous learning, reducing writing anxiety, or assessing language learning (Reardon 2017), assessing writing (Lam 2018), documenting personal and professional growth (Li & Tin 2013), teaching higher order thinking (Favarini & Atai 2015), exploring expectation and realization levels, or teaching in computer-mediated learning environments (Mastrogiacomi 2005) in higher education courses.

Given that students taking ELIV typically have no experience of working with portfolios, they are provided with a number of resources to aid them in this respect. Through Banfi (2003) they become familiar with the approach and the components expected in the production of the portfolios. The portfolio work is based on novels as trigger texts but students are expected to read and write other text types as portfolio components becoming familiar with the relevant conventions but also exploring different possible presentation formats (e.g. plain text, slides presentations, illustrated posters, Facebook pages). In particular, on the design of teaching tasks, the following materials are made available: Howard and Major (2004); Mukundan, Nimehchisalem and Hajimohammadi (2011); and McDonough, Shaw and Masuhara (2013).

Working with non-fiction is introduced with a discussion of the characteristics of different types of texts that students are already familiar with. Subsequently, a number of non-fiction pieces (e.g. essays, articles, papers) are analysed in more detail. Some articles from the *Economist* and *New Yorker* are used to introduce relevant current issues and support debates (see below). Articles by Crandall and Miller (2014) and Coleman (2014) are used to reflect on professional development issues and the process of journal article writing and publishing, respectively. Finally, Bryson (2003) is discussed as an example of popular science writing.

The discursive properties of each type of text are analysed in order to facilitate comprehension (and possibly production). Guiding questions for reading and analysing non-fiction are generated on the basis of classroom discussion and subsequently applied to other texts.

Concerning debates, the topics selected have changed over the years and they respond to student-teachers' interests, topical issues at different times as well as those presented by students on intercultural challenges or specific areas of interest for them as future educators. Other criteria for the selection of topics are the availability of interesting textual or video material as input and the potential for generating fruitful debates. Some topics used include varieties of English, the poor and the rich, new technologies, gender issues, political correctness, legality versus illegality, race and racism, censorship, death penalty, addictions and work-life balance. The source material for the discussion of topics is usually in English but could also be in Spanish; student-teachers are expected to search for ideas and supporting material regardless of the language in question. The response to this approach is generally positive; for example, student-teachers have expressed enthusiasm about the updated, relevant, controversial and culturally orientated topics which developed them as 'critical thinkers'. Also the opportunity for students to suggest their own topics allows constant updating of material related to the current concerns from the student-teacher perspective.

The topics and source materials used for the debates are then used as a springboard for the preparation of oral presentations and the writing of essays. Students are expected to prepare brief oral presentations on topics chosen from a selection provided by the lecturer, using a variety of source materials. Essay writing is carried out on the characteristics of essays and students are guided to write them. Sample essays are analysed to be used as models. Sections from various higher education manuals are used to support this work.

Other activities are introduced in response to particular issues or interests of different groups or opportunities that are available at different points in time. Among them are news of the day (commenting on current affairs in an informal context); organizing a writing competition for students; applying for a job (writing CVs and cover letters) and strategic career planning; sit-coms as teaching activities source material; or dealing with humour in the classroom.

Innovation

ELIV[1] expects students to employ the integrated skills and knowledge developed as part of other modules. Students report increasing confidence in skills such as following guidelines, presenting a topic, incorporating different types of materials and developing materials themselves:

> Even though I had created material of my own for my classes before, I had never made these types of activities before. I also felt that this was closely connected to the work being done in Methods 1 and 2 and applying what you see in one subject in another one is really useful. (Aldana)

ELIV builds on students' prior experience in previous modules but also departs from that tradition in significant ways. According to feedback gathered, students have reported being struck by differences in methodology, aims, teachers' roles in materials development, career development and learner autonomy. Active participation in the production of classroom materials with immediate peer feedback opportunities has been viewed as practical and invigorating. ELIV assumes that students have a sophisticated command of the language and significant metalinguistic and pedagogical knowledge and that in ELIV they put them to work. This makes the course somewhat unique in their training experience and to some extent addresses the question posed by several which is 'What else can I learn from Language?' For example, the portfolio offers the opportunity to focus on the results of production as well as the process.

ELIV provides opportunities for student-teachers to collaboratively apply their knowledge base in the design of different teaching tasks and other texts relevant to teachers, and to reflect on this practice. In this respect, it draws inspiration on the view of language presented in Freeman, Katz, Garcia Gómez and Burns (2015), with some caveats. The course highlights the importance of a specialized subset of language skills required to prepare and teach lessons. However, in this particular context, rather than focusing solely on English-for-teaching, the assumption is that students already possess a fairly high level of general English which they can develop more specifically for language for teaching purposes (Richards 2017a). In any case, the notion is an interesting one for students to reflect upon. For example, the analysis of novels includes a variety of activities the students have to design themselves. This active role in the process of teaching and learning that coupled with collaborative approaches has generated very positive feedback.

Instances of self- and peer correction of both written and spoken production are provided. Student-teachers apply approaches developed in ELIV to their own classrooms where their students share their work with their partners using peer review or blog posting, for example, to promote collaborative work positively experienced in ELIV classroom.

A range of text types relevant to language teachers (e.g. coursebooks, resource books for teachers, reference texts, journal papers, theses, collections of essays, newsletters) is presented and their main defining characteristics discussed. A departure from previous modules is the amount of non-fiction material students are expected to read. This is intended as an introduction to the type of material teachers should be familiar with as part of their practice, and as a sample of the texts they may need to write as part of their (autonomous) professional development. Student-teachers have reported that the use of technological tools in ELIV has direct applications to their work as online tutors as part of a rapidly expanding sector in language teaching.

ELIV aims at enhancing the language awareness of students in terms of subtler linguistic elements such as register, regional and social varieties of English, language for specific purposes (in this case, teaching, see Freeman et al. 2015) and academic purposes (see Lovat, Davies, & Plotnikof 1995). Vocabulary work focuses on reflecting on ways of selecting, organizing and storing lexical items rather than highlighting specific items to incorporate in productive vocabulary. Specific lexical issues are discussed when particular matters arise in class, for example, the correct use of forms of address, which lead to instances of incidental teaching. Student-teachers respond favourably to lexical growth and enhance their confidence at the moment of context-specific language production, for example, when preparing material for conferences. There is also increasing awareness of the multiple and complex skills that constitute the activity of professional life as a language (culture) teacher, writer and researcher. For example, as part of the development of academic skills, students are asked to find, select, use and properly cite bibliographical sources of different kinds to support their written and oral submissions. The innovative nature of the methodology used in ELIV requires the inclusion of an introductory section explicitly devoted to setting the ground and clarifying doubts. This section includes the presentation of the resources and tools to be used during the course, the exploration of text types (see further details below), and a reflection on the nature of teacher professional development conducted through the discussion of Crandall and Miller (2014). Although much of this does not sink in until later on in the module, the idea is for students to have the material available as a resource they can access autonomously when or if needed. The fostering of independence and creativity when working alone or collaboratively is a unique element of ELIV according to student-teachers.

Students are encouraged to develop their learning autonomy by preparing language pieces of professional relevance such as reports and reviews, or by assessing writing competition entries, trial teaching materials or abstracts for conferences. In so doing, they become aware of the nature of the course and its impact on their language and professional development:

> It was way more independent and focused on development of skills and strategies, rather than the usual work I had been used to. (Bianca)

My language, academic and professional skills developed a lot during the module. No doubt I succeeded in becoming an independent regular learner. (Silvia)

The approach

The different skills ELIV aims to develop are inextricably intertwined. It does not seem meaningful to separate them or attempt to develop them separately. The approach integrates linguistic, academic and professional skills as part of ELIV.

Central to the approach adopted in ELIV is the element of choice. Students have to make choices at every step of the way, for example, in terms of word limits, the portfolio components students pick to incorporate, or angles adopted in the writing of essays. Also, no prescribed list of acceptable sources is provided as one of the aims of ELIV is precisely for students to find and assess the quality of possible sources and select accordingly. There is also no prescribed format. For example, *culture capsules* can be presented in the form of lists, or in graphic organizers; as a combination of image and definition; with or without examples. These choices are fundamental to encourage students to reflect on their preferences as well as to tailor the tasks to the highly specific individual requirements of such students (Maley 2009). Creativity and originality, the best match of content and format, and adequate choices, are qualities that are valued in the assessment of these assignments.

As part of previous language modules, the student-teachers taking ELIV have typically experienced a wide range of error correction techniques (e.g. recast, prompt, metalinguistic feedback, explicit correction, clarification request, repetition for a review see Loewen 2007), as well as learnt about them to apply them in their teaching practice as part of the various methodology and practice modules they take. In this sense, error correction does not have a central part to play in ELIV. However, it is approached to encourage self- and peer correction, other than the highlighting of language errors produced by students in the work they submitted to encourage reflection. This process does not involve the writing and rewriting of the pieces submitted but, rather, involves the incorporation of my suggestions to improve future versions. Oral mistakes made in class are compiled, and a session each term, labelled language clinic, is devoted to error analysis generating an opportunity for reflecting on the different nature of errors (impeding vs. non-impeding, level-relevant, etc.). Students are also expected to include a reflection in their final exam on selected portfolio components and comment on how their work has evolved over the course of the three portfolios they produced.

Despite students' increasing familiarity with social networks (e.g. Facebook, Twitter, Instagram) and various phone apps, they display very limited experience, if any, in using it as part of their studies. Although ELIV in its early days incorporated technology in a number of ways (e.g. use of video material to present topics, a portfolio component that required students to produce an audio recording), in recent years the increased and varied availability of different technological applications and devices has greatly enhanced the possibilities in ELIV (on the various issues related to incorporating technology to teach English, see Dudeney & Hockly 2007; Dudeney, Hockly, & Pegrum 2013; Hockly 2016, Hockly & Dudeney 2016; Peachey 2016, 2017).

The technological innovations that have been introduced to ELIV over the years include the use of the following:

1. Communication between students and lecturer. An email group was used at first and, with the spread of mobile phones, a messaging group was introduced.
2. A repository of module materials. All module material (assignment rubrics, sample papers, readings, external links, etc.) is available electronically and lodged in a closed website; some large files are also made available via a shared electronic folder with bibliographical material; finally, videos are made available via YouTube.
3. Submission of student's work and of lecturer's guide. To submit their work, students upload assignments to the cloud. Some assignments and surveys are designed using e-forms.
4. Creative use of technology on the part of students. For various assignments students make very creative use of different online media including Facebook profiles, online applications for audio files and slides presentations (e.g. PowerPoint and Prezi).

The purposes of the introduction of technology have been

1. to familiarize students with these environments, that is to encourage first time encounters with platforms and applications that might play a major role in professional life after graduation like Google Docs;
2. to make module management more efficient and paperless – all student work and feedback are exchanged in electronic format. The course encourages the immersion in this 'digital practice' with the opportunity to adapt to it and experience first-hand its benefits to maximize the impact of teacher feedback – students can view each other's work and the feedback received. All student assignments are uploaded to and shared via the

cloud, allowing the students to 'learn from each other' in the words of one to encourage students to think of possible applications of technology in teaching – in the design of teaching tasks students often made use of technology, and to foster reflection on when, on how and to what end technology should be used.

The use of technology is not purely instrumental but, rather, it is incorporated in the debates and reading components, for example, via discussion of works such as James (2010) and Giles (2010). On the use of technology, former students have reported that after overcoming initial reservations and fears about new technological resources, they grew more confident and appreciated the impact collaborative production and learning and the sharing and availability of resources.

The fact that ELIV proposes a novel approach means that it generates a certain amount of discomfort on the part of students. I discuss below some possible reasons for this.

Work submitted is not assigned conventional grades. Students are provided with feedback but traditional numerical evaluation is not considered meaningful as the approach contemplated a diagnosis and subsequent process of development tailored to each student. Students are conventionally grade focused, and an adaptation period is required to accustom to open project feedback as a springboard to improving the next iteration as opposed to definitive grades marking the end of a task.

The format of feedback provided is also not what students expect. Rather than corrections or suggested improvements, students are provided with questions on which they can reflect, or certain points are highlighted for them to consider alternatives. This means that students have no specific 'right answer' provided but rather that they have to go over their work and think of possible alternatives. The following sample of response from student feedback illustrates the effect of this process on their personal approaches to their production.

> The assignments were reviewed online and (the feedback) included not only the highlighting of grammatical mistakes but also questions that raised the student's awareness of his/her own position about a particular issue and a profound reflection on his/her own creative process and choices. (Azul)
>
> (Feedback was) Really enriching! (Claudia)
>
> I found (feedback) useful because it triggered reflection. (Aldana)
>
> I always felt at ease when getting feedback from presentations. (Gabriela)
>
> (I found the feedback provided) Shocking at first: it was very thorough. We weren't used to getting useful comments. (Paula)

> I found it easy to understand because we were given feedback/comments on the digital copies. … I kept different drafts and I was able to check my progress continuously. (Mariana)

> For each part of the portfolio I was given feedback and opportunity for self-correction. (Fernanda)

The final exam also takes a different form from what students are familiar with. Typically, the final exam for English language improvement courses involves production in situ of a written text which, if passed, was followed by an oral examination. In both these instances students are expected to incorporate the words and expressions taught during the module. Instead of this, in ELIV, the written component is assessed during the year and the final exam consists of an oral presentation prepared by each student on a topic of their choice, plus a reflection on the portfolio work and their own evolution. Students have been positive about their autonomy and the nature of collaborative work with clear outcomes.

Students often express disconcertment as regards the level of freedom to make choices they have in the completion of ELIV assignments. Some student-teachers have expressed that the departure from previous language courses where 'written tests had been mandatory' was alarming, but as the purpose of the approach became clearer, they adapted.

Final remarks

Some general remarks can be made concerning the approach taken in ELIV. Critical to the work in this module is the development of future teachers' autonomy, critical learning and self-directed learning. At all times students are encouraged to consider the contexts they prepare material for (e.g. when designing teaching tasks, when writing a professional text such as a book review) and their purposes. Taking on board the different characteristics of students and their different levels of skills, the tasks provide opportunities for students to make choices and integrate skills. The design of teaching tasks allows for the glocalization of the material generating a space to reflect on how materials need to contemplate both local and global needs of their future students (see Katz & Snow 2009). Although all the students who have taken ELIV thus far are non-native speakers of English, the approach is equally pertinent to native and non-native aspiring teachers. As Maley (2009) indicates, tasks designed in this way can be appropriate for both groups

The development of the course is dialogic in nature, in particular when it comes to the provision of feedback and the assessment of attainment. In many ways, the development is innovative and, as such, distinct from student expectations; however, once the initial surprise is overcome, the result appears to have been positive.

Questions for change

1. What types of tasks can be designed to encourage critical thinking and integration of linguistic, academic and professional skills of student-teachers?
2. How should the contents of different disciplines and the development of skills be integrated in teacher education programmes?
3. In what ways can teacher education modules model those practices that student-teachers should become familiar with?
4. How can the real needs of student-teachers be incorporated into the curricular design of the programmes they undertake?

Acknowledgements

This work was partially completed during a stay at the University of California-Davis on a Fulbright and Ministry of Education of Argentina postdoctoral research scholarship from January to March 2019. The author would like to thank the editor of this volume, Darío Banegas, for his patience and support, and the comments and suggestions from an anonymous reviewer. As usual, all errors remain the author's responsibility.

Note

1　One of the innovations in the second edition of this module was the incorporation of assistant teachers (*adscriptas* in Spanish) which made a positive role to the module in terms of bridging the gap for the more disorientated students, managing some of the technological resources, doing a first read of assignments.

11

Developing Writing and Reflective Skills of First-Year Student-Teachers in Chile

Pamela Saavedra Jeldres and Mónica Campos Espinoza

Introduction

Writing portfolios have been a part of the teaching, learning and assessment of English as an alternative approach both in English as a foreign and second language (EFL/ESL) contexts (Nezakatgoo 2011). Therefore, teacher educators have included them as a strategy to develop writing and reflective skills in student-teachers. In Chile, however, portfolios in IELTE are primarily related to professional development in the didactics field rather than as a tool to improve English language proficiency. Writing portfolios in EFL contexts, like the Chilean setting, have proven to be beneficial due to the process-oriented nature of writing, which, through formative assessment and constant feedback, enhances performance in writing skills and reflection by evaluating one's own learning processes as writers (Aydin 2010; Burnaz 2011; Lam 2013; Lunar 2007; Nezakatgoo 2011; Nunes 2004).

Despite the popularity and effectiveness of writing portfolios in language education, there is a limited number of published studies on this topic in Latin America and Chile, country in which this chapter is set, and even fewer focused on the use of EFL writing portfolios with student-teachers specifically (Delmaestro 2005; Lunar 2007; Perdomo 2010; Saavedra & Campos 2018). In the particular case of IELTE programmes, portfolio keeping constitutes not only a strategy for learning but also a future strategy to be considered in their own pedagogical practice as future teachers of English.

This chapter seeks to present the writing portfolio strategy implemented with first-year student-teachers in the IELTE programme at Universidad Católica de Temuco, located in southern Chile. This teaching, learning and assessment tool is part of the Integrated Language courses I and II. According to the CEFR bands, the average entering proficiency level is A2 and the students achieve a level B1 by the end of the first year at university. Student-teachers who are enrolled in the programme are able to certify a C1 level through an official standardized test after five years of training. However, academic writing has proven to be the skill with the lowest attainment by students in such tests. Thus, as teacher educators of the programme we are constantly looking for new ways of strengthening student-teachers' writing skills.

IELTE programmes in Chile

In Chile, IELTE programmes aim to develop CK, PCK and GPK. Nonetheless, a critical aspect that underlies these broad areas of language teacher education in Chile is English language proficiency. In fact, since 2015, the Ministry of Education has imposed a level C1, according to the CEFR and national standards for IELTE programmes, as a graduation requirement.

Historically, IELTE programmes in Chile have followed an applied-linguistics model (Barahona 2016). However, the process of teaching writing has somehow been neglected or given a second place in most integrated skills language courses following the communicative approach at schools. A study carried out by Agencia de Calidad de la Educación (2017) shows that 68 per cent – seven out of ten students – do not reach the expected learning outcomes in English (B1) by the end of high school, whereas 40 per cent of the students who enter the university to study the English teaching program are A1 English level. Therefore, student-teachers need to enhance writing skills at university in order to achieve level C1, in compliance with graduation requirements.

Furthermore, the IELTE programme needs to encompass reflection as student-teachers have to identify their own weaknesses and strengths to learn from their own learning process. At the same time, this would contribute to achieving the pedagogical standard requirements for Chilean IELTE programmes and an evaluation that novice teachers in Chile are required to take upon graduation. This evaluation includes high levels of reflection skills.

This chapter describes an innovative strategy applied in the first year of the IELTE programme in the Integrated Language courses I and II, as part of a research study carried out in 2015–16 (Saavedra & Campos 2018). In addition to developing language proficiency, these language courses incorporate content knowledge from other courses in the programme, like grammar, semantics, applied linguistics, phonetics and DA, among others. Content knowledge allows them to make the right decisions when using the language as student-teachers. However, not only English language proficiency and content knowledge are enough for language courses; student-teachers have to build key transversal competencies for language teachers such as critical thinking and reflective skills.

This chapter focuses on the design, implementation and evaluation process of the strategy of a writing portfolio, using written corrective feedback to enhance writing and reflective skills from the beginning of teacher training. This process started off as a pilot project in the year 2015. During that year, an error analysis study was carried out in order to establish the main problems first-year students faced when writing in English, as well as the acquisition of correct structures that needed to be highlighted. That study became the starting point to planning a writing portfolio based on targeting students' needs.

Why a writing portfolio?

The IELTE programme at our university explicitly supports the process-oriented approach to develop writing skills, which also fits the framework of sociocultural theory, in terms of relating social interaction and mediation to individual development (Vygotsky, in Hyland & Hyland 2006b). The process-oriented approach is preferable for the first years of the programme since students enter university with a very low proficiency level (A2) and are not familiar with the process of writing. Accordingly, the different participants of the portfolio, the student-teachers, their peers and their teacher educators, play an important role in their growth as writers in EFL (Brown 2000). The writing portfolio (henceforth, WP) has had many definitions over time, but one that adjusts to our study defines it as 'a collection of texts which the student has had the opportunity to develop and reflect upon over a long period of time' (Burner 2014: 140). Along this line, Klenowski (2002) states that self-reflection, self-assessment, peer feedback, revision, and selection of texts are common activities in portfolios. This study kept track of student-teachers' progress and learning over their first year at university. Lam (2013) suggests that students performing their own revisions in the portfolio process could positively contribute to writing development.

The two central axes of our proposed strategy are (1) process-oriented approach and (2) alternative assessment. On one hand, the process-oriented approach is enriched by feedback; the opportunities for feedback increase through teaching and learning with portfolios. For example, there is the opportunity for several drafts of each piece of writing – enhanced by the possibility of revisiting and revising the piece of writing further during the semester (Hamp-Lyons & Condon 2000).

On the other hand, the portfolio constitutes an alternative type of assessment, since one of its main purposes is to assess students' progress over time (Burner 2014). Portfolio assessment is adopted instead of a traditional, product-oriented approach, not only because it strengthens the general quality of written drafts but also because it has a favourable impact on writing development (Lam 2013). The portfolio allows a visualization of the students' progress throughout the learning process according to the complexity and advancement of their educational performance (Barret 2009).

Framework for the writing portfolio

The writing portfolio strategy is based upon an instructional design. It integrates a framework and procedure clearly established for the organization of the learning and assessment tool. This strategy includes a variety of formative assessments, such as self-assessment, peer assessment, and systematic feedback from teachers and peers. Considering that portfolio writing assessment has its focus on the process of learning and evaluates students' progress overtime, it can be a more useful way of evaluation (Taki 2011).

The framework we have adopted for the organization of the portfolio has three main components:

1. Collection – multiple drafts from a same text
2. Delayed evaluation – the third (final) draft is evaluated
3. Reflection – self-assessment when writing a final draft and at the end of the process

First, the WP enables the writer to display a range of writing performances, in different genres and for different audiences and purposes. Secondly, an important characteristic is *delayed evaluation,* giving students both the opportunity and motivation to revise written products before a final evaluation is given. The use of portfolios provides a means for measuring development over time in ways that neither the teacher nor the student may have anticipated. Thirdly, a portfolio usually involves *reflection and self-assessment.* This means that portfolios can provide a means for measuring growth along specific parameters, such as linguistic accuracy or the ability to organize and develop an argument. Thus, a regular practice of reflection can encourage students to renew their compromise with their own learning process. To a certain extent, it turns to learners as owners of the process of learning for the sake of identifying, assessing and planning next directions (Huber & Hutchings 2004 in Zubizarreta 2009).

Reflecting and writing

Enhancing writing skills in English is not the only focal point of writing portfolios in EFL; reflection is also generally associated with the process function of the portfolio; however, reflection is not a goal in itself (Mansvelder-Longayroux, Beijaard, & Verloop 2007). Reflective skills are a crucial component in education programmes to make student-teachers aware of their own progress in terms of writing improvement. We, as teacher educators, believe that helping student-teachers to develop reflective skills can contribute to future processes of reflection within the context of the practice of teaching. The potential benefits of using the writing portfolio can be linked to the opportunity of making an interconnection between learning and the teaching processes in terms of writing growth (Romeo 2008 in Burner 2014).

A regular practice of reflection can encourage student-teachers to renew their commitment to their own process of learning. At the same time, it makes the student-teachers owners of the process of reflection on their learning process in order to identify, assess and plan next directions (Huber & Hutchings 2004 in Zubizarreta 2009).

For the purposes of this study, we have adopted the levels of critical reflection proposed by Zubizarreta (2009):

1. First Level: The most elementary reflections include simple labels, descriptions and so forth. Learners simply remember the what, when and how.
2. Second Level: Learners move beyond the remembering stage and demonstrate how someone analyses, interrelates and synthesizes materials. At this level the reflection is on the meaning of the text.
3. Third Level: Highest level of reflection, the learner not only remembers and reflects on the meaning of the materials and experiences but also discusses the next steps in the process of learning.

At each level of reflection it is important to think about and discuss gap analysis (a reflection on what the student-teacher has yet to learn as it relates to the purpose of the teacher educator).

The academic record of the portfolio helps self-awareness, reflection and, ultimately, learning, since it is based on student-teachers' own practical experiences in the process of writing in EFL. Nevertheless, this strategy can be enhanced by using systematic feedback, namely written corrective feedback to improve writing skills and language accuracy (Saavedra & Campos 2018).

How much feedback is appropriate?

Based on current research on second and foreign language writing, this programme has assumed that error treatment is an effective way to improve accuracy in FL writing (Bitchener & Knoch 2010; Chandler 2003; Ellis 2009; Ferris et al. 2013; Zheng & Yu 2018). However, there is always the recurring question of how much feedback is enough; should all grammar categories been addressed at once? Should we also give feedback on organization, ideas and content? How overwhelming would it be for a student-teacher to respond to everything at once? All of these questions, previously developed by scholars and researchers (Ferris 2006; Sheen 2007; Sheen, Wright, & Moldava 2009), have to be discussed in depth with the teacher educators and practitioners who are going to be engaged in the task of teaching how to write in EFL, so they feel empowered and taken into account. The most important part of this is to get consensus among the people involved in the teaching process.

For the first-year language courses of this IELTE programme, a specific approach has been selected as recommended by many authors (Ellis 2009; Ferris 2006; Lee 2011; Sheen 2007). Focused written corrective feedback is used and a limited number of five error types are marked on student-teachers' writing texts by means of coding

Focused or selective written corrective feedback has many advantages. Ellis (2009) indicates that 'learners are more likely to attend to corrections directed at a single (or a limited number of) error type(s) and more likely to develop a clearer understanding of the nature of the error and the correction needed' (p. 356). This is particularly useful for our student-teachers since they are at the lower levels of the programme and still have not studied semantics, applied linguistics or syntax, which makes it harder for them to make sense of all error categories; even if the teacher educator marks all of the errors comprehensively, the student-teachers would still not have the tools and knowledge to correct them successfully.

Furthermore, this approach is considered effective since 'it allows students to recognize patterns of errors, avoid being overwhelmed by teacher feedback, and develop independent editing skills in that they – and not the instructor – are then responsible for locating and addressing errors that are unmarked' (McMartin-Miller 2014: 25).

However, a focused approach is not considered viable over long periods of time since it might lead to the fossilization of errors (Scarcella & Oxford 1992). Thus, the focused approach is used only with the first-year students of this IELTE programme and a comprehensive approach – which targets all types of errors – is used with upper levels instead.

Against this backdrop, this study aims to answer the following questions:

1. To what extent do the writing portfolio and the use of written corrective feedback have an impact on student accuracy on specific targeted error categories?
2. What are student-teachers' perceptions towards the use of a writing portfolio to enhance writing skills?
3. To what extent can student-teachers reflect upon their own process of learning how to write in English?

The study

This study used a mixed-methods approach design in order to gain insight into the impact of corrective feedback and the strategy of the portfolio. As Brown (2014) suggests, quantitative and qualitative inquiry can support and inform each other.

The participants (N=34) were student-teachers in their second semester during the year 2016. They ranged in age from eighteen to thirty years; fourteen were women and twenty were men. Results from the Quick Placement Test reported that they had a pre-intermediate level of English – B1 according to the CEFR and were enrolled in their second compulsory English language course out of nine

Portfolio implementation

From the beginning, we committed ourselves to using the process approach to develop writing skills with our students, following its four stages: planning, writing, revising and editing of the text (Hyland 2003). However, during the implementation phase we realized we also needed to teach student-teachers different genres, their macro-structures and specific target language. The genre-based approach combines the teaching of writing with the identification and replication of textual structures (Hedgcock & Lee 2017).

The process was broken down into nine steps, which are described below (Figure 11.1). Step 1 is comprised of the presentation and exemplification of a specific genre. Then, the process approach was followed through – Steps 2 and 3 regarding the assignment of a task and prewriting activities, primarily outlining. Drafting (writing and revising stages) was made up of three steps: Step 4 included the writing of a first draft; in Step 5 peers' feedback and then teacher educators' feedback was given on general organization – macro and micro structure; and Step 6 involved the writing of the second draft. The editing stage comprised Steps 7 and 8. Step 7 consisted of the teacher educators' written corrective feedback to the second draft and Step 8 was editing the text and writing the final draft, which was graded. Finally, Step 9 focused on reflection at the end of each academic term, as well as every time the student-teachers had to hand in a final draft.

In the final stage of the process, student-teachers reflected on their learning outcomes, improvement and their identity as writers and future teachers of English. We have surmised, through the different implementations (since

Figure 11.1 The writing portfolio process

the year 2015) of this strategy, that it is reflection what gives the portfolio its effectiveness in the long term. When a student-teacher has done poorly during the semester or year, and at the end they can see, in effect, that they have not progressed as expected and they analyse their work and the reasons why they have not improved, this student-teacher is reflecting. On top of that, if the student-teachers assume their own responsibilities and commit and create a plan of action to improve, then the strategy is actually helpful for them. The adapted model in this strategy is summarized in Figure 11.1.

Portfolio contents

The writing portfolio included three or four different texts. The type of texts is mixed according to their level of proficiency (B1 – CEFR) and the writing production progression from the programme at the university. The texts belong to different genres both from the descriptive and narrative types.

As previously stated, there was a pilot project in the year 2015 and an error analysis study was carried out in order to have a better understanding of first-year student-teachers' strengths and limitations when writing in English. The error analysis focused primarily on accuracy. Thirteen recurrent errors emerged from the data analysis; these errors belonged to the broad categories of grammar, lexicon and mechanics (Stortch & Tapper 2000). Since the focused or selective approach of feedback (Ferris 2006) was chosen for this study, five linguistic categories out of the thirteen errors were selected considering the nature of the error and the capacity of student-teachers to correct these errors given their level of proficiency. These errors were as follows: (a) subject omission, (b) spelling, (c) subject-verb agreement, (d) use of capital letters and (e) use of the indefinite article.

Student-teachers received indirect written corrective feedback in the form of coding to highlight grammar inaccuracies (feedback of the second draft) and also commentary regarding the general layout and organization of their writing texts (feedback of the first draft).

Data collection and analysis

Different sources of data were used during the thirty-two weeks of the writing portfolio implementation. To determine whether the use of the writing portfolio and written corrective feedback had had an impact on accuracy, a pre-test and a post-test were applied in March and December 2016. These texts were part of the course – diagnostic/exit test, respectively – and at the same time they were also used for research purposes. Student-teachers had to write a new piece of writing and did not get feedback on it.

In addition, for the purpose of identifying student-teachers' perceptions towards the use of this technique, they had to complete a self-assessment (using a rubric) on their progress and performance in different areas affecting writing and reflective skills development (vocabulary, grammar, prewriting activities, text types, paragraph organization and reflection).

Finally, a total of eighty-eight texts from student-teachers' final reflections were analysed in order to hear their own voices. Student-teachers were asked to write a text guided by some questions so as to empower them to judge their progress critically over time and their attitude and work throughout the whole process. This procedure was repeated twice at the end of each academic term (July–December 2016).

Results

Results are presented following the three research questions posed for this study.

Research question 1: To what extent do the writing portfolio and the use of written corrective feedback have an impact on student accuracy on specific targeted error categories?

As Table 11.1 shows, there is a significant difference between the pre-test (M 4.21, SD 2.74) and post-test (M 1.70, SD 1.61). Descriptive data indicate that the frequency of errors decreased remarkably during the post-test; from a frequency close to five errors in the pre-test to two errors in the post-test. These are overall results consider the five targeted errors of the study. This indicates that the use of the writing portfolio contributes positively on language accuracy of specific grammatical categories when writing in EFL. The constant and methodical practice of writing through the process-oriented approach, where

Table 11.1 Pre- and Post-test Frequency of Errors

	Pre-test	Post-test
MEDIA	4.21	1.70
DS	2.704	1.610

students have the possibility of making mistakes, has an impact when writing new pieces, where no feedback is given (Bitchener & Knoch 2010; Chandler 2003; Ferris 2013).

On the other hand, from the data in Table 11.2, it can be observed that all targeted error categories had a significantly lower frequency of errors in the post-test compared to the pre-test. Besides this, there was a lower dispersion in the data. However, the error category of *subject-verb agreement* revealed the most dramatic decrease in the frequency of errors in the post-test compared to the pre-test.

This is a recurrent error in student-teachers throughout the programme; probably not only due to L1 interference (interlingual) – *people* in Spanish is a singular collective noun while in English it is plural – but also due to the lack of skills to identify the noun in complex noun phrases and therefore not applying the correct rules (intralingual). *Subject omission* was another error that was included in this study so it could be targeted early on to avoid fossilization. Surprisingly, results show that the frequency of recurrence in this category decreased. Student-teachers seemed to have internalized the rule after a year of targeted feedback.

Research question 2: What are student-teachers' perceptions towards the use of a writing portfolio to enhance writing and develop reflective skills?

Content analysis was conducted from the self-assessments and reflections from student-teachers and three broad themes emerged from the analysis: (1) writing skills improvement, (2) text type knowledge, and (3) a focus on the process.

First, there was a sense among student-teachers that their overall writing skills had improved, mainly in terms of grammar, vocabulary and punctuation. As some student-teachers put it:

> I think that the writing portfolio is a great idea to improve vocabulary, grammar and composition. (Camila)

> I think I have improved in many ways, like in my grammar or my coherence. I also understood the importance of the subject in each sentence, because if it doesn't have a subject nobody knows who I was talking about. (Felipe)

Secondly, student-teachers considered this strategy had given them a broader knowledge of different text types and genres; they claimed to have learnt the macrostructure of different genres and this contributed to their composition. Two student-teachers expressed:

Table 11.2 Comparison of Error Frequency between Pre-test and Post-test per Error Category

	Pre-test a	Post-test a	Pre-test b	Post-test b	Pre-test c	Post-test c	Pre-test d	Post-test d	Pre-test e	Post-test e
MEDIA	0.241	0.091	1.828	0.970	0.517	0.061	1.172	0.152	0.448	0.424
DS	0.511	0.2919	2.0541	1.1035	0.7847	0.2423	1.5369	0.3641	0.6859	0.6629

*Error categories: (a) subject omission, (b) spelling, (c) subject-verb agreement, (d) capital letters, (e) indefinite article

In my point of view, portfolios have given us knowledge about different kinds of written texts, which help us in our future job, not only as English teachers but also as speakers of a second language. (Claudia)

The portfolio is a good method to improve our English production. For me it has been very useful. I have learnt how to write different types of texts properly. (Eduardo)

Thirdly, student-teachers suggested that the focus on the process had a great utility for them. They identified two main aspects that were relevant in the process: systematic feedback from peers and teachers and the opportunity to make mistakes, which gave them a feeling of emotional support and confidence. Regarding this systematic feedback, two student-teachers said:

I had to check over and over again for new mistakes, sometimes I found mistakes like misspelling or wrong tenses, but with the teacher's corrections and advice I improved a lot. (Camila)

Having the possibility of having a draft and two corrected versions helps a lot to see your own mistakes and learn from them, so you can remember those and improve them in future writings. (Emanuel)

In relation to a feeling of confidence, a student-teacher stated:

The writing portfolio gave more trust about my writing skills. It's an amazing way to improve and learn vocabulary, also to recognize your own mistakes. (Claudia)

Research question 3: To what extent can student-teachers reflect upon their own process of learning how to write in English?

Considering the levels of reflection mentioned before, student-teachers from the first year are in an initial stage; reflections include simple labels and descriptions. They are able to remember the what, when and why (MacIsaac & Jackson 1994 in Zubizarreta 2009). Student-teachers' reflections show what they specifically learnt and in what areas they considered they had improved:

The portfolio has helped me to learn more types of texts, grammar and new vocabulary. It also helped me to be more confident at the moment of writing. (Samuel)

It pushed me to expand my vocabulary and be more careful with the organization. I learnt more about the structure of each format, and how to do a layout. (Victoria)

In the following quotation, one student-teacher presents a light of going beyond the what, but in the end he does not expand his own point of view:

> I think that writing portfolio is a great idea to improve vocabulary, grammar, composition and organization, but I feel I am not giving my best on this project. (Emanuel)

We were and we still are firmly convinced that the promotion of reflection will improve not only writing skills, but also teaching ones. A recent study (Tagle, Díaz, Briesmaster, Ubilla, & Etchegaray 2017) focused on pre-service EFL teachers' beliefs about teaching writing states that teacher candidates acquire their ideas and knowledge concerning the teaching of writing with the help of university training. From this view, the observation of their own teachers' strategies would help them with the construction of the representations in the area of teaching writing skills.

Conclusion

Teaching writing to IELTE student-teachers is a challenging task for two reasons: on the one hand, they need to enhance their proficiency in the language and on the other, they are learning how to teach. Besides, developing writing skills with low-proficient student-teachers is another important variable to take into account. The implementation of a writing portfolio has proven to be an effective strategy to accomplish this goal through its process-oriented nature, which allows students to improve with multiple drafting and systematic feedback from both tutors and peers. The focus on the process rather than the product has a positive effect primarily on low-proficient students. In addition to the teaching and learning contribution of the portfolio, it also comprises an alternative assessment method in itself. The formative potential of this methodology allows student-teachers to visualize and reflect upon their own learning process in different instances throughout an academic term and, at the same time, sets the ground for gaining confidence in writing with the premise of delayed evaluation. The whole process of writing and reflection is a never-ending cycle that is student-centred; they need to become responsible for their own learning and the role of the teacher educator and peers is just to support student-teachers in their commitment to learn and improve. The main goal of the writing portfolio is to empower student-teachers by providing them with the appropriate content knowledge to make informed decisions, an appropriate proficiency level and enhancing self-reflexive skills to become self-editors of their work as writers of an FL.

Questions for change

1. How can we help our student-teachers reach upper levels of reflection without giving guiding questions?
2. Would student-teachers engage in deep learning if the tasks are more meaningful for them?
3. How can we enhance peer feedback to contribute to student-teachers' process of learning?

12

Empowering Chilean Student-Teachers to Become Highly Capable English Language Educators

Malba Barahona and Ricardo Benítez

Introduction

Historically, ELTE programmes in Chile have tended to draw their curricula from applied linguistic perspectives, placing a particular emphasis on English language proficiency and a broad semiotic knowledge of the English language (Barahona 2016). Although recently reformed national standards for teaching programmes have made explicit the need to integrate practical and pedagogical curricular activities (Abrahams & Silva Ríos 2017), most Chilean ELTE programmes sustain a clear emphasis on the development of student-teachers' proficiency in English. This is reflected in the priorities of student coursework, relative number of hours and learning activities in the curricular structure of local programmes (Martin 2016). Furthermore, the current standards for graduates of ELTE programmes in Chile similarly establish that graduate teachers should hold an advanced level of proficiency that is equivalent to C1 level from the CEFR.

However, based on a developing body of research, ELTE programmes in South America are being increasingly challenged to find more effective ways to help future teachers achieve higher levels of proficiency and integrate content knowledge for teaching English (Banegas 2017a; Kamhi-Stein, Díaz Maggioli, & de Oliveira 2017). This is our motivation to write this chapter, in which, we as committed English language educators, reflect on the design and implementation of an *Advanced English* (AE) module for prospective teachers of English as an effective way to empower future teachers of English. The AE module is based on a sociocultural perspective of learning (Lantolf 2000), which sees learning and teaching as a social goal-oriented activity in which teachers act as mediators and empower students to be active and independent thinkers (Lantolf & Thorne 2006). Therefore, language learning not only involves the acquisition of linguistic items and development of skills but also comprises an activity in which learning takes place through social interaction. Thus, our role as English language teacher educators consists in creating opportunities for student-teachers to engage in activities that are meaningful, realistic and culturally contextualized.

In this chapter, based on a self-study research methodology (Lassonde, Galman, & Kosnik 2009) and also drawing on student-teachers' voices, we explore our implementation of a thematic advanced (C1 CEFR) English module in a Chilean ELTE programme that integrates all four language skills (speaking, listening, reading, and writing). This module enhances practical English-language-learning experiences that contribute to strengthening student-teachers' confidence and their preparation for their teaching careers through tasks that integrate controversial issues, relevant contents and complex linguistic demands. The learning experiences detailed here offer an instance of a form of heightened engagement in cross-cultural understanding and cultural sensitivity, one that can potentially contribute to higher levels of proficiency and confidence. This provides a foundation for the further consideration of the pedagogical and practical challenges that English language teacher educators face in designing an advanced language module which aspires to integrating elevated levels of students' engagement.

Having a sociocultural understanding of language learning in mind (Vygotsky 1978), we argue that an AE language module for future teachers of English can be effectively framed within what we would describe as a social learning pedagogy design. Social learning pedagogy is an educational approach that considers knowledge and content as connected to authentic tasks within the learning processes (Barahona & Martin 2014). This design requires an alignment of learning outcomes, tasks, assessment and timely scaffolding. The social emphasis is engendered through the integration of a wide range of opportunities created for students to represent and co-construct knowledge for an authentic audience, giving them a sense of voice and purpose in their processes of language development.

Theoretical perspectives of language and language teaching at an advanced level

Our perspective of English language learning and teaching is mainly drawn from two theoretical perspectives: SFL (Halliday 1980) and a sociocultural approach

(Lantolf & Thorne 2006; Vygotsky 1978). From a functional perspective, learning a language requires to learn how to mean in that language (Halliday & Matthiessen 1999). Thus, as Byrnes (2009) claims, 'language learning is not a skill that can be enhanced through decontextualized and content-less learning strategies' (p. 6), but it should be framed by meaning. This implies that students learn about the language through language use. From Vygotsky's sociocultural theory, we consider the concepts of the zone of proximal development (Vygotsky 1978) and scaffolding (Byrnes, Weger, & Sprang 2006). In this sense, language learning is considered a social activity which is culturally based (Lantolf & Poehner 2008; Lantolf & Thorne 2006). In other words, there is a dialectic relationship between individual learning and the sociocultural context. This perspective acknowledges that timely scaffolding contributes to overcoming the limitations of individual learning. Scaffolding empowers students and enables them to complete the assigned tasks successfully. This sociocultural approach provides a framework to understand the role of culture and cultural artefacts as tools that can mediate positive learning outcomes based on the adoption of a sound educational design (Thorne & Payne 2005).

Thus, we consider that the confluence of SFL and sociocultural theory allows us to examine and enhance FL learning at an advanced level of proficiency (Byrnes 2009). SFL provides a framework to analyse how meaning is made through language use. In turn, sociocultural theory provides an understanding that language learning is the result of social interaction through a process of socialization and acculturation. From these theoretical underpinnings, we believe that English language learning at an advanced level is not represented by the attainment of structures and the processing of input, but rather it is characterized by the co-construction and internalization of knowledge as part of a social activity. In this sense, learners co-construct knowledge while engaged in collaborative dialogue that focuses on form and meaning at the same time. Our task as teacher educators of an advanced module is to provide meaningful opportunities to student-teachers to accomplish a task or a goal. Language is a tool that develops from the activity required to accomplish a task or goal and not merely as a system to be implemented after acquisition.

Another important assumption that underlies our teaching approach refers to the inseparability of language and culture. From this perspective, language is 'an integrated part of society, culture and the psyche' (Risager 2005: 185). However, a valid question emerges: What forms of culture are associated with the English language? In this current globalized world, the English language is an international language (Risager, 2005); for this reason, it is considered a communication tool that may be used by anybody anywhere in the world. In this sense, in the context of teaching English, it is important to consider the complex functions of the use of English by diverse people in different contexts around the world. Therefore, teaching English should contribute to developing multilingual awareness and intercultural competence.

The following section contextualizes the ELTE programme and the AE module we explore in this chapter.

The ELTE programme

This ELTE programme is nine semesters long and its curriculum includes four main areas: English language proficiency, linguistics, didactics and practicum, and culture. The two areas that are more extensive in terms of hours per week are English language proficiency and didactics and practicum. The compulsory English language core courses are aligned with differing levels of English proficiency according to the CEFR: beginners (A1), pre-intermediate (A2), intermediate (B1), intermediate advanced (C1), and writing and speaking for professional purposes (C2).

The teaching and learning experiences we describe in this chapter are the 2017 version of the AE module, a ten-hour-a-week module offered in the second semester of third year in the ELTE programme. Student-teachers enrolled in this module were fifty-three third-year students (twenty- to twenty-three-years old) divided into two parallel groups taught by the authors of this chapter who are two experienced English language teacher educators.

Advanced English (AE) module

Syllabus

For the 2017 version, we designed this module to engage student-teachers in challenging tasks and helped them construct knowledge as part of a global community of teachers of English. The essence of the design of the subject is the articulation and alignment of the learning outcomes with meaningful tasks and a coherent assessment scheme. It was expected that learning outcomes (see Table 12.1) would be achieved throughout the following topics divided into four units: gender issues, history and economy education; food and technology policies; animal testing and the arts; and current issues.

Table 12.1 Summary of Main Learning Outcomes and Units

Learning outcomes
By the end of the semester students will be able to:
Apply the English phonological and morphosyntactic systems for meaning making in a wide range of contexts at level B2/C1.
Use oral communication features depending on monological and dialogical communicative situations.
Use rhetorical features to write short argumentative essays.
Demonstrate understanding oral and written texts related to various current affairs.
Produce written and oral texts according to determined rhetorical situations at B2 / C1 level.

Prior to the beginning of the second semester of 2017, the students' interest in a number of topics was surveyed online. This survey included several topics, and the students were asked to rank their preferences from the more interesting to the less interesting topics. Once all the students completed the survey, the topics were arbitrarily distributed among the four units.

Language teaching approach, methodology and resources

Following a sociocultural and functional understanding of language learning, our teaching was framed by three main approaches: task-based, project-based and content-based approach. In this sense, we planned our lessons to provide opportunities for student-teachers to develop the language communicatively and learn content at the same time. In our module, student-teachers worked in either pairs or groups performing tasks that increased collaboration and interaction among them. These tasks were activities that demanded understanding, producing, manipulating and interacting in/with authentic language with emphasis on meaning to attain objectives (Bygate, Skehan, & Swain 2001; Nunan 2004). Examples of tasks and projects used in this module can be seen in Tables 12.2 and 12.3.

The teaching resources used were authentic (e.g. interviews, TED Talks, documentaries, newspaper articles, blogs, podcasts, online documents, book chapters, journal articles). For our lessons we designed worksheets using the resources around tasks and projects as presented in Tables 12.2 and 12.3 that included something to talk about, something to listen to, something to read about, and something to write about.

Table 12.2 Task Samples

Speaking tasks	Role-play

Student A (Interviewer): S/he is a journalist for a most renowned social medium and is doing a report on the impact of some educational policies. S/he might like to derive other questions from the answer given by the interviewee/ Student B.

Student B (Interviewee): A distinguished academic whose main research work is on educational policy.

Group Discussions
Agree on a definition of gender inequality using three concepts.

Group work
1. Read the concepts assigned, negotiate and then explain their meanings to the class, and provide examples.
2. Agree on a definition of gender inequality using three concepts.
3. Agree on a definition of identity as a group and some artefacts and cultural practices that characterize that identity.

Reading tasks	Read the first two pages (1 & 2) of Tannen's article *Marked Women, Unmarked Men* respond to the following:

1. Justify the title.
2. Purpose of the text.
3. Relation of the content to linguistics.
4. This article can/can't have the same impact today as the one it had back in 1993. Give reasons.

Pair work: Now read the remaining two pages (3 & 4) of the article and formulate at least four questions (factual, lexical, rhetorical-discursive and extra textual questions). The whole class should participate by answering the questions you formulated.

Writing tasks	Write a 400-500-word argumentative essay on one of the topics discussed in class. Choose a topic that you can argue either a position or a solution. Ensure that you support your claims with evidence.

Following are some examples of topics/issues you could discuss:
- There is no longer any real need for equal opportunity initiatives for women in the workplace, because there is now equal access for all based on merit.
- The world's oldest continuing culture is not valued in Australia because it denies its past.
- Should sexual preference be a civil right or a personal preference?
- The Second World War made the United States a superpower.

Table 12.2 (Continued)

Listening/ viewing tasks	a) Before you watch
	1. On a map of Australia locate the Torres Strait and Murray Island.
	2. Discuss and define Land Rights. Find out what a Native Title is.
	3. Discuss and find out who Eddie Mabo is and why he is important to Australian history generally and more specifically the history of indigenous land rights in Australia.
	b) While you watch
	Watch the video clip and take notes so you can answer the following questions:
	1. What relation is Douglas Bon to Eddie Mabo? How does he describe this relationship?
	2. Why does Douglas say it is important to retain and maintain the land?
	c) After you watch
	1. Research the life of Eddie Mabo and create a poster display. Make sure you research his work on land rights and his personal life.
	2. Research and discuss the Mabo case. Imagine you are a newspaper journalist attending the court case that is shown in the clip. Write a short editorial, commenting on the decision, its importance and the impact you think it will have on Australia.

Assessment tasks

The module considered ten graded tasks: one reading test, one listening test, two *Use of English tests* (focus on accurate use of morphosyntactic structures), four mini-essays and two speaking projects. These tasks covered all four linguistic skills separately, plus *Use of English tests* which allowed the syllabus to align with the level of CAE exam.

Topics for these mini-essays were chosen from the units described in Table 12.2. However, the topic selected by student-teachers most frequently was related to gender issues. In Figure 12.1, one of the mini-essays is provided as an example in which a student-teacher analysed the provision of gender-neutral bathrooms on their campus.

Just as listening activities, reading comprehension was formatively assessed by having the student-teachers perform a series of tasks. Among them, answering four types of questions on the assigned texts (factual, lexical, rhetorical-discursive and extra textual); formulating questions based on the texts; making a timeline poster and presenting it to the class; outlining mind maps; and underlining topic-specific vocabulary. *Factual questions* ask about specific things

Table 12.3 Speaking Project Sample

Speaking project: Analysing films

Student-teachers (in groups of four) will select a movie (from the English-speaking world) to explore one key cultural representation evidenced in politics, economy, religion, culture and ideology.

Student-teachers in the group will work in this project and prepare a presentation with the outcomes of the project. It should include the following aspects:

1. Select a relevant two-minute segment of the movie to show to the audience. This segment must reflect the main issue portrayed in the film.

2. An overview of the film – film review

What is the theme of the movie?

Who are the characters?

When and where does it take place?

Structure of the story

Director-actors

Technical features

3. Analysis of the film as a cultural artefact. Pick one of the following factors that play an important role in the film. Choose among political, economic, religious, social and ideological factors.

How does the film reflect the factor you identified?

What ideas and values are embedded in this film? And, how are these messages conveyed?

What hopes, preferences, or ideas of success does the film communicate? What do these values (and thus this artefact) reveal about a specific community? About society as a whole?

Presentation: Student-teachers will have a choice as to how they present the outcomes of their project. The presentations will be made to the class and must be fifteen minutes long. Each member has to be able to give a two-minute speech during the presentation. After your presentation, they will be asked some questions by the audience.

Examples on how to present the project.

Create a learning activity to teach the essentials of the film

Perform the alternative ending of the movie in front of the class

Make a video (four minutes maximum) – alternative ending, or a section of the analysis.

Conduct an interview with someone that works/ is affected by the issue analysed in the film

Present your movie project as a TV show

Create a story board

Create a quiz show or a game

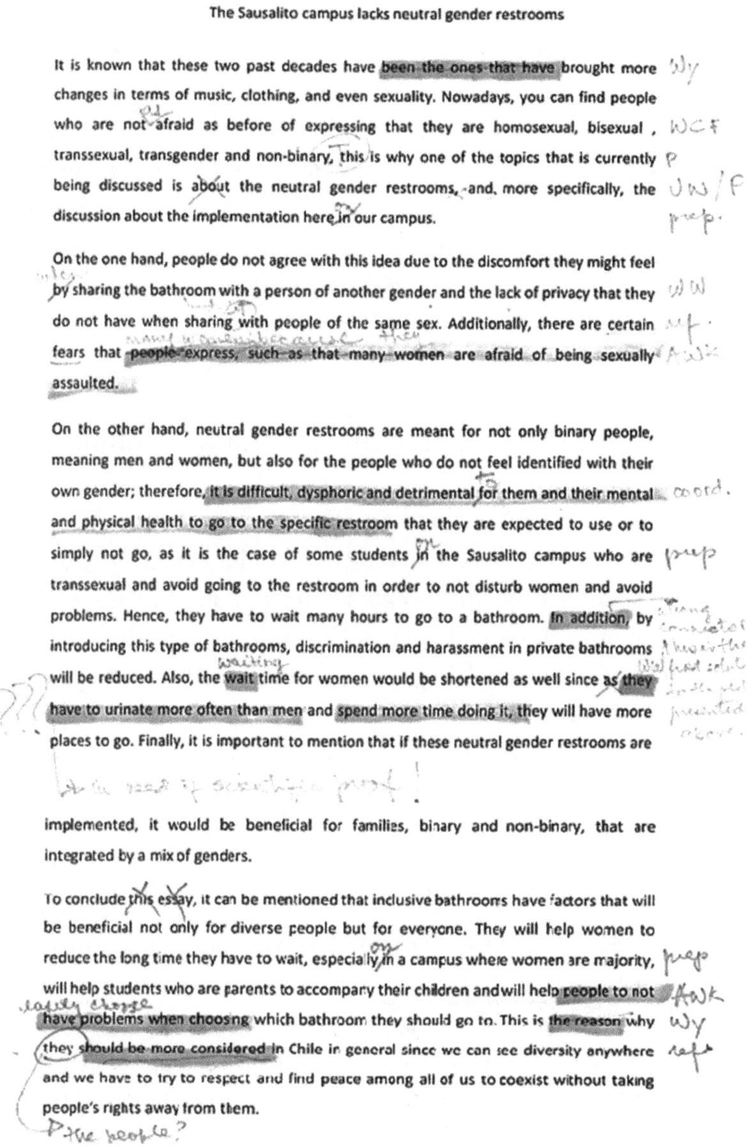

The Sausalito campus lacks neutral gender restrooms

It is known that these two past decades have ~~been the ones that have~~ brought more changes in terms of music, clothing, and even sexuality. Nowadays, you can find people who are not afraid as before of expressing that they are homosexual, bisexual , transsexual, transgender and non-binary, this is why one of the topics that is currently being discussed is about the neutral gender restrooms, and, more specifically, the discussion about the implementation here in our campus.

On the one hand, people do not agree with this idea due to the discomfort they might feel by sharing the bathroom with a person of another gender and the lack of privacy that they do not have when sharing with people of the same sex. Additionally, there are certain fears that ~~people express, such as that many women~~ are afraid of being sexually assaulted.

On the other hand, neutral gender restrooms are meant for not only binary people, meaning men and women, but also for the people who do not feel identified with their own gender; therefore, it is difficult, dysphoric and detrimental for them and their mental and physical health to go to the specific restroom that they are expected to use or to simply not go, as it is the case of some students in the Sausalito campus who are transsexual and avoid going to the restroom in order to not disturb women and avoid problems. Hence, they have to wait many hours to go to a bathroom. In addition, by introducing this type of bathrooms, discrimination and harassment in private bathrooms will be reduced. Also, the wait time for women would be shortened as well since as they have to urinate more often than men and spend more time doing it, they will have more places to go. Finally, it is important to mention that if these neutral gender restrooms are

implemented, it would be beneficial for families, binary and non-binary, that are integrated by a mix of genders.

To conclude this essay, it can be mentioned that inclusive bathrooms have factors that will be beneficial not only for diverse people but for everyone. They will help women to reduce the long time they have to wait, especially in a campus where women are majority, will help students who are parents to accompany their children and will help people to not have problems when choosing which bathroom they should go to. This is the reason why they should be more considered in Chile in general since we can see diversity anywhere and we have to try to respect and find peace among all of us to coexist without taking people's rights away from them.

Figure 12.1 Sample of a student-teacher's mini-essay (abbreviations on the margin correspond to a correction code)

that can be found in the text, with no other support than the text itself; *lexical questions* ask about specific words, terms or nominal phrases found in the text and supposed to be answered with the help of the co-text; *rhetorical-discursive questions* ask about the rhetorical strategies used by the author, the purpose of the writing or the author's intention either in a certain passage or in the whole text, the cohesion between sentences and the coherence between one paragraph and the next; *extra textual questions* ask about the reader's prior knowledge, the intertextual associations the reader may make, the reader's intention after reading the text, and everything that transcends it (e.g. whether or not they are interested in delving into the topic with the aid of subsequent reading input).

Complex grammatical structures such as parallelism, inversion, fronting, and nominalization were also included in this module. These structures were not taught explicitly, but they were part of the materials and tasks student-teachers had to accomplish.

Student-teachers' responses to the AE module

We considered a high level of student-teachers' participation in the design of the module. Thus, we surveyed them about how the module was developing during the semester. We applied two questionnaires: one, by the middle of the semester, and another, at the end. These instruments collected their perceptions about topics, activities, methodology and assessment. In this section, we present student-teachers' unaltered responses to these questionnaires categorized according to main themes: student-teachers' engagement, topics, activities, English language proficiency, assessment and critical thinking.

Student-teachers' engagement

The activities were designed to be challenging, both linguistically and thematically, and the student-teachers had a positive reaction to them, especially because they seemed to generate very efficacious group dynamics. Both teacher educators tried to create a relaxing classroom atmosphere by having the student-teachers express their ideas freely. This reduced their anxiety at speaking and turned the lessons into a democratic instance. A factor that helped student-teachers feel at ease and develop a stronger sense of confidence was their contribution to the selection of topics covered in this module. As the following student-teacher reports, they became enthusiastic in class:

> To be honest, I think this was the first semester in the program in which I participate so actively in classes because we covered topics that I am interested, and I feel comfortable to talk about. It was great that we were asked about the themes for this class. (Carla, Excerpt 1)

Topics

In the second survey, student-teachers were asked about the most significant topics for them during the semester. Most considered the topic of gender issues significant as expressed in the following responses:

> Gender issues helped me to understand how male chauvinism is thought, how we normalize certain situations that are simply not fair. (Carlos, Excerpt 2)

> I think that this topic took on new relevance in light of recent events and the appearance of the #MeToo on social media. (Cristina, Excerpt 3)

Student-teachers expressed that they had gained a broader understanding of the topic of gender issues and felt better able to support a position about gender inequality:

> Yes, I feel like if I get in a debate or argument about gender inequality I would be able to point out specific issues and raise awareness with thought provoking questions. (Maura, Excerpt 4)

Other student-teachers responded by saying that the topic of gender issues is something that teachers must be aware of, that must be taught to new generations and that it helped them make informed opinions.

The Arts and Australian history also emerged among the significant topics. Student-teachers commented that they were significant because they were related to their interests and could be powerful tools to influence changes in society. Student-teachers affirmed that through engaging tasks they could develop a broader understanding of major milestones in Australian culture and to link it to Chilean reality. In this sense, not only was topic selection facilitative of the learning process but also the teaching approach was. In fact, many expressed their gratification at having a different way of dealing with topics, skills and class management.

Class activities

Most student-teachers responded that they felt mostly engaged with the activities proposed by this module. In both surveys, most of them considered that developing *Speaking Projects* were the most effective activity because they helped them make learning more meaningful, it enhanced collaborative work and decrease their anxiety levels:

[they were] very well designed. We were able to create our own type of presentation that gave us freedom in doing it and also made different topics understandable. (Lucía, Excerpt 5)

My classmates and I were able to create projects in which we were both the protagonists and the creative minds. (Pablo, Excerpt 6)

Because it was most friendly for our anxiety issues having the opportunity to prepare something, being almost an expert and able to defend your argument. (Amanda, Excerpt 7)

The second most frequent activity mentioned was essay writing as it helped them expand knowledge by doing research about a topic (Figure 12.1), express their own points of view and increase topic-specific vocabulary. The third most favoured activity was having in-class discussions as they not only helped them develop their speaking skills but also were

a good way to share our opinions, and it is enriching as I learn to value other people´s opinion. (Marcos, Excerpt 8)

English language proficiency

Student-teachers reported that throughout the semester they developed effective strategies to acquire topic-specific vocabulary, idiomatic expressions and complex grammatical structures. In addition, they perceived that they had improved their writing skills and gained confidence in speaking:

I think I have expanded my vocabulary a lot in a short time as several times in the integrated skills worksheets I was asked to explain some terms or I have to look for the meaning of new words that appeared in the texts. And to accomplish the tasks, we needed to command the language and the contents. (Paulina, Excerpt 9)

It also helped me to improve my writing skills since we had feedback from the teacher before handing the different essays. (Jorge, Excerpt 10)

Assessment

Student-teachers reported that the most effective assessment tasks were essays among speaking projects, and use of English and reading comprehension tests:

Essays gave me more time to reflect and write my opinions, and I believe it was great to have this opportunity to write with no pressure of time. (Emilia, Excerpt 11)

The essays, (…), were also really effective because we could do research about the topic, and check what was wrong and improve it in the next one and, in some of them, we had the chance to have someone else revise it before submission which also makes a difference and helps us correct our mistakes more effectively (Maria, Excerpt 12)

Other responses referred to encouraging reflection, a deeper understanding of the topics, acquiring vocabulary and assessing the writing process instead of the final product.

Speaking Projects 1 and 2 were reported as the second most effective assessment tasks. Student-teachers considered that these assessments were the key to learning as they had freedom to carry them out; they could conduct research on their own, could engage in collaborative work and could integrate the four linguistic skills.

Critical thinking

The module helped the student-teachers develop their critical thinking in that they could analyse the topics from different perspectives:

Now I try to question others' positions on a topic and also my own opinions about it before stating who is right or wrong. (Juan, Excerpt 13)

I remember that during the unit of gender issues, we watched a TED talk of a man promoting feminism, we read an article by Deborah Tannen about why women are marked and we read an article about a black man against homosexuality. We could perceive similar issues from different perspectives and, by doing so, we could get a broader view of it. For the unit about Australia and the one about Education we were also able to identify different aspects of certain issues. I think that the fact that we have been able to deal with all these issues from different points of view have been very helpful for me. (Augusta, Excerpt 14)

Class discussions have helped me develop critical thinking, since we were constantly clashing in the ideas we, as a class, had about different issues. These different perspectives gave me ideas that I could later develop in essays. (Pamela, Excerpt 15)

Discussion and challenges

One of the purposes of embracing the design of this module was to help shape a teaching/learning community where all its members would benefit, and, at the same time, the student-teachers' professional career would be furthered and empowered by our modelling the teaching process. As members of the Department of English teaching staff of PUCV we are convinced that the teaching model we designed can be replicated in the student-teachers' own teaching practices. In addition, motivation to participate as student members of this community was strengthened not only with the organization of the module but also with the opportunity to share their perceptions of the way the module was being developed. Another teaching purpose was to receive the students' feedback on how they had been taught the language and how they would respond to a fresh teaching approach. As the first survey and assessment tasks revealed, the positive responses informed that our approach was accurate, that we were achieving the objectives set for the module and that the competence-based curriculum was being closely followed. The second survey corroborated both our own perceptions and those of our student-teachers.

The module included generally neglected or superficially treated topics such as the history of Australia and gender issues. At the moment the module was taking place, gender issues was a trending topic in Chile (still is), and most of the student-teachers would advocate for equal rights between men and women (they still do). These two topics – Australia and gender issues – helped them discuss and support their arguments in a respectful ambiance. Evidently, these topics and those concerning history and current world events contributed to giving them a multicultural perspective as well. The student-teachers' writing skills were also enriched, judging from the results obtained from the mini-essays. These mini-essays seemed to have prepared them for the following level of English, whose syllabus contents seek to have them adopt both professional attitudes towards writing and formal composition behaviours. Grammar and the use of English took up less classroom time than did other contents, but these features were also relevant to the student-teachers' knowledge of English because their level of English must be internationally certified in C1 before they graduate.

Not only were the materials engaging but also meaningful to their future professional career; this was coupled with the freedom to choose topics within a vast range of options, the freedom to choose their partners to work in groups and the freedom to entertain informed opinions. This freedom contributed to their active participation in class and to an enthusiastic welcome of the topics. By the same token, the approach adopted for this module was the students' exposition to new methods and activities and, ultimately, to new ways of doing things, as compared to previous levels of English proficiency that make up the language core of the ELTE programme. We presume that most assessment tasks, for example, were new to the student-teachers, because they were applied in a very stress-free manner: oral presentations, which caused them to form very cohesive groups with three or four of their classmates, and take-home written tests, which caused them to look up extra information.

Undoubtedly, this module was not without its challenges. First, the class sizes (twenty student-teachers in one parallel module; twenty-five in the other) were a demanding job. Sometimes we would get the two parallel modules together for different activities, thereby having a class of over fifty students in one classroom. Group work engaged in collaborative tasks was the way we approached this challenge. This contributed to increasing student-teachers' time on task and peer support.

Another challenge that we faced while teaching this module was related to our own beliefs and experiences as teacher educators. In this sense, through this module we learnt to be more flexible and to challenge ourselves to implement an approach that integrated linguistic skills, cultural contents and tasks. With limited time, we did our best to embrace a learning design that allowed our student-teachers to advance their command of English and learn about crucial topics that empowered them as committed teachers of English.

A third challenge was to make sure the competencies set in the syllabus were achieved including the level of language proficiency. In fact, a permanent tension during the module was to integrate strategies so that student-teachers could succeed in CAE exam without affecting the other demanding learning outcomes. In fact, aligning learning outcomes, topics, grammatical structures and skills was not easy. However, we believe that the module design proved to be successful.

Conclusions

In this chapter, we have reflected on the pedagogical and practical challenges of an advanced language module for future English teachers in Chile. This module was coherent with a social pedagogy, employing an explicit sociocultural understanding of language learning. This is reflected in the alignment of learning outcomes, tasks, assessment, scaffolding and the use of a wide range of resources. The dialectic relationship between the individual learning and the sociocultural context was engendered through the constant challenge of co-constructing content and active participation in the tasks. This design proved to promote high level of student-teachers' engagement and empower student-teachers to understand sociocultural context of English language as a global communication tool.

This experience also demonstrated that this design can effectively contribute to developing productive and receptive skills of English learning effectively at an advanced level. The design of complex tasks proved to challenge and engage student-teachers in their own learning. However, if task completion is aided with such expectation setting and timely scaffolding, the learning experience can be positive and productive. Our student-teachers could develop a collaborative attitude towards overcoming difficulties, aligning their individual needs to the collective sociocultural context and becoming empowered English teachers. We strongly believe that experiences like this one have the potentiality to shape and change student-teachers' beliefs in language learning and impact their future teaching practices across a diverse range of contexts. In this sense, we argue that ELTE programmes should move towards less compartmentalization of content knowledge and move towards more integration of language development and teaching methods.

Questions for change

1. What is the impact of standardized tests on the design of AE courses for prospective teachers of English?
2. What are the challenges for student-teachers to engage in their own learning?
3. How can teacher educators align learning outcomes with grammar structures, skills and strategies more effectively?
4. What are the challenges for teacher-educators teaching advanced levels of proficiency?

13

English Language Proficiency of Non-Native Student-Teachers in Turkey

Müzeyyen Nazlı Güngör

Introduction

Non-native English-speaking teachers (NNESTs) constitute a wide majority of English language teachers around the world (Canagarajah 1999; Medgyes 2017). Recent studies focus on NNESTs' preparation on two main themes: knowing how (being able to do something with the language) and knowing what (knowing about the language) (Freeman 2017; Martinez Agudo 2017; Tarone & Allwright 2005). While the first theme is related to PCK – the pedagogical knowledge applied in the field – the latter centres around content knowledge (subject-matter knowledge) (Banegas 2009; Richards 2017a). Work on content knowledge draws on the notion that 'a teacher's confidence is most dependent on his or her own degree of language competence' (Murdoch 1994: 258) because it deals with language proficiency skills that an English language teacher is required to master in the target language (Kamhi-Stein 2009). Recent studies (Banegas 2009; Borg 2006b; Kamhi-Stein 2009; Tsang 2017; Woodgate-Jones 2008) have shown that NNESTs view language proficiency as the most important element of teacher education programmes. As noted by Medgyes (2017), second language teacher education programmes are, therefore, designed to link content knowledge with pedagogical CK and GPK.

As it is explained in various studies (Freeman 2017; Richards 2017a; Tarone & Allwright 2005), one of the components of teachers' knowledge base is content knowledge because English language teachers are expected to teach language skills (reading, writing, listening and speaking) and components (grammar and vocabulary) competently. Thus, professional competency in ELT is closely related to content knowledge, teaching skills and the ability to teach in

English (Murdoch 1994; Richards 2017). Content knowledge refers to teachers' understanding of the teaching subject that can be learnt from disciplines such as linguistics, advanced language skills and components, and literature, among others. Richards (2017) asserts that the mastery of language and the ability to use it are vital for effective lesson delivery and management. Freeman (2017) also agrees that teaching language through language has required a number of interrelated elements: content knowledge, pedagogical knowledge and ability, and discourse skills. For Freeman (2017), the language in FL classes plays two main roles: (1) as the lesson content and (2) the means of teaching and content. In other words, a language teacher needs high degree of ELP to scaffold students' learning and mediate the talk during activities. It is also necessary to become a role model in using and practising the language during activities, managing the classroom through dialogues and building interaction among students. Richards (2017), for example, lists a number of classroom acts and activities that require high ELP for effective instruction such as explaining the aims of the lesson, giving instructions, using English for classroom management, asking and answering questions, simplifying or paraphrasing the message, explaining meanings through metaphors and synonyms, leading activities, or giving feedback on students' performances.

In light of these directions, this chapter focuses on the ways content knowledge is approached in IELTE programmes and how non-native student-teachers are scaffolded to develop knowledge of and about the English language in Turkey. The following sections provide an overview of the research on language-proficiency-related problems of NNESTs and describe the recent approaches that IELTE programmes have employed to address the issue of NNESTs.

NNESTs' ELP levels

As explained above, teachers' ELP plays an important role in determining the effectiveness of teaching. Taken together, research findings (Butler 2004; Copland, Garton, & Burns 2014; Cullen 2002; Murdoch 1994; Kamhi-Stein 2009) have shown that ELP has been mainly concerned with teachers' self-perceptions, instructional practices and pedagogical skills, motivation, confidence, and identity. Kamhi-Stein (2014) and Woodgate-Jones (2008), for instance, have reported a strong relationship among language proficiency, teaching practices and self-perceptions of language teachers. In their study Kamhi-Stein and Mahboob (2005) also found that NNESTs related their ELP to effective instruction delivery in the classroom. Similarly, Eslami and Fatahi (2008) investigated the relationship between Iranian English language teachers' self-reported English proficiency and their self-efficacy regarding abilities to teach English. Their findings reveal a positive relationship between perceived level of ELP and sense of self-efficacy. To be more specific, a NNEST's teaching skill has been described as influential in a number of teaching dimensions (Cullen 2002; Richards 2017). More specifically, a teacher with low proficiency level is likely to have difficulty with basic instructional procedures such as giving instructions, asking questions on activities, explaining the meaning of a word, using complex and long literary texts with students, consulting dictionaries, or adapting language content in a coursebook to tailor it according to students' needs. In other words, low-level ELP restricts NNESTs in the choice of instructional activities in the classroom. Therefore, as Kamhi-Stein (2014) emphasizes, the level of ELP affects how NNESTs position themselves in the classroom. Considering the examples above, a teacher with high-level ELP is found to be more self-confident, able to teach more effectively, use the target language more communicatively in the classroom, and communicate with students more successfully (Banegas 2009: Kamhi-Stein 2014; Medgyes 2017; Richards 2017).

The importance of developing ELP is central to many NNESTs from all around the world particularly in Europe (Copland, Garton, & Burns 2014; Smit & Dafouz 2012), Asia (Kam 2002; Zein 2017), and America (Bale 2016; Tedick 2013) since recent studies reveal that many NNESTs still have problems with their ELP levels. In East Asian countries such as Bangladesh, Malaysia, Vietnam, Thailand, Singapore, Indonesia, although English is being introduced in primary schools, this policy has not been successfully implemented due to many factors, one of which is primary English teachers' inadequate command of English (Hamid 2010; Kam 2002; Zein 2017). This situation, unfortunately, limits the use of English for communication purposes suggested in the curriculum and the integration of language skills into classroom practices. In a similar vein, Butler (2004) investigated the self-evaluations of NNESTs' English proficiencies in Korea, Taiwan and Japan. These studies show that the NNESTs do not find their current proficiency levels satisfactory enough to teach English communicatively. As a result, it is argued that the kinds and levels of English proficiency NNESTs need to teach English under the existing language policy emphasizing communicative language teaching should be identified (Butler 2004). In his study with fifteen experienced Argentinian NNESTs, Banegas (2009) also found out that the participating teachers viewed content knowledge as the most salient aspect of the knowledge base in their initial teacher education. Their beliefs revealed that in order to be a model for learners, student-teachers needed to be equipped with background in the culture of the target language and high ELP. Hence, in the study it was suggested that due to teachers' low-level ELP, IELTE programmes focus on English grammar, advanced language skills and linguistics courses more. In another study by Medgyes (2017), 198 Hungarian NNESTs were asked to identify the difficulties in English and evaluate their IELTE programmes. According to the results, vocabulary, speaking and oral fluency were considered to be the most problematic areas. Medgyes (2017) elaborated on the results stating that that these teachers had problems with slang words, idioms, phrasal verbs and synonyms. These deficits in teachers' vocabulary repertoire may cause problems in their classroom teaching skills such as making error corrections, managing classrooms, simplifying the language according to learners' levels, and choosing instructional materials (Medgyes 2017; Richards 2017). Moreover, NNESTs with low ELP may have the tendency to be coursebook slaves without trying to change, omit or insert anything (Medgyes 2017). The lack of authentic communication skills in the target language may also cause NNESTs to simply switch into L1 for fear of being unable to deal with problematic situations effectively. In addition, NNESTs were found to be more heavy-handed while marking and correcting errors and most of them were unable to catch lexical errors in learners' English language usage (Medgyes 2017).

Similar to these findings, Hadjioannou and Hutchinson (2010) assert that student-teachers cannot teach the grammar topics in which their subject-matter knowledge is lacking; as a result, their quality of grammar teaching experience suffers. In their qualitative case study with thirty-one student-teachers in the United States, it was found that as a result of their microteaching practices in grammar teaching, they began to notice the grammar topics more and made connections between the grammatical concepts and how they could help learners understand these topics. Furthermore, Barkhuizen (1997) revealed in his study that South African student-teachers were concerned with and anxious about their low ELP. In his qualitative study with twenty-nine non-native student-teachers (Arabic, Spanish, French, German, Japanese) in the United States, Bale (2016) found out that using the target language competently in teaching English contributed to both their understanding of the role of English as content and medium of instruction and the expansion of their pedagogical and professional skills.

As Freeman and Johnson (1998) state, language teachers must be seen as learners of language teaching and the factors affecting and contributing to their language learning must be considered in local teacher education programmes. What is meant by the local teacher education here is rooted in the sociocultural theory in language teacher education. Accordingly, the knowledge base must be grounded in teacher learning within the social, cultural and institutional contexts in which learning and teacher learning occur. Moving from this notion, Turkey is considered as one of the expanding circle countries (Medgyes 2017) where English is accepted as an FL and language teachers have almost no chance to interact with native speakers to develop their language proficiency. Hence, IELTE programmes are the sole settings for them to improve and practice their ELP. As it is the case in many expanding circle countries (Greece, Hong Kong, Japan, Russia), language teaching problems stemming from the language proficiency deficit of Turkish English language teachers have received a great deal of attention in various studies.

Developing ELP in IELTE in Turkey

IELTE programmes in Turkey use a concurrent model for all levels of education (Eurydice 2009). According to this model, student-teachers receive subject training, pedagogical subjects and a certain amount of practicum credit during their four-year undergraduate studies. These programmes educate English language student-teachers for primary, secondary and tertiary levels (Seferoğlu 2006). Most IELTE programmes in Turkey require one-year preparatory education that educates student-teachers for the department in terms of language proficiency (Demirbaş 2011; Özmen, Çakır, & Cephe 2018). Upon their enrolment in the university, student-teachers are required to take an ELP examination at the beginning of the year. Although the conduction of these examinations varies among universities, in general students are to be tested in language proficiency skills and components (Coşkun & Daloğlu 2010). If they pass the exam, they start their four-year education in the department. If they fail, then they take a one-year compulsory preparatory course solely focusing on language skills and language component courses. Student-teachers in this preparatory education are introduced to authentic video and audio materials to practise presentation and pronunciation skills, and so they have the chance to develop writing, reading and listening skills (Demirbaş 2011).

After successfully completing the preparatory year, student-teachers continue their education in the IELTE programme. All the IELTE programmes in Turkey followed the curriculum the Council of Higher Education (CoHE) issued back in 2006 until 2018, when a revised version was introduced as a framework for all the IELTE programmes in Turkey. This previous curriculum was different from the new one in terms of reduced course hours in some skills, the variety and content of the courses in content knowledge, pedagogical content knowledge, pedagogical knowledge and general knowledge skills (Table 13.1). With the newly launched IELTE curriculum (CoHE 2018), the scope of the Bachelor's degree curriculum in IELTE has become 240 ECTS (European Credit Transfer System) credits (CoHE 2018). Out of 240 credits, 65 credits are offered for content knowledge courses, 42 credits are for general culture and for PCK courses, and 91 credits are for GPK courses. The categorization of the courses in both versions of the curriculum is as follows:

Table 13.1 The 2006 and 2018 IELTE Curricula in Turkey

	The Previous (2006) IELTE Curriculum	The New (2018) IELTE Curriculum
Content knowledge	• Advanced Reading and Writing Skills I, II • Listening and Pronunciation I, II • Oral Communication Skills I, II • Contextual Grammar I, II • Lexicology • Linguistics I, II • English Literature I, II • Turkish – English Translation • English – Turkish Translation • Public Speaking • English in Mass Media	• Reading Skills I, II • Writing Skills I, II • Listening and Pronunciation I, II • Oral Communication Skills I, II • Structure of English • English Literature I, II • Linguistics I, II • Critical Reading and Writing • Translation Studies
Pedagogical content knowledge	• Approaches in ELT I, II • Language Acquisition • Teaching English to Young Learners I, II • Teaching Language Skills I, II • Special Teaching Methods I, II • Literature and Language Teaching I, II • Drama • Materials Adaptation and Syllabus Design in ELT • Testing and Evaluation in ELT	• Approaches to English Language Learning and Teaching I, II • English Language Teaching Curriculum • Language Acquisition • Teaching English to Young Learners I, II • Teaching English Language Skills I, II • Literature and Language Teaching I, II • Syllabus Design in ELT • Testing and Evaluation in ELT

(Continued)

Table 13.1 (Continued)

	The Previous (2006) IELTE Curriculum	The New (2018) IELTE Curriculum
General pedagogical knowledge	• Introduction to Education • Educational Sociology • Educational Psychology • Effective Communication Skills • Instructional Technologies and Materials Evaluation in Education • Instructional Principles and Methods • Classroom Management • Testing and Evaluation • Turkish Educational System and School Management • School Experience • Practice Teaching • Special Education and Inclusion • Guidance	• Introduction to Education • Educational Sociology • Educational Psychology • Educational Philosophy • Instructional Technologies • Instructional Principles and Methods • Research Methods in Education • Classroom Management • Ethics in Education • Testing and Evaluation in Education • Turkish Educational System and School Management • Practice Teaching I, II • Special Education and Inclusion • Guidance at Schools
General knowledge	• Principles of Ataturk and History of Turkish Revolution • Second Foreign Language I, II, III • Information Technologies in Education • Turkish I, II (Written and Oral Expression) • History of Turkish Education • Research Methods	• Principles of Ataturk and History of Turkish Revolution • Foreign Language I, II • Information Technologies • Turkish I, II • History of Turkish Education • Community Service
Elective courses	• Community Service • Career Planning in ELT • Pragmatics • Semantics • Sociolinguistics • Discourse Analysis	• English in Mass Media • Pragmatics and Language Teaching • Language and Society • World Englishes and Culture • English Coursebook Evaluation • Drama in ELT • Materials Design in ELT • New Approaches in ELT • Teaching Lexicon • Testing Learning • Sociolinguistics and Language Teaching • Discourse Analysis and Language Teaching • Teaching Integrated Language Skills

The aims of content knowledge courses are to develop student-teachers' cognitive skills (summarizing, synthesizing, analysing, referring, guessing, evaluating) in literary texts, help them gain reading and writing habits, familiarize them with authentic audio and visual texts, perform presentation skills in public, and raise their self-confidence as a teacher. In general, the medium of communication in all these courses is English. Teacher educators both follow the latest course descriptions and bring authentic materials for extracurricular studies. Along with the content knowledge courses, general pedagogical, pedagogical content knowledge, general knowledge and elective courses provide student-teachers with the opportunity to transfer their content knowledge skills into the field. Specifically, student-teachers in this concurrent model use their English language skills in microteaching presentations and real classes, the cooperation with peers while getting prepared for presentations, reflections in and on their self- and peer performances, and methodology courses and practicum experience in which they teach English to different age groups and populations (Coşkun & Daloğlu 2010; Seferoğlu 2006).

Despite the heavy load in terms of course variety and hours, NNESTs in Turkey still stress the challenges they have experienced in teaching both at pre-service and in-service contexts due to their limited proficiency levels. The notion that IELTE programmes need to deal with issues of student-teachers' language proficiency-related problems, as well as issues of offering opportunities to develop student-teachers' ELP levels, has received strong support in the national literature (Akcan 2016; Altan 2006; Çetinavcı & Yavuz 2010; Coşkun & Daloğlu 2010; Erozan 2005: Kırkgöz 2009; Kömür 2010; Özmen, Çakır, & Cephe 2018; Şallı-Çopur 2008; Seferoğlu 2006; Yavuz & Zehir Topkaya 2013). Coşkun and Daloğlu (2010) evaluated the effectiveness of one of the IELTE programmes in Turkey from student-teachers' and teacher educators' perspectives. While student-teachers focused on the practicum component and delivery of the courses, teacher educators thought that the programme neglected developing student-teachers' ELP levels. They argued that some student-teachers were not ready for the second-year courses of the programme, which required more complex written production, due to their low-level ELP. They further admitted that the number of courses was not sufficient to develop their ELP levels and that for this reason student-teachers needed to either be offered more content knowledge courses or take one-year preparatory education before they enrol in the programme. Erozan (2005) also evaluated the language improvement courses in an IELTE programme in Turkey through questionnaires, interviews, classroom observations, and examination of the significant documents. She suggested that the component of the content knowledge courses involve more practice through the active use of authentic materials, appropriate activities and methods, and continuity and coherence between other language skill courses.

Similarly, Şallı-Çopur (2008) investigated how competent graduate prospective English teachers found themselves and how successful they found the IELTE programme in Turkey. Although these teachers found themselves competent enough in most of the skills, they expressed the need to further develop the competencies of language knowledge and spoken use of English. Another study by Yavuz and Zehir Topkaya (2013) highlighted the necessity of standardization in preparatory education across the country and concluded that the content knowledge needed to be emphasized and developed by extending the skill courses throughout the four-year programme. They further discussed that student-teachers especially in EFL countries cannot perceive themselves as competent language teachers without sufficient ELP levels. It was implied that IELTE programmes needed to be revaluated regarding content, procedures and teaching competencies of the novice teachers and to be divided according to the needs of primary and secondary students' needs in basic education (Yavuz & Zehir Topkaya 2013).

Emphasis on issues of language proficiency levels of student-teachers has also come from detailed analysis of interviews, questionnaires and observation in the microteaching and practicum contexts. For example, Kömür (2010) conducted a study with thirty-nine senior student-teachers to investigate the relationship between teaching knowledge, self-rating of competencies and their practicum experience. More recently, Akcan (2016) conducted a study with non-native novice language teachers and collected data through a questionnaire and focus group interviews. In her study, emphasis was placed on novice teachers' needs for more explicit guidance from the supervisors to improve their language proficiency and teaching skills. It was also stated that those teachers needed guidance as to the ways and opportunities to develop their ELP levels. Similar to Akcan (2016), Kömür (2010) also supports the notion that language proficiency should play an important role in IELTE and that student-teachers should be given more explicit feedback to improve their ELP levels. Specifically, Çetinavcı and Yavuz (2010) investigated the language proficiency of 144 NNESTs in Turkey through a questionnaire and state staff FL proficiency exam. Their findings indicated that there was either deterioration or no positive change in these teachers' grammatical and lexical knowledge of English during their initial years of teacher education. Therefore, they argue that initial teacher education programmes should be revised so as to improve student-teachers' ELP levels. Altan (2006), exploring the ways to prepare English language teachers for new standards and policies in the twenty-first century, suggests embedding language proficiency enhancement activities into IELTE programmes while, at the same time, capitalizing on the challenges that Turkish English language teachers experience. He acknowledges that the ability to use the language in real-life contexts for social and professional purposes is required of English language teachers in Turkey to understand the contemporary media in the target language and to interact effectively. More recently, Özmen, Çakır and Cephe (2018), investigating the 851 NNESTs' perception of English accent and culture in Turkey, revealed that these teachers mostly had problems with pronunciation skills. While they emphasize the need to revise the IELTE curriculum, they also argue that it is teacher educators' role and responsibility to scaffold student-teachers to improve their ELP.

Özmen (2012), examining the impact of IELTE programmes in Turkey on student-teachers' belief development, found out that the first year of the IELTE programme that consisted of content knowledge courses were reported to have the least impact on student-teachers' academic achievement. This is because of the delivery of these courses and their traditional view of learning an FL; however, they found these courses critical in developing their academic language skills. In other words, student-teachers were observed to follow rote learning, memorization and short-term study habits as major learning strategies. Özmen (2012) reasons that this situation could stem from the grammar-based national examination policy, which has been applied from primary level of education to tertiary levels. English language student-teachers in Turkey take high-stakes examinations before their enrolment in any IELTE programme (Çetinavcı & Yavuz 2010). These examinations consist of multiple-choice questions and assess reading, vocabulary and grammar knowledge through artificial and isolated contexts. Student-teachers who are prepared for these examinations throughout their fourth year of high-school education follow certain exam strategies by focusing on grammar and vocabulary building. Not surprisingly, such examination policy leaves negative washback on developing student-teachers' communicative language skills and ELP levels. In addition to the problems in the delivery of the skill courses, teacher educators' insufficient feedback strategies and less effective facilitator roles, and student-teachers' previously held language-learning beliefs make the language proficiency development process difficult for student-teachers in IELTE programme.

Steps towards the development of ELP

Educating NNESTs with regard to CK, PCK and GPK for a more communicative teaching atmosphere has received growing attention in the field. This notion draws on Murdoch's rationale (1994: 254): 'Language proficiency will always represent the bedrock of their professional confidence.' In other words, language teachers view opportunities to improve their ELP as vital to their professional identity and development. Given the highly expressed need for more opportunities to develop ELP levels of NNESTs in Turkey, it is possible to identify the following issues as central to in IELTE programmes, teacher educators, and NNESTs in preparation.

Firstly, the curriculum in IELTE programmes should challenge and help NNESTs develop a sense of self-confidence and professional legitimacy (Kamhi-Stein 2009). To this end, as Altan (2006) suggests, the rationale behind educating NNESTs should change from initial teacher education only to life-long professional development. In this way, when they become novices, they will be able to experience a wider use of English in daily life and academic contexts through seminars, in-service trainings, and professional organizations (Freeman 2017; Özmen 2012).

Secondly, it is thought that teacher educators play a great role in helping NNESTs develop positive self-identities (Akcan 2016; Kamhi-Stein 2009; Kömür 2010; Richards 2017), particularly by providing student-teachers with opportunities to develop and practise their language skills through various authentic audio and video materials, and effective feedback during the activities. Hence, the quality of content knowledge courses can be increased in the first and second year of the IELTE programmes (Coşkun & Daloğlu 2010). As regards quality, instead of employing memorization and other traditional techniques, student-teachers should be provided with more opportunities to perform their productive skills such as oral presentations, role-plays and drama. Educators in these courses should carefully detect the language deficits and needs of student-teachers and develop activities that are congruent with these deficits and needs throughout the programme.

Teacher educators can also scaffold NNESTs by integrating a language development component into other CK and PCK courses (Murdoch 1994; Richards 2017). To be specific, assignments, microteaching lesson plans, video recordings of microteaching performances, diaries and other documents can be utilized as reflection materials that help NNESTs evaluate themselves, understand their basic mistakes, raise their awareness in the deficits of language skills and components, and discuss alternative ways to improve problematic areas. Cullen describes this approach as 'a command of classroom language' in which lesson transcripts and microteaching lesson plans are used as tools for developing ELP (as cited in Richards 2017: 27). Teacher educators may ask student-teachers to read aloud or role-play these transcripts in PCK courses. Then, student-teachers may redesign the lesson plans by considering language proficiency and pedagogy components. Nemtchinova, Mahboob, Eslami and Doğançay-Aktuna (2010) also suggest the use of role-play and game activities to improve student-teachers' both teaching and language skills. As Coşkun and Daloğlu (2010) highlight, the components of an IELTE programme should reflect the harmony of both theory and practice.

Thirdly, IELTE programmes should apply a communicative preparatory exemption examination which focuses on the integrated use of the four skills. Those who fail the examination should receive one-year English preparatory education. In her study, Demirbas (2011) revealed that student-teachers who received a one-year preparatory course at a large state university in Turkey were found to be more successful than those who did not especially in terms of reading and writing skills. To gain a deeper insight into effectiveness of English language preparatory education on student-teachers' ELP levels, the content of preparatory education, the instructors' background in the proficiency, the selection of materials and implementation of the skill-based examinations should also be analysed through various data collection methods. In this respect, Kırkgöz (2009: 679) states: 'Effective foreign language education is predicated significantly on the training of teachers. Without a strong contingent of professionally competent and well-trained teachers, there will always be a gap between policy rhetoric and classroom reality'. Hence, educating professionally competent and self-confident teachers will affect, respectively, the education of their students.

Fourthly, current thinking in the field emphasizes the notion that student-teachers' motivation, self-confidence and willingness play a prominent role in overcoming ELP-related teaching and learning problems (Kamhi-Stein 2014; Medgyes 2017; Nemtchinova et al. 2010). These scholars emphasize that self-directed strategies may help them develop better language skills and proficiency levels, and may boost their confidence as a teacher. To start with the speaking skill, it is suggested that student-teachers practise their pronunciation by reading passages containing problematic sounds. Alternatively, they may play 'just a minute' game in which they try to speak about a hot topic without hesitating, stammering or repeating the same words for exactly one minute (Medgyes 2017). They may even record their own monologue and listen to it to detect problematic sounds or expressions. Another opportunity is to attend international conferences and talk to colleagues about the field.

A new trend in organizing international conferences is webinars, which saves money and time for many professionals and organizers in the world. IATEFL, for example, organizes free monthly webinars on English language and language teaching. Webinars may serve as a good opportunity to engage in text messages in the chat box, listen to the speaker and join the discussion online. This may both enhance student-teachers' conversational strategies and broaden their horizons in the field. As for the listening skill, the most convenient technique may be watching TV series, video clips or news on BBC or CNN. While listening to these programmes, student-teachers may take notes about who and where they are, what they are doing and their relationship to each other. Özmen, Çakır and Cephe (2018) provided strong support for the fact that upon their graduation NNESTs considered the Internet and other online materials as the primary source to develop their speaking and listening skills in English. They may even focus on one type of a language element (collocations, phrasal verbs, etc.) and jot down every part of speech as they hear it.

Considering the limitations of an expanding circle country and the teachers' teaching experiences mainly for preparing students for high-stakes exams in the country, the Internet and online sources are perceived to be the most effective and affordable way to practise English language skills by NNESTs. To develop reading and writing skills, Kamhi-Stein (2014) suggests a useful technique called 'macro-text deconstruction strategies'. Specifically, NNESTs select an article from a well-known journal such as TESOL Quarterly or ELT Journal. They may try to identify as many text structures, vocabulary items and clauses as necessary to understand how well-written articles are designed. By paying attention to academic vocabulary, one can take articles as examples to shed light on their writing skills. Another technique is that student-teachers use dictionaries when they come across a word or idiom they have not heard or seen before, because reading skills cannot be improved without lexical background. Particularly, using corpora such as the British National Corpus, the Oxford English Corpus and the Corpus of Contemporary American English will enhance student-teachers' understanding of native speakers' use of words and word families in contexts.

Finally, Altan (2006) and Kamhi-Stein (2014) suggest that student-teachers be informed about national and international teacher associations and professional organizations such as INGED, IATEFL and TESOL. This may be realized in various courses such as career planning or ELF in IELTE programmes. Through these associations, they can be informed about professional development opportunities in which English is used as the means of communication to teach, develop job-advertising practices and meet many professionals in the field.

Conclusion

The relationship between student-teachers' ELP levels and their ability to teach is often found to be problematic and complex for non-native student-teachers who are aware of their limitations in ELP and teacher educators in IELTE programmes. In this chapter, I have drawn attention to non-native student-teachers' increasing need for developing ELP levels in an EFL context and opportunities to be employed by teacher educators and IELTE programmes in Turkey. Overall, while IELTE programmes are found to be successful in educating non-native student-teachers regarding pedagogical skills, they are reported to be limited in terms of developing ELP levels and enriching content knowledge courses. Although teachers do not have to be native speakers to teach the language effectively, high degree of ELP in oral and written skills is required in our globalized world (Freeman 2017). Yet, how high this proficiency should be depends on a variety of factors such as the context where English is taught, the skills which are being practised, the aims of students' learning English and students' level of English (Kamhi-Stein 2014; Nemtchinova et al. 2010).

To conclude, language proficiency and teaching ability are not the same. The deficit view of knowing *what* without *how* or vice versa fails to recognize the importance and sociocultural aspect of language teaching and learning in diverse contexts. An alternative perspective provided by Freeman (2017) is to perceive teaching English for specific purposes as an effective way to help NNESTs improve their classroom English proficiency. He advocates that the traditional view of native speakerism, in which NNESTs have outmoded ideas of fluency in general language use, should be forgotten. In other words, it is argued that while providing PCK for student-teachers, it is also necessary to improve their classroom ELP that will support them in the teaching profession. In this respect, there is an urgent need for studies which focus on NNESTs' classroom discourse, their beliefs about developing ELP in expanding circles, how non-native student-teachers' language proficiency needs are met and affected in local teaching contexts, and how IELTE programmes address this issue. Non-native student-teachers in expanding circle countries need to view their ELP education as part of their life-long professional development rather than an absolute end.

Questions for change

1. What are the major ELP-related problems you have encountered in teaching English? What are your strategies to overcome them? Which strategy in this chapter appeals to you most?
2. Do you think having a high ELP guarantees the ability to teach? Why/not?
3. What other skills, values and dispositions, do you think, you need to develop to be a competent teacher in the global world?
4. Have you ever transferred your own language-learning strategies into your teaching skills? How does it contribute to your teaching practice?
5. How does IELTE in Turkey differ from your context? What are the successful and less successful features of IELTE programmes in your context?

14

Literacy in the IELTE Curriculum through a Cultural Component

María Alejandra Soto and Ricardo Martín Ramírez

Introduction

Reading and writing courses are frequently a central component of IELTE curricula. Usually, the design of this type of course entails a careful consideration of the topics, genres and task formats that aspiring language teachers should most likely engage in and, especially, a clear theoretical basis to support any pedagogical decision taken in relation to curricular adjustments. In the case of the course described here, introducing such adjustments to our syllabus implied a detailed analysis of the reading and writing practices our student-teachers engage in so as to promote their effectiveness through their intersection with culture.

Reading is often taken for granted by those who read on a regular basis. However, it is a complex and multifaceted activity that requires deep understanding of the processes involved. As such it is desirable that teacher educators be aware of the complexities that arise when teaching to read in a second language and the theoretical underpinnings necessary to justify pedagogical decisions. In the same vein, writing is a multimodal and multidimensional activity that has particular affordances as a means of representation and as a form of communication. Nonetheless, it is usually considered a secondary symbolic system due to the importance given to speech and to the misconception that writing is a gift that only a few possess. In this sense, we (all upcoming uses of this inclusive pronoun *we* should be interpreted as a direct reference to the authors of this chapter) agree that a comprehensive approach to both reading and writing should focus on the fact that these two are dialogic skills that can actually be learnt.

Due to the traditional operative modes in which reading and writing classes are usually structured in IELTE programmes in Argentina, student-teachers seldom find a space to reflect upon their own linguistic processes while adhering to a critical thinking matrix. For this reason, it is vital that teacher educators do not oversimplify the nature of the reading and writing spectrum but rather help student-teachers grapple with the benefits of developing rhetorical awareness insofar as it may provide them with a dynamic intellectual tool for decoding different discourses and (literary) genres. We are convinced that by introducing the notion of rhetorical awareness at an early stage in an IELTE programme, student-teachers can navigate different semantic fields and (literary) genres feeling more at ease; develop intercultural awareness and critical thinking skills alongside; and challenge the pervasiveness of ethnocentric perspectives as they embark on meaningful reading and writing projects. Relatedly, we believe that 'language is the principal means whereby we conduct our social lives' (Kramsch 1998: 3) and that in communication language is the vehicle through which culture is realized in a multiplicity of complex symbolic ways. In other words, language is culture.

This said, in this contribution we pose that reading and writing courses as literacy practices should focus not only on the hard core of language courses (i.e. coding and decoding a good number of written texts or finely analysing literary pieces) but rather on a variety of literacies and social contexts in which language use is materialized. In view of this, this chapter explores how reading and writing are taught as semiotic systems at the IELTE programme at the Faculty of Humanities, Arts and Social Sciences (Autonomous University of Entre Ríos, Argentina), specifically within the Taller Integrador de Habilidades Lingüísticas (TIHL) (in English, Workshop on Language Skills) module. To accomplish this task, throughout this chapter we contend that the incorporation of the cultural dimension in a reading and writing curriculum may contribute to boosting learner engagement and language proficiency. Although the contents of this chapter ensue from our own reflections and experiences as ELT educators in Argentina, we believe that our contribution might resonate or prove insightful for teachers in language classrooms in other IELTE contexts around the world.

Teacher cognitions and classroom practices

Introducing changes into course syllabi and/or teacher practices frequently implies the development of a complete new mindset on the part of the teacher educators in charge of the TIHL module mentioned *a priori*. In our particular case, this meant challenging the traditional course format adopted along the years, while examining and problematizing our deep-rooted practices.

The extensive body of literature that exists on the topic of teacher cognition gives relevance to the role that such cognitions play in the way teachers understand the processes of teaching and learning. Borg (2006a) defines cognition as 'an inclusive term referring to the complex, practically-oriented, personalized, and context-sensitive networks of knowledge, thoughts and beliefs that language teachers draw on their work' (p. 272), which are in turn deeply influenced by the social, institutional and physical contexts where teachers carry out their practices.

Similarly, on discussing teacher cognition from a sociocultural perspective, Johnson (2009) refers to cognitions in relation to those social activities teachers engage in when they are part of a community of practice:

> Teacher's knowledge and beliefs are constructed through and by the normative ways of thinking, talking, and acting that have been historically and culturally embedded in the communities of practice in which they participate (as both learners and teachers). This suggests that the normative ways of acting and interacting and the values, assumptions, and attitudes that are embedded in the classrooms where teachers were once students, in the teacher education programs where they receive their professional credentialing, and in the schools where they work, shape the complex ways in which they come to think about themselves, their students, the activities of L2 teaching, and the L2 teaching-learning process. (Johnson 2009: 17)

Study outcomes, however, show that the relationship between the network interrelating teacher cognitions and teacher actual classroom practices is not always congruent, and that there may be inconsistencies between what teachers *say* they do and what they *actually do* in class (e.g. Hos & Kekec 2014; Imran & Wyatt 2015; Oranje & Smith 2018; Zhu & Shu 2017). In close connection to this and to the main concern of this chapter, a study on the role of culture in an EFL context conducted by Salcedo and Sacchi (2014) shows that many a time such tensions arise as a direct consequence of *contextual* factors, irrespective of what teachers might believe is best for their classes. In other words, even though teachers might recognize and state the value of, for example, integrating a cultural component in their English lessons, their stated beliefs and their practices go separate ways due to contextual constraints such as the rigidity of the school curriculum, the textbook used, insufficient class time, or an inadequate preparation to teach such contents:

> Teachers also reported that their classroom practices were highly influenced by contextual factors that sometimes did not allow for an exploration of cultural

aspects in their lessons. This finding suggests that despite believing that teaching culture is important, when faced with contextual constraints, the focal participants continue to choose the teaching of linguistic aspects of the language over cultural aspects. (Salcedo & Sacchi 2014: 89–90)

Borg contends that an understanding of the mismatches between teachers' *stated* cognitions and their actual practices should entail a deeper interpretation of 'how cognition, context and practice are mutually informing' (Borg 2006a: 275–6), and of how the dynamic interactions among cognitions define the teaching process. In addition, changes in teacher behaviour do not necessarily involve changes in teacher cognitions, and vice versa. In other words, according to this author the influence of context might lead to two different types of alterations in teacher behaviour: (a) changes in teachers' cognitions, which occur as a result of what happens in the classroom; and (b) changes in teachers' practices, which might take place without producing any alterations in teachers' cognitions.

The relevance of understanding our own cognitions, therefore, resides in how these influence our instructional decisions and how they articulate with the principles underlying our curricular choices. But, clearly, this understanding is only possible if we are first able to reflect upon our established practices in order to uncover cognitions and thus implement hoped-for changes.

Theorizing our practices

In his seminal work on language teaching, far back in 1983, H. H. Stern claimed that 'theory is implicit in the practice of language teaching' and that it materializes in the way teachers plan their courses or in their everyday classroom routines (Stern 1983: 23). If the main goal for TIHL, then, was to leave behind a theory of language that typically centres round 'the matrix of four skills and three elements (grammatical structure, vocabulary, phonology / graphology)' (CEFR 2001: 31) in order to adopt a cultural perspective, a process of analysis and reflection was imperative. We understood that this process would have to entail discussing, articulating and understanding our *personal* theories regarding teaching and learning how to read and write at an IELTE programme, and how to back up the perhaps intuitive feeling that a change in our entrenched practices was necessary.

A central problem we had to face was, precisely, making the real reasons underpinning our didactic decisions explicit. A second related problem involved the need to establish how far such reasons, whether driven by theory or merely intuitive, were congruent with our actual teaching. Engaging in this reflective exercise meant addressing these broad questions that we will in tandem attempt to answer in the wording of this chapter:

1. Are the contents we are teaching significant for student-teachers and their future practices?
2. Are the contents we are teaching integrated into broader teaching practices and other curricular areas?
3. Are we making sure that our student-teachers recognize the intrinsic relationship between language and culture?
4. Are we teacher educators transmitting *good* teaching models in our own teaching practices?

These questions led us to a consideration of more specific issues concerning the main characteristics of our classroom environment and its dynamics; the dimensions of this setting; the problems and needs observed; the potentialities that the teaching situation offered to us in terms of the scope for improvement. We concluded that finding answers would necessarily involve looking back at relevant up-to-date professional theories to analyse and, perhaps, challenge and/or recontextualize them; and, especially, looking deep into our *personal theories*, that is, those emerging as a direct consequence of our on-the-job experience. In other words, in order to introduce insightful changes into our syllabus, we would have to theorize our practices so as to practise what we theorize (Kumaravadivelu 2009).

It was clear to us that engaging in some form of critical reflection would enable our own cognitions to emerge and thus help us find support to the perceived need that a cultural component for our reading and writing course was essential. Before any change could be introduced to our syllabus, therefore, a necessary first step was to scrutinize our usual classroom practices to articulate whether they correlated with the approach adopted and our (implicit) understandings of reading and particularly writing.

Our TIHL

The TIHL module here described belongs to the first year of a four-year undergraduate IELTE programme at the Faculty of Humanities, Arts and Social Sciences (Autonomous University of Entre Ríos, Argentina). The module was originally conceived as a foundation course for other ensuing language courses. As such, it was meant to help student-teachers either reach or consolidate an intermediate level in language proficiency, roughly equivalent to the independent user B1/B2 levels, as described in the CEFR (2001). Although this class was also initially expected to involve the integrated development of the four macro skills (listening and speaking, reading and writing), eventually, engaging learners in detailed reading and writing tasks became the main course goal.

Generally speaking, however, our student-teachers experience great difficulty in successfully completing such tasks, in the first place, given the great heterogeneity of their previous contact with the target language; and, secondly, due to factors springing from their often limited knowledge of: (a) the language system itself, (b) the writing process and/or (c) effective reading and writing strategies.

As teacher educators in charge of the design of the course, we have thus been faced with the challenge of adopting a suitable approach that would allow us not only to enhance the learners' already existing subject-matter knowledge but also to facilitate the initial development of reading and writing skills in the L2. It was clear to us that to accomplish this we would have to provide student-teachers with opportunities to acquire the necessary literacy involved in the production of genres traditionally expected of Year 1 student-teachers.

The course structure

Student-teachers who enrol in TIHL fulfil a requirement for Year 1 learners at the IELTE programme in our college. The course comprises a weekly three-hour workshop during two fifteen-week semesters, and it is designed to help students become effective readers and writers by featuring assignments that allow them to explore their personal and academic interests.

Most of the lessons in this course centre on workshop-style activities, including writing conferencing, drafting, peer review and editing. Although there are mini-lectures on a variety of writing-related topics, the majority of class time is spent engaging in collaborative discussions and writing activities. Some of the lessons are also conducted in seminar format, which means that teachers and learners engage in discussions about reading and, especially, writing assignments, and examine the rhetorical strategies used to persuade audiences. During the different lessons teacher educators encourage student-teachers to raise questions, pose problems, interpret readings, challenge each other's ideas and develop strategies for successfully completing writing assignments.

The course also asks student-teachers to engage with different genres written for a range of audiences (Riestra, Goicoechea, & Tapia 2014), such as newspaper and magazine articles, short stories and the like. Writing is conceived as an interactive process that emphasizes multiple drafting and constant revision, and that gives learners practice in critical thinking, reinforcing the notion that writing conventions differ according to their rhetorical situations. In other words, the course emphasizes writing as a recursive, developmental process in which learners explore and generate ideas in order to address a rhetorical problem presented by a writing task. They do so through the use of strategies and extensive planning in close collaboration with others, and as a response to focused feedback from their instructors and their peers (Hyland 2016). We always begin by focusing students on the writing process and their own practices as writers.

The class uses a portfolio system. This consists in the compilation of a series of successive polished drafts of writing assignments, which are regularly turned in for both peer review and instructor comments, but which do not receive any formal grades until the end of the academic year, when student-teachers submit their final portfolio showcasing their very best work. The adoption of this system ensures that student-teachers have plenty of time to get feedback on their work so as to revise and polish their pieces in order to redraft them. It is expected that through this approach learners will be able to identify their strengths and weaknesses and thus improve the overall quality of their writing.

The undergirding approach

To provide our course with a suitable theoretical framework we initially adopted an eclectic approach, combining the main notions underpinning Badger and White's (2000) process-genre approach and the key ideas deriving from Halliday's context of situation, that is 'the environment in which meanings are being exchanged' (Halliday & Hasan 1985) or, in other words, the idea that language varies according to the situation in which it is used. A process-genre approach to writing entails understanding writing as

> knowledge about language (as in product and genre approaches), knowledge of
> the context in which writing happens and especially the purpose for the writing
> (as in genre approaches), and skill in using language (as in process approaches).
> (Badger & White 2000: 157)

Incorporating a Hallidayan view of language, that is, one that sees language as a resource for making meaning in a particular context of use rather than as a set of fixed rules and structures, encompasses teaching writing through a consideration of 'the semiotic parameters of the context in which the discourse is located: field, tenor and mode' (Halliday 2003: 18). This approach characterizes writing as involving an analysis of the situation in terms of purpose, audience and organization, together with a focus on those language features that will more likely enable learners to meet the purpose and the audience's expectations by being functional to the particular writing task set. At the same time, the linguistic choices made will contribute to the conveyance of meaning at three different levels: (1) the content of the text or ideational meanings (field); (2) interpersonal meanings that construe the different attitudes, role relationships and evaluation in a text (tenor); and, finally, (3) textual meanings that construct the flow of information in a text (mode) (Halliday & Hasan 1985; Halliday & Matthiessen 2014).

The materialization of the approach adopted

In line with the above, the TIHL was traditionally organized around three core writing contents: informal letters or emails, narratives, and brief argumentative pieces. As explained before, student-teachers typically engaged in a series of tasks involving a number of recursive steps.

In the initial stages of the writing process, there was much scaffolding pair or small group work. Student-teachers first engaged in language awareness activities that generally involved genre-oriented tasks with a view to determining the situation for writing, the writer's purpose, an idea of the target reader and their relation to the writer, the type of information to include, and so on. This prewriting stage also included reading and the analysis of sample texts, and answering questions related to the information included in the samples. Attention was often paid to stylistic features, for example, by highlighting or underlining typical phrases, or by reflecting upon possible spoken equivalents, which would help raise awareness of vocabulary and sentence complexity. This first set of tasks aimed at generating, assessing and organizing ideas for writing through the employment of different techniques and strategies (e.g. brainstorming, word-mapping, clustering or quickwriting).

After a first draft was completed, learners would begin the process of rewriting by revising their production through the application of appropriate strategies, such as proofreading, reorganizing and assessing information. To revise and proofread their drafts, learners were expected to share their outcomes with peers so that they would give each other feedback. In order to guide this stage, they were provided with strategies for peer assessment through the use of assessment rubrics. In addition, all these drafts and redrafts were part of a feedback loop in the hands of the course instructors.

The perceived need for a cultural component

Central to the process described above was what Hyland (2016) describes as a reader-oriented approach, which subsumes Halliday's interpersonal function and which understands writing as 'an interactive, as well as cognitive, activity which employs accepted resources for the purpose of sharing meanings in (that) context' (p. 30). As time went by, however, we realized that our students needed more input for the initial stages of the writing process, most specifically for the generation of ideas. We became aware that neither the articles selected for prewriting tasks nor the use of sample materials to analyse the different genres were helping our learners engage at a more personal level so as to develop a deeper understanding of the language. We came to the realization that the writing samples employed would, more often than not, be adopted by learners as fixed templates on which to base their own drafts. In other words, we concluded that implementing a process-genre approach was suitable but that using the same types of genres over and over again was counterproductive as our learners would stick to them instead of producing more creative pieces. At the same time, one related constraint was the fact that the texts selected would usually involve a strong focus on the more rigid aspects of language (mainly grammar) thus hindering both the possibility for learners to represent themselves in their texts or the articulation of a more personal stance (Hyland 2016).

Most importantly, the analysis of classroom practices, coupled with the reflective process course instructors were going through, led us to notice that there is more to the teaching of reading and writing as social practices. We learnt that there is a cultural dimension that is often neglected and that should be re-enacted if we want our students to understand that twenty-first-century literacy necessarily entails culturally situated learning scenarios. We too realized that we should move away from a traditional structural approach to language teaching towards a wider enriching framework around the notion of *language-culture*.

One way we found to accomplish this challenging mission was by introducing reading and writing tasks that aimed at having student-teachers develop rhetorical awareness. We decided that we wanted them to learn the basic elements that intervene in the analysis of a specific rhetorical context and thus develop a deeper sensitivity to writing arguments. We know that in doing this students enrich their ability to read, think critically and write or speak about significant issues that have social consequences. In other words, we would ask our student-teachers to interact with a good number of different texts in which they were supposed to identify the constituting elements of a rhetorical situation (ethos, pathos, logos). We placed emphasis on this type of initial activity given that it provides student-teachers with a valuable opportunity to challenge their cultural perceptions around a selected topic for discussion. Shortly after doing that, we would expose them to pre-, while- and post-guiding questions to generate and confirm reading and writing hypotheses. We would principally focus on the use of literary writings for we believe these texts can introduce the student-teachers to a possibly unknown literary genre, thus allowing them to become familiar with specific literary jargon (which they would otherwise grasp only when exposed to a specific literature class in a later stage of their teacher education programme). As a way of decentring or flipping the traditional classroom structure, we would finally ask them to carry out small informal research projects at home to later discuss their findings in class. Additionally, to allow for *kairotic* reinterpretations of the texts selected, we would ask the student-teachers to partake in a multimodal remix; that is, we would allow for students to design a short digital presentation on the topics covered in class. In this regard, we believe that digital literacies should also be embraced in the reading and writing class since they are descriptive of the kind of learning experiences that students partake in on a daily basis.

After working in this way, we felt it was worth asking ourselves if there is a specific moment for their development of rhetorical awareness in the reading and writing class. In this respect, Yancey (2004) holds that *there is* such a moment and that, usually, most meaningful literacy happenings for people's lives take place outside schools, even more so today due to the ever-evolving Internet and the noticeable need for people to disclose daily written interactions on social media:

> Today, we are witnessing a parallel creation, that of a writing public made plural, and as in the case of the development of a reading public, it's taking place largely outside of school – and this in an age of universal education. (Yancey 2004: 300)

For this reason and in order to bring the outside into the inside, we believe that other than the traditional ways of having students tackle the notion of rhetorical analysis while working with different texts, they should likewise embrace the world of digital literacies insofar as these are descriptive of the kind of technology-mediated learning experiences they partake on a daily basis. This said, in our

TIHL class the students engage into the analysis of rhetorical situations while interacting with digital texts we have created ad hoc; utilize specific apps and websites for developing the aforementioned skills; interact with each other on discussion boards to build a community of practice and a bedrock of ideas around what constitutes a 'good writer'; and are required to describe their learning process as part of their writing portfolio towards the end of the course.

Literary explorations

Culture teaching derives from social and cultural anthropology, which aim to provide a comprehensive description of the way of life of a society. There is no question that culture, at least on paper, is part of most modern language curriculums. Although the fields of language education and culture have both made important strides during the past quarter of a century, they have often wandered alone, along separate paths. This separation is evidenced in educational approaches to the teaching of foreign and second languages that do not explicitly and consistently incorporate the intercultural component and, also, in the dearth of university courses, specifically within IELTE programmes, where those engaged in intercultural matters work in separate networks as if intentionally detached from language teachers.

Every so often, language teachers express an interest in culture as part of the language experience. However, they often treat culture as supplemental or incidental to the real task and usually ignore intercultural concerns that come along, that is, the dynamic tension between the target language and culture, and one's own. This may be relatable to the fact that, more often than not, we take language for granted, unaware that our native tongue is not merely a neutral communication system but rather a pervasive medium that directly influences every aspect of our lives. This may probably have to do with the fact that we seldom need to reflect on our use of language for it has been there for as long as we can remember. And therein lies the power of a different linguistic experience. If while providing a chance to learn about another way of communication, another way of life, we expose students to a reading and writing class that provokes a good number of questions about one's own language, culture and world view, then their knowledge would be tremendously augmented through language use. It is a point in fact that language permits contemplating the impossible and exploring the unfathomable.

To accomplish this, we, teacher educators and student-teachers, need to become more culturally competent. We need to understand more completely the cultural dimension of language. Language does serve as a tool for communication, but in addition it is a system of representation for perception and thinking. This function of language provides us with verbal categories and prototypes that guide our formation of concepts and categorization of objects; it directs how we experience reality. This may be a good way to avoid the typical kind of thinking that can lead to becoming a 'fluent fool' (Bennet 1997), that is someone who speaks an FL well but does not understand the social or philosophical content of that language.

Developing intercultural competence is a shared challenge for language educators and interculturalists alike and, certainly, its attainment promises rewards. Intercultural competence offers the possibility of transcending the limitations of one's singular view of the world. Those who have never experienced another culture nor striven hard to communicate using a second or FL are often unaware of the milieu in which they have always existed. That is why contact with other world views in the classroom is so important: it can result in a shift of perspective, along with a concomitant appreciation for the diversity and richness of human beings.

When students interact with literary texts they are usually confronted with the task of having to decode the meaning behind the lines that given characters enunciate, the intentionality underlying a specific fragment, the rhetorical situation that encapsulates a target chapter and whatnot. It is in interacting with these kinds of tasks that contextualized reading and writing practices can help them tackle different types of literary genres in order to develop high order thinking skills. We are making reference here to reading and writing skills like reading for gist, summarizing, annotating, interpreting, identifying ways in which author or narrator signify, explaining, composing, debating and the like. Indeed, we are here advocating for the development of critical thinking skills not solely in connection with discipline-specific topics and tasks but more specifically in connection to Barnett's self- and world domains – that is criticality and critical cultural awareness in relation to the internal and external worlds (Barnett 1997 as quoted in Porto & Byram 2015). This compendium of critical thinking skills may allow for the transition of an inexperienced writer into one that can dare go for more meaningful writing enterprises, such as writing a paper or a future thesis dissertation (Beaufort 2012). We believe that by practising all these in a literature-driven reading and writing class, student-teachers can develop rhetorical awareness, identify different hierarchies as they tap into the macro structure of a text, assess and utilize information accordingly to those hierarchies, and develop a sensitivity towards the use of format, design and structure when it comes, for example, to analysing the most important arguments put forward by the author of a given text. Most importantly, perhaps, we believe that it is through the systematic incorporation of this cultural element that we can foster our students' development of the ability to understand and interact effectively with people from diverse cultural backgrounds, unmistakably different from solely the British or American ones, while helping bridge the gap between the academic concerns of school life and the students' own worlds of experience.

Conclusions

All the sections in this chapter were conceived in the belief that to understand what makes effective reading and writing enterprises, it may be necessary to examine how we, teacher educators, approach the teaching of reading and writing. It is our opinion that these are complex intellectual activities that cannot be reduced to learning recipes, and that in order to make our own *imprimatur* on the reading and writing field, we suggest that exploring the scope of literature to spur on the development of reading and writing skills may render into a fruitful experience for a number of reasons. To mention a few, reading literary texts allows student-teachers to explore and question their own positionality around a given topic. This is beneficial for a future educator inasmuch as it helps them perceive their own teacher's cognitions and identity. Furthermore, by analysing the basic elements that configure a rhetorical situation, student-teachers learn to identify the intentionality underlying the composition of a message and become more prone to develop critical thinking skills. Similarly, working with literary texts allows for the development of creative reading and writing skills for they confront the reader with a given scenario that is usually open to interpretation, and above all, allow the reader to explore the prospective and healing power of narratives.

We hold the view that now more than ever we have to promote intercultural tolerance in our classrooms through the use of relevant (literary) texts. We consider that we teachers should address intercultural topics in our lessons taking into account the social and cultural background of our students and bearing in mind that it is a teacher's job to adapt those materials and methodology according to the audience. We are living through times of world crises and violence outbreaks, and thus we have to ensure that a strong organic wave of non-violence and rationality prevails in this fragile context. We have to embrace that sense of responsibility and create and exchange ideas for the betterment of our societies. We feel it is time to expand our horizons and include themes and topics like cooperation, diversity, equity, peace and conflict resolution, tolerance, and mediation in our curriculums.

It is our conclusion these are the kinds of questions we should be posing in our teaching practices regardless of whether we have an answer for them or not. We support the idea that education is about empowering others through cognition and not just by passing on information. And that it is the ultimate weapon that we can use to combat the vertical patterns that educational systems usually disclose and put in play against the more noble sides of education.

Questions for change

1. How can the introduction of a cultural component in IELTE programmes help overcome the rigidity of approaches focused solely on the development of subject matter and PCK?
2. How can the intersection of culture and language take into consideration aspiring teachers prior learning experiences?
3. How can the exploration of literary texts in your IELTE language classes promote critical thinking, intercultural awareness and student-teacher self-expression?
4. What challenges might the introduction of a change like the one portrayed in this chapter present to teacher educators in your context?

Conclusion

Darío Luis Banegas

In the Introduction, I posed a few initial questions: How much English should a teacher of English know to teach it effectively as another language? How much about English should a teacher know? Should they know about syntax, phonology and pragmatics? How does that affect a teacher's professional identity? The chapters in this volume have discussed these questions among others and have shown that such questions gravitate in ELTE programmes and teacher educators' situated practices around the world.

In this concluding chapter, I discuss three broad areas around content knowledge in ELTE: (1) how content knowledge can be supported, (2) how content knowledge can be researched and (3) how I envisage the development of content knowledge. These broad areas signal that the role of content knowledge in the ELTE curriculum is to set in place the confidence, curiosity, agency, so that the English teacher has a sense of user expertise in the same way that excellent science teachers are scientists, and history teachers are historians.

Supporting content knowledge

The success of language teacher education programmes hinges on content knowledge and the teaching strategies to transpose it. According to Ball, Thames and Phelps (2008: 404),

> Teachers must know the subject they teach. Indeed, there may be nothing more foundational to teacher competency. The reason is simple: Teachers who do not themselves know a subject well are not likely to have the knowledge they need to help students learn this content. At the same time, however, just knowing a subject well may not be sufficient for teaching.

If we transpolate this quote to the field of ELTE, it may be concurred that ELTE programmes should be calibrated in such a way that future teachers are provided with a comprehensive approach which integrates what to teach and how to teach it. A common thread running across the chapters included in this volume is that of congruent teaching or modelling practices since teacher educators' pedagogical decisions, syllabi, reading material, tasks, and assessment practices are aligned with how student-teachers are expected to teach English. In this volume, Chappell has summarized the role that ELTE programmes and teacher educators have as he believes that

> we should be concerned with supporting our students to successfully communicate across a range of different communicative events, for example, enjoying a casual conversation with a visitor to their country, presenting their work in a seminar, collaborating with university peers on a research project, writing an email to a customer, and writing a report for a school assignment. This necessitates more than knowledge about the different forms language takes. It requires understandings of how different combinations of language forms function to make particular meanings in particular social and cultural contexts. (Chappell, this volume, p. 32)

How student-teachers can be supported take a number of varied and complementary strategies and tools. The chapters show that conspicuous efforts are made around the world to support content knowledge as a pillar in the ELTE domain. In light of both traditional and new directions, the authors included in this volume have signalled several frameworks and specific strategies to reinforce the weight and impact that content knowledge has in student-teachers' trajectories while studying at an ELTE programme and after graduation. A comprehensive revision of the chapters in this volume shows that content knowledge in ELTE hinges on systematic functional linguistics and genre pedagogy as well as on language awareness. Both frameworks indicate that language is studied from a descriptive stance and that language teaching and learning are concentrated in what language users do with English.

Drawing on SFL and genre pedagogy, Chapters 2, 3, 4, 8, 12 and 14 highlight the relevance of approaching language as a meaning-making system to fulfil different social functions. Through these chapters we have been shown that a functional perspective does not reject form; on the contrary, form is the element through which meanings are encoded and therefore both form and meaning bear equal importance. However, what these chapters reveal is that student-teachers need to be prepared to encode meanings through a range of forms since language is a system of choices and therefore student-teachers need to be proficient at using several forms to complete functions such as describing, narrating or explaining among others. In addition, it is remarked that grammar in ELTE cannot be detached from ELTE aims. Thus, pedagogical grammar should be encouraged and in so doing student-teachers learn grammar themselves while learning how to teach grammar. This connection is vital to ensure that student-teachers can visibilize more tangibly the impact of SFG in their future practices and the connections that studies on grammar can have on everyday language teaching.

Closely linked to SFG, genre pedagogy emerges as a solid direction to follow in order to organize grammar learning and holistic language improvement in ELTE. Genre pedagogy is an approach that helps learners, particularly bilingual learners or ESL instruction, to develop academic literacy through the production of specialized texts, that is persuasive essays (Ramos 2015), in upper elementary and secondary school as well as in higher education, especially in EMI settings. In a study on preparing history teachers to teach language, Schall-Leckrone (2017) observes that in SFL-informed genre pedagogy:

(1) Grammar is considered to be a meaning making resource, and (2) texts are considered to be semantic choices in a social context. In other words, genres, from an SFL perspective, are identified by recurrent organizational and linguistic features (grammar patterns) and understood by the way in which they accomplish a particular purpose in a social or academic context. (p. 362)

Thus, student-teachers can be supported in their development of academic literacy by drawing their attention to authentic texts from specific disciplines. In this regard, authenticity is another helpful concept in which content knowledge rests. Authenticity as discussed in Chapters 7 and 12 in this volume refers to sources of input, tasks, purposes and topics. In Chapters 1, 4, 13 and 14 we can find instances of authentic topics which come from current affairs or areas such as historical linguistics, literature and cultural studies. In Chapter 4, genre pedagogy and authenticity are merged through the practice of helping student-teachers create a corpus that can guide them in their learning of grammar in context. Already established corpora such as the British National Corpus (BNC) or the Corpus of Contemporary American English (COCA) can help future teachers understand language use through examination of real-life language use. In fact, several EFL coursebooks are constructed around English language corpora.

Drawing student-teachers' attention to the language of specific texts and genres comes to cement the vital need to develop language awareness in ELTE. In this volume, Chapters 4, 5, 6, 7, 8 and 9 address language awareness from different but complementary perspectives. Through pedagogical grammar, for instance, student-teachers can incorporate metalanguage to reflect on their own understanding of grammar and acquire specific terminology that they may not teach to their learners but which can strengthen them professionally. Language awareness can also appear in activities which draw student-teachers' attention to different alphabets and phonemes. At a macro level, language awareness can also serve student-teachers to detect hidden agendas and warrants in discourse, whether it is political, social or educational. If ELT promotes that learners can discover language rules and meanings by themselves through awareness-raising activities, it stands to reason that future teachers develop and explore first-hand language awareness at a more advanced level.

Language awareness development can be recorded in journals (Chapters 10 and 12) and portfolios (Chapter 11). Drawing on approaches that promote integrated learning and skills, both language and cognitive, these two tools can be become powerful resources for student-teachers and teacher educators to measure impact of specific ELTE modules and strategies and to reflect on learning trajectories. At the same time, portfolios may constitute a valid assessment tool through which processes are given more prominent attention.

In conclusion, it may be agreed that supporting content knowledge in ELTE entails treating language as a semiotic system that is embedded in particular cultural and social contexts that student-teachers should be made aware of.

Researching content knowledge

This volume has shown that teacher and ecological approaches to researching content knowledge are possible and needed in ELTE. Based on the experiences described in this volume, teacher educator inquiry could be conceptualized as inherently context-responsive, organic, situated and firmly rooted in a careful and detailed understanding of the processes that support teaching and learning. In this framework, teacher educator inquiry often exhibits a qualitative, exploratory nature captured through student-teachers' voices, day-to-day teaching and personal introspection. It is of paramount importance to understand that teacher educators are in a privileged position as they can research their own modules, and by engaging in research in their own programmes, they become examples of educators who do research to transform their own practices.

What do we mean by teacher research? As the chapters show, teacher research is research carried out by teachers for teachers. In this volume, it is teacher educators examining or systematizing reflection and evaluation upon their own modules. In teacher research, action research (AR), exploratory action research (EAR) and exploratory practice (EP) are often subsumed to account for the research opportunities that are closer to teachers' realities. Should teacher educators be willing to engage in teacher research for understanding their classrooms and developing professionally, research literacy needs to be sought and prioritized. According to Xerri and Pioquinto (2018),

> Research literacy does not only consist of the technical knowledge and skills required to engage with and in research. Besides knowing how to critically engage with published research, design research instruments, and conduct a study, teachers also need to develop attitudes and beliefs in relation to research that will enable them to position themselves as research-engaged professionals. To do this, teachers need various kinds of support, including one that goes beyond the traditional forms of teacher training popular in ELT. The main objective of this support is to empower teachers to see themselves as capable of finding answers to the questions they have about their context, their practices, their students, and their professional identity. (Xerri & Pioquinto 2018: vii)

In ELTE, teacher research bears to clear features: (1) small-scale studies and (2) qualitative approaches. Studies carried out by teacher educators are often small scale in nature since the aim is for teachers to understand their own contexts for possible transformations. They usually consist of examining one class, a group of parallel groups, or, less frequently, one class over longer periods of time. In these small-scale studies, qualitative approaches are preferred as through them teachers can gain deeper and situated insights, and therefore data collection instruments such as journals, peer classroom observations, surveys, questionnaires, multimodal resources and interviews can become invaluable research resources (e.g. Villacañas de Castro 2017). Such instruments together with teaching materials, lecture notes and slides, and student-teachers' evidences of learning (e.g. mid-term exams, reports, essays, forum posts) constitute instances of ecological research, that is research that it firmly rooted in a particular setting and in which data come from the regular teaching and learning processes. In ecological research, learning tasks and outcomes also become research data (e.g. Banegas 2017b; Edwards & Burns 2016).

In researching content knowledge, teacher educators pay particular attention to student-teachers' linguistic and identity development since content knowledge modules may exert a tremendous influence on how student-teachers perceive themselves as L2 language users and teachers. As I discussed in the introductory chapter to this volume, more often than not language teacher effectiveness depends on ELP and ability to scaffold learning through metalanguage and language awareness strategies. In this collection, for example, Chapters 5, 10 and 13 include student-teachers' voices which suggest that systematic work on content knowledge and ELP provides student-teachers with tools to shape their professional identity.

In relation to what else deserves our attention, the questions for change raised at the end of each chapter may signal possible area worth investigating. Drawing on the questions found in each chapter, the list below condenses those questions which I think are most relevant for a comprehensive understanding of content knowledge in ELTE:

1. Do teacher educators think that historical background knowledge about English is necessary for language teachers and learners?
2. What are student-teachers' conceptions of language and language learning?
3. Should there be a balance between form-based and meaning-based models in ELTE?
4. What are the effects of corpora-based pedagogy in teacher preparation?
5. Can content-based grammar teaching work with elementary language learners?
6. What's the impact of reflections on one's own language for EFL/ESL teaching?
7. For ELTE programme planners/designers: To what extent does your programme focus upon the curriculum designs and pedagogies oriented towards training language (English) skills, and/or content knowledge and skills in literature analysis and translation?
8. In what ways do student-teachers develop their pragmatic competence?
9. What kinds of texts are supported and reproduced by ELTE programmes and higher education institutions?
10. How do factors such as motivation, personality traits, self-esteem and cultural identity affect the acquisition/learning of English pronunciation of student-teachers?
11. How should the contents of different disciplines and the development of skills be integrated in teacher education programmes?
12. How can we enhance peer feedback to contribute to students' process of learning?
13. What are the challenges for teacher-educators teaching advanced levels of proficiency?

14. Do teacher educators transform their own language-learning strategies into teaching skills?
15. How can the exploration of literary texts in IELTE language improvement classes promote critical thinking, intercultural awareness and student-teacher self-expression?

The questions listed above seem to indicate that content knowledge should embrace a holistic and comprehensive attitude in terms of implementation and research in ELTE. What is striking is that all the questions direct teacher educators' attention to the impact, short term as well as long term, that content knowledge modules and practices may have in student-teachers' professional competences. This special feature emphasizes that content knowledge modules cannot ignore the primary purpose of ELTE programmes: the education of language teachers, not linguists.

Future directions

In times of superdiversity (Coehlo Liberali 2017), transversal competencies and phenomenon-based learning (Symeonidis & Schwarz 2016), and interdisciplinarity (Arneback & Blåsjö 2017), a reconfiguration of content knowledge in ELTE entails a change in the teacher knowledge base of language education. In this section I put forward some ideas in relation to content knowledge in ELTE and, at a macro level, ELTE knowledge base overall.

Perhaps, the chapters concentrated on English language improvement (Chapters 10–14) signal where the future is going. On the one hand, I see that ELP is by definition an issue that needs to be operationalized through holistic proposals where language skills, critical thinking skills and teaching competencies are intertwined with ELTE contents and topics that relate to educational and citizenship. In so doing, student-teachers explore first-hand the dynamics of interdisciplinary learning where different areas of knowledge contribute to their education in terms of ELP à la par with their teaching skills. On the other hand, realistic aims should be set in terms of the level of proficiency student-teachers are expected to have. While it is always desirable that they become their best version possible as L2 users, it would be misleading to think that they should acquire high levels of proficiency particularly when ELTE programmes have dissimilar entry levels in, for example, EFL contexts. Le (2018) reminds us that it is still false to equate ELP to teaching performance as this myth is a remnant of native speakerism since the underlying warrant is that only proficient L2 speakers can become competent teachers. However, here what is actually desired is the graduation of language teachers who are both proficient L2 users *and* effective teachers. Yet, the pressing needs to have qualified teachers across the world may make ELTE programmes compromise ELP proficiency. After all, novice teachers have the rest of their professional career to improve their English, and it is there where governments and universities need to step in to organize language improvement courses or ELTE courses that, if delivered through the medium of English, allow teachers to improve both their teaching and language skills.

In this volume we have agreed that currently, content knowledge includes ELP and English as a system. Chapters 1–9 concentrated on the different subsystems that a language has. They also show a trend that should be more forcefully embraced by ELTE programmes: that modules such as pragmatics, phonetics or grammar should be conceived and delivered in such a way that they respond to the aim of educating English language teachers with a primary function: teaching English as another language. In this sense, I strongly encourage teacher educators in charge of such modules to let their syllabi be informed by PCK. As teacher educators lead modules on SFG or historical linguistics, they can always bring in tasks that make explicit connections to ELT. For example, in Argentina, when I taught a module on SFG, I asked the student-teachers to bring the coursebooks and other teaching materials they were using in the practicum to analyse how SFG was present there and how they could scaffold, for example, the teaching of writing skills, even at elementary levels, through the help of SFG. More recently, on a sociolinguistics module, I introduced the concepts of code switching and translanguaging, and the student-teachers had to observe and record lessons to analyse these concepts in practice and then develop lesson plans that would incorporate them as teaching approaches.

In the same manner that ELP modules have amalgamated different areas of knowledge, English as a system modules could adopt a holistic and trans- and interdisciplinary perspective to transform themselves into modules that, following phenomenon- and problem-based learning, allow student-teachers to explore and examine language as a unity. In addition, these modules could adopt a CLIL approach with the aim of providing student-teachers with authentic instances of content and language learning at the same time. These modules also have a responsibility in developing student-teachers' ELP, and therefore teacher-educators need to plan their lessons, not just lectures, in such a way that both content and language are scaffolded.

Final words

The volume has particularly considered student-teachers' perceptions. This focus reminded me of Le (2018) and his definition of pedagogical learner knowledge:

> Pedagogical learner knowledge is defined as teachers' knowledge of the learners in all their richness and complexity with which they develop their personal and interpersonal skills as well as sensitivity and ability to accommodate their subject-matter knowledge and knowledge of L2 teaching to their learners' varied learning trajectories. This knowledge informs teachers of ways of capitalizing on the learners' different personal histories, beliefs, identities, emotions, and other personal and affective factors that shape their agency in second language learning. By doing that, they turn the challenge of learner diversity into a pedagogical advantage for both student learning and their professional development. (p. 7)

While Le has a different population in mind, mainly teachers' learners at the places where they exercise teaching as a socially situated practice, the concept of pedagogical learner knowledge can be transpolated to ELTE with the aim of reminding ourselves who our student-teachers are and how we can calibrate our content knowledge modules so that they respond to our student-teachers' immediate needs particularly after graduation: teaching. In this volume, we have shown how teacher educators understand that complex task and reflect and act on it.

May this volume help with such a multifaceted, challenging, but, awesome quest.

References

Abrahams, M. J., & Silva Ríos, P. (2017). What happens with English in Chile? Challenges in teacher preparation. In L. Kamhi-Stein, G. Díaz Maggioli, & L. C. de Oliveira (Eds.), *English Language Teaching in South America: Policy, Preparation and Practices*. Bristol: Multilingual Matters.

Abrams, Z. (2014). Using film to provide a context for teaching L2 pragmatics. *System*, *46*(1), 55–64.

Agencia de Calidad de la Educación (2017). Informe de Resultados Estudio Nacional Inglés III Medio 2017. Retrieved from http://archivos.agenciaeducacion.cl/Info rme_Estudio_Nacional_Ingles_III.pdf

Akcan, S. (2016). Novice non-native English teachers' reflections on their teacher education programmes and their first years of teaching. *Profile Issues in Teachers Professional Development*, *18*(1), 55–70.

Alcón-Soler, E. (2012). Teachability and bilingual effects on third language knowledge of refusals. *Intercultural Pragmatics*, *9*, 511–41.

Alcón-Soler, E., & Martínez-Flor, A. (2008). *Investigating Pragmatics in Foreign Language Learning, Teaching and Testing*. Bristol: Multilingual Matters.

Altan, M. Z. (2006). Preparation of foreign language teachers in Turkey: A challenge for the 21st century. *Dil Dergisi*, *134*(1), 49–54.

Anderson, L., Kathwohl, D., Airasian, P., Cruikshank, K., Mayer, R., Pintrich, P., Rahths, J., & Wittrock, M. (Eds.). (2001). *A Taxonomy for Learning, Teaching and Assessing: A Revision of Bloom's Taxonomy of Educational Objectives*. New York: Longman.

Andrews, S. (2003). Teacher language awareness and the professional knowledge base of the L2 teacher. *Language Awareness*, *12*(2), 81–95.

Arana, V. F., Blázquez, B. A., Lagos, I., & Valls, L. S. (2016). Dictado y transcripción fonética: El material audiovisual como alternativa en la clase de pronunciación. In G. D. Leiton (Ed.), *III Jornadas Internacionales de Didáctica de la Fonética de las Lenguas Extranjeras* (pp. 4–14). San Antonio de Areco: Universidad Nacional de San Martín.

Arana, V., Blázquez, B. A., Labastía, L., & Lagos, I. (2017). *Introducción a la Lengua Inglesa: Dicción* (2nd ed.). General Roca: Publifadecs.

Arneback, E., & Blåsjö, M. (2017). Doing interdisciplinarity in teacher education. Resources for learning through writing in two educational programmes. *Education Inquiry*, *8*(4), 299–317.

Austin, J. L. (1962). *How to Do Things with Words*. Oxford: Oxford University Press.

Aydin, S. (2010). EFL writers' perceptions of portfolio keeping. *Assessing Writing*, *15*, 194–203.

Azar, B. S., & Hagen, B. A. (2016). *Understanding and using English* (5th ed.). New York, NY: Pearson.

Badger, R., & White, G. (2000). A process genre approach to teaching writing. *ELT Journal, 54*(2), 153–60.

Baker, A. (2006). *Tree or Three? An Elementary Pronunciation Course* (2nd ed.). Cambridge: Cambridge University Press.

Bale, J. (2016). Language proficiency in an era of accountability: Using the target language to learn how to teach. *Journal of Teacher Education, 67*(5), 392–407.

Ball, D. L., Thames, M. H., & Phelps, G. (2008). Content knowledge for teaching: What makes it special? *Journal of Teacher Education, 59*(5), 389–407.

Ball, P. (2015). CLIL, English teachers and the three dimensions of content. *Modern English Teacher, 24*(2), 15–19.

Banegas, D. L. (2009). Content knowledge in teacher education: Where professionalisation lies. *ELTED Journal, 12*, 44–51.

Banegas, D. L. (Ed.). (2017a). *Initial English Language Teacher Education: International Perspectives on Research, Curriculum and Practice*. London and New York: Bloomsbury.

Banegas, D. L. (2017b). Teaching linguistics to low-level English language users in a teacher education programme: An action research study. *Language Learning Journal*, DOI: 10.1080/09571736.2017.1370604

Banfi, C. (2003). Portfolios: Providing the opportunity to integrate advanced language, academic and professional skills. *ELT Journal, 57*(1), 34–42.

Banfi, C. (2013). Tradición, autonomía, innovación y reforma en la enseñanza superior en lenguas en la Ciudad de Buenos Aires. *Lenguas V;vas, 9*, 27–62.

Barahona, M. (2016). *English Language Teacher Education in Chile: A Cultural Historical Activity Theory Perspective*. Abingdon: Routledge.

Barahona, M., & Martin, M. (2014). Effective social learning pedagogy in Spanish language teaching: Integrating podcasting and blogging to teach current affairs. In C. Travis, J. Hajek, C. Nettelbeck, E. Beckmann & A. Lloyd-Smith (Eds.), *Practices and Policies: Current Research in Languages and Culture Education. Selected Proceedings of the Second National LCNAU Colloquium, Canberra 3–5 July 2013.* (pp. 485–96). Melbourne: Languages and Culture Network for Australian Universities.

Bardovi-Harlig, K. (2013), Developing L2 pragmatics. *Language Learning, 63*, 68–86.

Bardovi-Harlig, K., & Mahan-Taylor, R. (2003). *Teaching Pragmatics*. Washington: Office of English Programs, U.S. Department of State.

Barkhuizen, G. (1997). Predicted problems of elementary school ESL teachers: Implications for teacher education. *TESL Reporter, 30*(1), 17–26.

Barnett, R. (1997). *Higher Education: A Critical Business*. London: Open University Press.

Barret. J. (2009). Create your own electronic portfolio. *Learning & Leading with Technology, 27*(7), 14–21.

Bartels, N. (Ed.). (2005). *Applied Linguistics and Language Teacher Education*. New York: Springer.

Bathia, V. K. (2004). *Worlds of Written Discourse: A Genre-Based View*. London: Continuum.

Bathia, V. K., Flowerdew, J., & Jones, R. H., (Eds.). (2007). *Advances in Discourse Studies*. London and New York: Routledge.

Bauer, L. (2007). *The Linguistics Student's Handbook*. Edinburgh: Edinburgh University Press.

Baugh, A., & Cable, T. (2013). *A History of the English Language* (6th ed.). Oxford: Routledge.

Bazerman, C. (1994). Systems of genre and the enactment of social intentions. In A. Freedman & P. Medway (Eds.), *Rethinking Genre* (pp. 79–101). London: Taylor & Francis.

Bazerman, C. (2004). Speech acts, genres, and activity systems: How texts organize activity and people. In C. Bazerman & P. Prior (Eds.), *What Writing does and how it does it* (pp. 309–39). Mahwah: Lawrence Erlbaum.

Beaufort, A. (2012). College writing and beyond: Five years later. *Composition Forum*, *26*, 1–13.

Bennet, M. J. (1997). How not to be a fluent fool. Understanding the cultural dimension of language. *New Ways in Teaching Culture in TESOL*, 16–21.

Biber, D., Conrad, S., & Leech, G. (2002). *Longman Student Grammar of Spoken and Written English*. Essex: Pearson Education Limited.

Birnbaum, R. et al. (Producers) & Ratner, B. (Director). (1998). *Rush hour* [DVD]. United States: New Line Cinema.

Bitchener, J., & Knoch, U. (2010). The contribution of written corrective feedback to language development: A ten month investigation. *Applied Linguistics*, *31*(2), 193–214.

Bitchener, J., Young, S., & Cameron, D. (2005). The effect of different types of corrective feedback on ESL student writing. *Journal of Second Language Writing*, *14*, 191–205.

Blanco, A. O. (1970). Symposium on the training of teachers. *The English Language Journal – Revista de la Lengua Inglesa*, *1*(1), 26–45.

Blommaert, J. (2010). *The Sociolinguistics of Globalisation*. Cambridge: Cambridge University Press.

Bloor, T., & Bloor, M. (2013). *The Functional Analysis of English* (3rd ed.). London: Routledge.

Boccia, C., Brain, V., Dorado, L., Farías, A., Gauna, B., Hassan, S., & Perera de Saravia, G. (2013). *Working with Texts in the EFL Classroom*. Mendoza: Editorial Universidad Nacional de Cuyo, EDIUNC.

Bohlke, D. (2014). Fluency-oriented second language teaching. In M. Celce-Murcia, D. M. Brinton & M. A. Snow (Eds.), *Teaching English as a Second or Foreign Language* (4th ed., pp. 121–35). Boston, MA: National Geographic Learning Heinle Cengage Learning.

Borg, S. (2006a). *Teacher Cognition and Language Education*. London: Continuum.

Borg, S. (2006b). The distinctive characteristics of foreign language teachers. *Language Teaching Research, 10*(1), 3–31.

Borg, S. (2013). Language teacher education. In J. Simpson (Ed.), *The Routledge Handbook of Applied Linguistics* (pp. 215–28). London and New York: Routledge.

Bourdieu, P. (1991). *Language and Symbolic Power*. Cambridge, MA: Harvard University Press.

Brinton, D. M., & Snow, M. A. (2017). The evolving architecture of content-based instruction. In M. A. Snow & D. M. Brinton (Eds.), *The Content-Based Classroom: New Perspectives on Integrating Language and Content* (2nd ed., pp. 2–20). Ann Arbor, MI: University of Michigan Press.

British Council. (2015). Education intelligence. English in Ecuador: An examination of policy, perceptions and influencing factors. Retrieved from https://ei.britishcouncil .org/sites/default/files/latin-america-research/English%20in%20Ecuador.pdf

Brown, H. (2000). *Principles of Language Learning and Teaching* (4th ed.). New York: Longman.

Brown, J. (2014). *Mixed Methods Research for TESOL*. Edinburgh: Edinburgh University Press

Brown, K. (Ed.). (2006). *Encyclopaedia of Language and Linguistics* (2nd ed.). Oxford: Elsevier.

Bryson, B. (2003). *A short history of nearly everything*. London: Black Swan.

Burbano, M. D. (2011). Communicative competence: Myth or reality when learning English as a foreign language. Unpublished master's thesis, University of Cuenca, Cuenca, Ecuador.

Burnaz, Y. (2011). Perception of EFL learners towards portfolios as a method of alternative assessment: A case study at a Turkish university. Unpublished doctoral thesis, Middle East Technical University, Turkey. Retrieved from: http://citeseerx.ist .psu.edu/viewdoc/download?doi=10.1.1.460.9966&rep=rep1&type=pdf

Burner, T. (2014) The potential formative benefits of portfolio assessment in second and foreign language writing contexts: A review of the literature. *Studies in Educational Evaluation, 43*, 139–49.

Burns, A., Joyce, H., & Gollin, S. (1996). *"I see what you mean": Using Spoken Discourse in the Classroom: A Handbook for Teachers*. Sydney: NCELTR, Macquarie University.

Butler, Y. G. (2004). What level of English proficiency do elementary school teachers need to attain to teach EFL? Case studies from Korea, Taiwan, and Japan. *TESOL Quarterly, 38*(2), 245–78.

Bygate, M., Skehan, P., & Swain, M. (2001). Introduction. In M. Bygate, P. Skehan & M. Swain (Eds.), *Researching Pedagogic Tasks: Second Language Learning, Teaching and Testing* (pp. 1–20). New York: Pearson Education.

Byrnes, H. (2009). *Advanced Language Learning: The Contribution of Halliday and Vygotsky*. London: Bloomsbury.

Byrnes, H., Weger, H. D., & Sprang, K. A. (2006). *Educating for Advanced Foreign Language Capacities: Constructs, Curriculum, Instruction, Assessment.* Washington DC: Georgetown University Press.

Cable, T. (2013). *A companion to Baugh & Cable's a history of the English language* (4th ed.). Boston: Pearson Education.

Campos, R., & Hernández, A. M. (2013). *Mexicanos y los idiomas extranjeros: Encuesta nacional en viviendas.* Mexico: Consulta Mitofsky.

Canagarajah, A. S. (1999). *Resisting Linguistic Imperialism in English Teaching.* Oxford: Oxford University Press.

Canagarajah, A. S. (2007). Lingua franca English, multilingual communities, and language acquisition. *Modern Language Journal, 91,* 923–39.

Canagarajah, A. S. (2009). The plurilingual tradition and the English language in South Asia. *AILA Review, 22*(1), 5–22.

Canagarajah, A. S. (2011). Translanguaging in the classroom: Emerging issues for research and pedagogy. *Applied Linguistics Review, 2*(1), 1–28.

Canagarajah, A. S. (2013). *Translingual Practice: Global Englishes and Cosmopolitan Relations.* New York: Routledge.

Carley, P., Mees, I. M., & Collins, B. (2018). *English Phonetics and Pronunciation Practice.* Abingdon: Routledge.

Celce-Murcia, M., & Larsen-Freeman, D. (2016). *The Grammar Book: An ESL/EFL Teacher's Course* (3rd ed.). Boston, MA: Heinle-Cengage.

Celce-Murcia, M., & Olshtain, E. (2000). *Discourse and Context in Language Teaching: A guide for Language Teachers.* Cambridge: Cambridge University Press.

Celce-Murcia, M., Brinton, D. M., & Goodwin, J. M. (2010). *Teaching Pronunciation: A Course Book and Reference Guide.* New York: Cambridge University Press.

Çetinavcı, U. R., & Yavuz, A. (2010). Language proficiency level of English language teacher trainees in Turkey. *The International Journal of Research in Teacher Education, 1*(4), 26–54.

Chalak, A. (2015). The effects of explicit and implicit pragmatic instruction on Iranian EFL learners' production of suggestion speech act in the context of distance learning. *Journal of Applied Linguistics and Language Research, 4,* 275–84.

Chandler, J. (2003). The efficacy of various kinds of error feedback for improvement in the accuracy and fluency of L2 student writing. *Journal of Second Language Writing, 12,* 267–96.

Chappell, P. (2017). Interrogating your wisdom of practice to improve classroom practices. *ELT Journal, 71*(4), 1–13.

Chappell, P. J. (2014). *Group Work in the English Language Curriculum: Sociocultural and Ecological Perspectives on Second Language Classroom Learning.* London: Palgrave Macmillan.

Chomsky, N. (1988). *Language and Problems of Knowledge: The Managua Lectures (Vol. 16).* Cambridge, MA: MIT press.

Clayton, D., & Drummond, R. (2018). *Language Diversity and World Englishes.* Cambridge: Cambridge University Press.

Cobuild. (2011). *Collins Cobuild English Grammar* (3rd ed.). New York: Harper Collins.

Coelho Liberali, F. (2017). Globalisation, superdiversity, language learning and teacher education in Brazil. In D. L. Banegas (Ed.), *Initial English Language Teacher Education: International Perspectives on Research, Curriculum and Practice* (pp. 177–91). London and New York: Bloomsbury.

Cohen, A. (2008). Teaching and assessing L2 pragmatics: What can we expect from learners? *Language Teaching, 41*(2), 213–35.

Cohen, A. (2016). The teaching of pragmatics by native and nonnative language teachers: What they know and what they report doing. *Studies in Second Language Learning and Teaching, 6*(4), 561–85.

Cohen, A. (2017). Teaching and learning second language pragmatics. In E. Hinkel (Ed.), *Handbook of Research in Second Language Teaching and Learning* (pp. 428–52). New York: Routledge.

CohenMiller, A. S., Merril, M. & Shamatov, D. (2018). Effective teaching strategies: A brief overview. *Pedagogical Dialog, 1*, 32–52.

Coleman, J. A. (2014) How to get published in English: Advice from the outgoing editor-in-chief. *System, 42*, 404–11.

Collins, B., & Mees, I. M. (2013). *Practical Phonetics and Phonology: A Resource Book for Students* (3rd ed.). Abingdon: Routledge.

Collins, J. W., & O'Brien, N. P. (Eds.). (2003). *Greenwood Dictionary of Education.* Westport: Greenwood.

Conrad, S. (2000). Will corpus linguistics revolutionize grammar teaching in the 21st century? *TESOL Quarterly, 34*, 548–60.

Copland, F., Garton, S., & Burns, A. (2014). Challenges in teaching English to young learners: Global perspectives and local realities. *TESOL Quarterly, 48*, 738–62.

Coşkun , A., & Daloğlu, A. (2010). Evaluating an English language teacher education program through Peacock's model. *Australian Journal of Teacher Education, 35*(6), 24–42.

Council of Europe. Modern Languages Division. (2001). *Common European Framework of Reference for Languages: Learning, Teaching, Assessment.* Cambridge: Cambridge University Press.

Council of Higher Education. (2018). İngilizce öğretmenliği programı. Retrieved from http://www.yok.gov.tr/documents/10279/41805112/Ingilizce_Ogretmenligi_Lisans_Programi.pdf

Coyle, D., Hood, P., Marsh, D. (2010). *Content and Language Integrated Learning.* Cambridge: Cambridge University Press.

Crandall, J., & S. F. Miller (2014) Effective professional development for language teachers. In M. Celce-Murcia, D. M. Brinton & M. A. Snow (Eds.), *Teaching English as a Second or Foreign Language* (4th ed., pp. 630–48). Boston, MA: National Geographic Learning/Heinle Cengage.

Cross, R. (2010). Language teaching as sociocultural activity. *Modern Language Journal*, *94*(3), 434–52.

Cross, R. (2018). The "subject" of Freeman & Johnson's reconceived knowledge base of second language teacher education. *Language Teaching Research*, doi: 10.1177/1362168818777521

Cruttenden, A. (2014). *Gimson's pronunciation of English* (8th ed.). Abingdon: Routledge.

Crystal, D. (2003). *The Cambridge Encyclopedia of the English Language* (2nd ed.). Cambridge: Cambridge University Press.

Crystal, D. (2010). *The Cambridge Encyclopedia of Language* (3rd ed.). Cambridge: Cambridge University Press.

Crystal, D. (2012a). A global language. In P. Seargeant & J. Swann (Eds.), *English in the World: History, Diversity, Change* (pp. 152–77). Abingdon: Routledge.

Crystal, D. (2012b). *Spell it Out: The Curious, Enthralling, and Extraordinary Story of English Spelling*. New York: St. Martin's press.

Cullen, R. (2002). The use of lesson transcripts for developing teachers' classroom language. In H. Trappes-Lomaz & G. Ferguson (Eds.), *Language in Language Teacher Education* (pp. 219–35). Amsterdam: John Benjamins.

Cushing-Leubner, J., & Bigelow, M. (2014). Principled eclecticism and the holistic approach to language teaching and learning. In S. Çelik (Ed.), *Approaches and Principles in English as a Foreign Language (EFL) Education* (pp. 254–63). Ankara: Egiten.

D'Angelo, J. (2012). WE-informed EIL curriculum at Chukyo: Towards a functional, educated, multilingual outcome. In A. Matsuda (Ed.), *Principles and Practices of Teaching English as an International Language* (pp. 121–39). Toronto: Multilingual Matters.

De la Fuente, M. J., & Goldenburg, C. (2018). Understanding the role of L1 in instructed second language acquisition: Effects of using L1 in the L2 classroom. Paper presented at American Association of Applied Linguistics, Chicago, Illinois.

Delmaestro, A. (2005). El portafolio como estrategia de evaluación en la enseñanza de lenguas extranjeras: Fundamentos teóricos y orientaciones procedimentales. *Lingua Americana*, *16*, 43–68.

Demirbas, M. N. (2011). The comparison of Gazi University ELT freshmen's receptive and productive skill performances. Unpublished master's thesis, Gazi University, Ankara, Turkey.

Department of Linguistics, The Ohio State University (Eds.). (2016). *Language Files: Materials for an Introduction to Language and Linguistics* (12th ed.). Columbus, OH: The Ohio State University.

Derewianka, B. (2011). *A New Grammar Companion for Teachers*. Newtown: Primary English Teaching Association.

Derewianka, B., & Jones, P. (2010). From traditional grammar to functional grammar: bridging the divide. *NALDIC Quarterly*, *8*(1), 6–17.

Derwing, T. M. (2017). L2 fluency development. In S. Loewen & M. Sato (Eds.), *The Routledge Handbook of Instructed Second Language Acquisition* (pp. 246–59). New York and Abingdon: Taylor & Francis.

Derwing, T. M., & Munro, M. J. (2015). *Pronunciation Fundamentals: Evidence-based Perspectives for L2 Teaching and Research.* Amsterdam: John Benjamins.

Dewey, J. (1933). *How We Think: A Restatement of the Reflective Thinking to the Educative Process.* New York: Heath.

Diamond, J. (2010). The benefits of multilingualism. *Science, 330*(6002), 332–33.

Diaz-Maggioli, G., & Painter-Farrell, L., (2016). *Lessons Learned: First Steps Towards Reflective Reaching in ELT.* Montevideo: Richmond.

Donnini Rodrigues, L. A., de Pietri, E., Sanchez, H. S., & Kuchah, K. (2018). The role of experienced teachers in the development of pre-service language teachers' professional identity: Revisiting school memories and constructing future teacher selves. *International Journal of Educational Research, 88*, 146–55.

Dudeney, G., & Hockly, N. (2007). *How to Teach English with Technology.* Harlow: Pearson.

Dudeney, G., Hockly, N., & Pegrum M. (2013). *Digital Literacies.* New York: Routledge.

Drew, P. (2005). Conversation analysis. In K. Fitch & R. Sanders (Eds.), *Handbook of Language and Social Interaction* (pp. 71–102). New York: Lawrence Erlbaum.

Echevarría, J., Vogt, M. E., & Short, D. (2017). *Making Content Comprehensible for English Learners: The SIOP® Model* (5th ed.). Boston: Allyn & Bacon.

Ecuador tiene falencias en enseñanza del inglés, promedio en escuelas y colegios es de 13/20 (2012). Retrieved from http://www.ecuadorinmediato.com/index.php?mod ule=Noticias&func=news_user_view&id=17747

Educational Testing Service (2018). Test and score data summary forTOEFL iBT Tests. Retrieved from http://www.ets.org/s/toefl/pdf/94227_unlweb.pdf

Edwards, E., & Burns, A. (2016). Language teacher–researcher identity negotiation: An ecological perspective. *TESOL Quarterly, 50*(3), 735–45.

Eggins, S. (2004). *An Introduction to Systemic Functional Linguistics.* London: Continuum.

Ellis, R., (2003). *Task-based Language Learning and Teaching.* Oxford: Oxford University Press.

Ellis, R. (2009). A typology of written corrective feedback types. *ELT Journal, 62*(2), 97–107.

Ene, E., & Upton, T. A. (2018). Synchronous and asynchronous teacher electronic feedback and learner uptake in ESL composition. *Journal of Second Language Writing, 41*, 1–13.

Eom, S. B., Wen, H. J., & Ashill, N. (2006). The determinants of students' perceived learning outcomes and satisfaction in university online education: An empirical investigation. *Decision Sciences Journal of Innovative Education, 4*, 215–35.

Erozan, F. (2005). Evaluating the language improvement courses in the undergraduate ELT curriculum at Eastern Mediterranean University: A case study. Unpublished doctoral dissertation, Middle East Technical University, Ankara, Turkey.

Eslami, Z. R., & Fatahi, A. (2008). Teachers' sense of self-efficacy, English proficiency, and instructional strategies: A study of nonnative EFL teachers in Iran. *TESL-EJ*, *11*(4), 1–19.

Estebas-Vilaplana, E. E. (2009). *Teach Yourself English Pronunciation: An Interactive Course for Spanish Speakers*. La Coruña: Netbiblo.

Eurydice (2009). Indicators on initial teacher education. Retrieved from http://www .sdcentras.lt/pla/res/Indicators%20on%20Initial%20Teacher%20Education.pdf

Fairclough, N. (2003). *Analysing Discourse: Text Analysis for Social Research*. London: Routledge.

Fairclough, N. (2010). *Critical Discourse Analysis: The Critical Study of Language*. Harlow: Longman.

Fairclough, N. (2013). *Language and Power*. New York: Routledge.

Faravani, A., & Atai, M. (2015). Portfolio assessment and the enhancement of higher order thinking through multiple intelligence and dialogic feedback. *Issues in Language Teaching 4*(1), 1–25.

Ferris, D. (2006). Does error feedback help student writers? New evidence on short- and-long-term effects of written error correction. In K. Hyland & F. Hyland (Eds.), *Feedback in Second Language Writing: Contexts and Issues* (pp. 81–104). Cambridge: Cambridge University Press.

Ferris, D., Liu, H., Sinha, A., & Senna, M. (2013). Written corrective feedback for individual L2 writers. *Journal of Second Language Writing, 22*, 307–29.

Fortanet-Gómez, I. (2013). *CLIL in Higher Education: Towards a Multilingual Language Policy*. Bristol: Multilingual Matters.

Freeman, D. (2017). The case for teachers' classroom English proficiency. *RELC Journal, 48*(1), 31–52.

Freeman, D., & Johnson, K. E. (1998). Reconceptualizing the knowledge-base of language teacher education. *TESOL Quarterly, 32*(3), 397–417.

Freeman, D., Katz, A., Garcia Gómez, P., & Burns, A. (2015). English-for-teaching: Rethinking teacher proficiency in the classroom. *ELT Journal, 69*(2), 129–39.

Frodesen, J., & Wald, M. (2016). *Exploring Options in Academic Writing: Effective Vocabulary and Grammar Use*. Ann Arbor: University of Michigan Press.

Gaido, A., Oliva, M. B., Calvo, A., & Ríus, N. (2016). *English Grammar: Basic Notions on Systemic-Functional Grammar*. Córdoba: FL Copias.

García, O., Ibarra Johnson, S., & Seltzer, K. (2017). *The Translanguaging Classroom: Leveraging Student Bilingualism for Learning*. Philadelphia: Caslon.

García, O., & Wei, L. (2014). *Translanguaging: Language, Bilingualism and Education*. New York: Palgrave Macmillan.

Gareis, E., Merkin, R., & Goldman, J. (2011). Intercultural friendship: Linking communication variables and friendship success. *Journal of Intercultural Communication Research, 40*(2), 153–71.

Ghio, E., & Fernández, M. D. (2005). *Manual de lingüística sistémico funcional: El enfoque de M. A. K. Halliday y R. Hasan: Aplicaciones a la lengua española*. Santa Fe: Universidad Nacional del Litoral.

Ghirardotto, M. V., Canavosio, A. de los Á., & Giménez, F. (2013). El uso de material auténtico: Un desafío en la clase de fonética y fonología. In G. Bombelli & L. Soler (Eds.), *Oralidad: Miradas plurilingües desde la fonética y la fonología* (pp. 294–304). Córdoba: Buena Vista Editores.

Giles, M. (2010). A world of connections A special report on social networking. The Economist. Jan 30th. Retrieved from https://www.economist.com/special-report /2010/01/28/a-world-of-connections

Giménez, F., & Aguirre Sotelo, E. (2015). Tareas de autocorrección: Herramientas útiles en el área de pronunciación del inglés. In P. L. Luchini, M. A. García Jurado & U. Kickhöfel Alves (Eds.), *Fonética y fonología: Articulación entre enseñanza e investigación* (pp. 222–30). Mar del Plata: Universidad Nacional de Mar del Plata.

Golombek, P. R. (2015). Redrawing the boundaries of language teacher cognition. Language teacher educations' emotions, cognition, and activity. *Modern Language Journal, 99*(3), 470–84.

Graham, C. (2003). *Small Talk: More jazz chants.* Oxford: Oxford University Press.

Gramley, S. (2012). *The History of English: An Introduction.* Oxford: Routledge.

Grasso, M. (2017). Reflecting upon students' problems in phonemic dictations. In Proceedings of the Phonetics Teaching and Learning Conference (pp. 54–58). London: UCL.

Greenpeace International (2018). Rang-tan: The story of dirty palm oil [video file]. Retrieved from https://www.youtube.com/watch?v=TQQXstNh45g&t=2s (13 September, 2018).

Grice, H. P. (1975). Logic and conversation. In P. Cole & J. Morgan (Eds.), *Speech Acts* (pp. 41–58). New York: Academic Press.

Gumperz, J., & Hymes, D. H. (1986). *Directions in Sociolinguistics: Ethnography of Communications.* Oxford and New York: Basil-Blackwell.

Hadjioannou, X., & Hutchinson, M. C. (2010). Putting the "G" back in English. *English Teaching: Practice and Critique, 9*(3), 90–105.

Halliday, M. A. K. (1980). The contribution of developmental linguistics to the interpretation of language as a system. In E. Hovdhaugen (Ed.), *The Nordic Languages and Modern Linguistics* (pp. 1–18). Oslo: Universitetsforlaget.

Halliday, M. A. K. (1985). *An Introduction to Functional Grammar.* London: Arnold.

Halliday, M. A. K. (1993). Towards a language-based theory of learning. *Linguistics and Education, 5*(2), 93–116.

Halliday, M. A. K. (2002). On grammar. In J. Webster (Ed.), *The Collected Works of MAK Halliday, Vol. 1.* London: Continuum.

Halliday, M. A. K. (2003). On language and linguistics. In J. Webster (Ed.), *The Collected Works of M.A.K. Halliday, Vol. 3.* London and New York: Continuum.

Halliday, M.A.K. (2004). Three aspects of children's language development: Learning language, learning through language, learning about language. In J. J. Webster (Ed.), *The Language of Early Childhood: M. A. K. Halliday* (pp. 308–26). London: Continuum.

Halliday, M. A. K., & Greaves, W. S. (2008). *Intonation in the Grammar of English*. London: Equinox.

Halliday, M. A. K., & Hasan, R. (1976). *Cohesion in English*. London: Longman.

Halliday, M. A .K., & Hasan, R. (1985). *Language, Context and Text: A Social Semiotic Perspective*. Geelong: Deakin University Press.

Halliday, M. A. K., & Matthiessen, C. (1999). *Construing Experience Through Meaning: A Language-Based Approach to Cognition*. London: Cassell.

Halliday, M. A. K., & Matthiessen, C. M. I. M. (2014). *Halliday's Introduction to Functional Grammar* (4th ed.). Abingdon: Routledge.

Hamid, M. O. (2010). Globalisation, English for everyone and English teacher capacity: language policy discourses and realities in Bangladesh. *Current Issues in Language Planning, 11*(4), 289–310.

Hamp-Lyons, L., & Condon, W. (2000). *Assessing the Portfolio: Principles for Practice, Theory and Research*. Cresskill: Hampton Press.

Harbour, K., Evanovich, L., Sweigart, C., & Hughes, L. (2015). A brief review of effective teaching practices that maximize student engagement. *Preventing School Failure: Alternative Education for Children and Youth, 59*(1), 5–13.

Hardin, K. (2013). What goes unsaid: Expression of complaints and advice about health in Eastern Ecuador. *Intercultural Pragmatics, 10*(4), 569–91.

Harmer, J. (2012). *Essential Teacher Knowledge: Core Concepts in English Language Teaching*. Harlow: Pearson.

Harsch, C. (2017). Proficiency. *ELT Journal, 71*(2), 250–53.

Hasenfratz, R., & Jambeck, T. (2011). *Reading Old English: A Primer and First Reader*. Morgantown, WV: West Virginia University Press.

Hawkins, M., & Norton, B. (2009). Critical language teacher education. In A. Burns & J. C. Richards (Eds.), *Cambridge Guide to Second Language Teacher Education* (pp. 30–39). Cambridge: Cambridge University Press.

Hayes, M., & Burkette, A. (Eds.). (2017). *Approaches to Teaching the History of the English Language: Pedagogy in Practice*. Oxford: Oxford University Press.

He, C., & Yan, C. (2011). Exploring authenticity of microteaching in pre-service teacher education programmes. *Teaching Education, 22*(3), 291–302.

He, D., & Zhang, Q. (2010). Native speaker norms and China English: From the perspective of learners and teachers in China. *TESOL Quarterly, 44*(4), 769–89.

Hedgcock, J., & Lee, H. (2017). An exploratory study of academic literacy socialization: Building genre awareness in a teacher education program. *Journal of English for Academic Purposes, 26*, 17–18.

Heras, G. (2014). Designing and piloting part of an introductory pragmatics workbook for 3rd level students of the English degree course, University of Cuenca. Unpublished master's thesis, University of Cuenca, Cuenca, Ecuador.

Hino, N. (2012). Endonormative models of EIL for the expanding circle. In A. Matsuda (Ed.), *Principles and Practices of Teaching English as an International Language* (pp. 28–43). Bristol: Multilingual Matters.

Historia Universitaria (2018), Retrieved from: https://www.buap.mx/historia_
universitaria

Hockly, N., & G. Dudeney (2016). Current and future digital trends in ELT. *RELC Journal, 49*(2), 164–78.

Hockly, N. (2016). *Learning Technologies*. Oxford: Oxford University Press.

Holliday, A. (2006). Native-speakerism. *ELT Journal, 60*(4), 385–87.

hooks, b. (1994). *Teaching to Transgress*. New York: Routledge.

Hos, R., & Kekec, M. (2014). The mismatch between non-native English as a foreign language (EFL) teachers' grammar beliefs and classroom practices. *Journal of Language Teaching and Research, 5*(1), 80–87.

Houck, N., & Tatsuki, D. (2011). *Pragmatics from Research to Practice*: New Directions. Alexandria: TESOL.

Howard, J., & J. Major (2004). Guidelines for designing effective English language teaching materials. *The TESOLANZ Journal, 12*, 50–58.

Hualde, J. I. (2014). *Los sonidos del español*. Cambridge: Cambridge University Press.

Huerta, B. (2005). Génesis y desarrollo en la enseñanza de lenguas en la BUAP. *Revista Tiempo Universitario, 8*(3).

Humphrey, S.L., Droga, L. & Feez, S. (2012). *Grammar and Meaning*. Newtown: Primary English Teaching Association.

Hyland, K. (2003). *Second Language Writing*. Cambridge and New York: Cambridge University Press.

Hyland, K. (2008). Genre and academic writing in the disciplines. *Language Teaching, 41*(4), 543–62.

Hyland, K. (2016). *Teaching and Researching Writing* (3rd ed.). New York: Routledge.

Hyland, K., & Hyland, F. (2006a). *Feedback in Second Language Writing: Contexts and Issues*. Cambridge: Cambridge University Press.

Hyland, K., & Hyland, F. (2006b). Feedback on second language students' writing. *Language Teaching, 39*(2), 83–101.

IELTE LEI. Discourse Analysis (2009). Programas LEI. (Cuatrimestral) Facultad de Lenguas. Benemérita Universidad Autónoma de Puebla.

Ignatieva, N. (2011). Verbal processes in student academic writing in Spanish from a systemic functional perspective. *Lenguaje, 39*, 447–67.

Ignatieva, N., & Rodríguez Vergara, D. (Eds). (2016). *Lingüística sistémico funcional en México: Aplicaciones e implicaciones*. México. UNAM.

Imran, S., & Wyatt, M. (2015). Pakistani university English teachers' cognitions and classroom practices regarding their use of the learners' first languages. *Asian EFL Journal, 17*(1), 138–79.

Ishihara, N., & Cohen, A. (2010). *Teaching and Learning Pragmatics: Where Language and Culture Meet*. Harlow: Longman.

Ishihara, N., & Maeda, M. (2010). *Advanced Japanese: Communication in Context* [Kotobato bunka no kousaten]. London: Routledge.

Ismaili, M. (2013). The effectiveness of using movies in the EFL classroom: A study conducted at South East European University. *Academic Journal of Interdisciplinary Studies, 2*(4), 121–32.

Iyeiri, Y. (Ed.). (2016). *Korekara no eigokyoiku: Eigoshikenkyu tono taiwa* [Can knowing the history of English help in the teaching of English?] Osaka: Osaka Books.

Jackendoff, R. (2003, November). The structure of language: Why it matters to education. In Talk for conference on Learning and the Brain, Linguistic Society of America, Cambridge, November (pp. 5–8).

James, J. (2010). New technologies in developing countries: A critique of the One-Laptop-Per-Child Program. *Social Science Computer Review, 28*(3), 381–90.

Jenkins, J. (2000). *The Phonology of English as an International Language.* Oxford: Oxford University Press.

Jenkins, J. (2007). *English as a Lingua Franca: Attitude and Identity.* Oxford: Oxford University Press.

Jenkins, J. (2009). Exploring attitudes towards English as a lingua franca in the East Asian context. In K. Murata & J. Jenkins (Eds.), *Global Englishes in Asian Contexts: Current and Future Debates* (pp. 40–56). Basingstoke: Palgrave.

Jenkins, J., Cogo, A., & Dewey, M. (2011). Review of developments in research into English as a lingua franca. *Language Teaching, 44*(3), 281–315.

Johnson, K. E. (2000). *Teacher Education: Case Studies in TESOL Practice.* Alexandria: TESOL.

Johnson, K. E. (2009). *Second Language Teacher Education: A Sociocultural Perspective.* New York and Abingdon: Routledge.

Johnson, N. H., & de Haan, J. (2013). Strategic interaction 2.0: Instructed intercultural pragmatics in an EFL context. *International Journal of Strategic Information Technology and Applications, 4*(1), 49–62.

Kachru, B. B. (1985). The bilinguals' creativity. *Annual Review of Applied Linguistics, 6,* 20–33.

Kachru, B. B. (1986). *The Alchemy of English: The Spread, Functions, and Models of Non-Native Englishes.* Chicago: University of Illinois Press.

Kam, H. W. (2002). English language teaching in East Asia today: An overview. *Asia Pacific Journal of Education, 22*(2), 1–22.

Kamhi-Stein, L. D. (2009). Teacher preparation and non-native English-speaking educators. In A. Burns & J. Richards (Eds.), *The Cambridge Guide to Second Language Teacher Education* (pp. 91–101). Cambridge: Cambridge University Press.

Kamhi-Stein, L. D. (2014). Non-native English-speaking teachers in the profession. In M. Celce-Murcia, D. M. Brinton & M. A. Snow (Eds.), *Teaching English as a Second or Foreign Language* (4th ed., pp. 486–600). Boston: Cengage.

Kamhi-Stein, L. D., Díaz Maggioli, G., & de Oliveira, L. C. (Eds.). (2017). *English Language Teaching in South America: Policy, Preparation and Practices.* Bristol: Multilingual Matters.

Kamhi-Stein, L. D., & Mahboob, A. (2005). Language proficiency and NNES professionals: Findings from TIRF-Funded research initiatives. Paper presented at 39th Annual TESOL Convention, San Antonio, Texas.

Kaplan-Weinger, J., & Ullman C. (2015). *Methods for the Ethnography of Communication: Language in Use in Schools and Communities.* New York: Routledge.

Kasper, G. (1997). Can pragmatic competence be taught? Honolulu: University of Hawai'i, Second Language Teaching & Curriculum Center. Retrieved from: http://www.nflrc.hawaii.edu/NetWorks/NW06/

Kasper, G., & Rose, K. (1999). Pragmatics and SLA. *Annual Review of Applied Linguistics, 19,* 81–104.

Kasper, G., & Rose, K. (2002). *Pragmatic Development in a Second Language.* Malden: Blackwell Publishing Inc.

Katz, A., & M. A. Snow (2009). Standards and second language teacher education. In A. Burns & J. Richards (Eds.), *The Cambridge Guide to Second Language Teacher Education* (pp. 66–76). New York: Cambridge University Press.

Kirkgöz, Y. (2009). Globalization and English language policy in Turkey. *Educational Policy, 23*(5), 663–84.

Klenowski, V. (2002). *Developing Portfolios for Learning and Assessment.* London and New York: Routledge Falmer.

Kömür, Ş. (2010). Teaching knowledge and teacher competencies: A case study of Turkish preservice English teachers. *Teaching Education, 21*(3), 279–96.

Kömür, Ş., & Ş. S. Çimen (2017). Exploring pre-service English teachers' course expectations and their realization levels through portfolios. *International Online Journal of Education and Teaching, 4*(4), 449–56.

König, J., Lammerding, S., Nold, G., Rohde, A., Strauß, S., & Tachtsoglou, S. (2016). Teachers' professional knowledge for teaching English as a foreign language: Assessing the outcomes of teacher education. *Journal of Teacher Education, 67*(4), 320–37.

Kramsch, C. (1998). *Language and Culture.* Oxford: Oxford University Press.

Kress, G., & van Leeuween, T. (1996). *Reading Images: The Grammar of Visual Design.* London: Routledge.

Kress, G., & van Leeuwen, T. (2001). *Multimodal Discourse: The Modes and Media of Contemporary Communication.* London: Arnold.

Kristeva, J. (1986). Word, dialogue, and the novel. In T. Moi (Ed.), *The Kristeva Reader* (pp. 35–61). New York: Columbia University Press.

Kubota, R. (2012). The politics of EIL: towards border-crossing communication in and beyond English. In. A. Matsuda (Ed.), *Principles and Practices of Teaching English as an International Language* (pp. 55–69). Bristol: Multilingual Matters.

Kumaravadivelu, B. (2009). *Understanding Language Teaching. From Method to Postmethod.* New York and Abingdon: Routledge.

Kwai-peng, S. F. (2016). Exploring cross-cultural pragmatic judgment of two groups of EFL teachers on formal written requests. *Theory and Practice in Language Studies, 6*(4), 693–705.

Lam, R. (2013). Two portfolio systems: EFL students' perceptions of writing ability, text improvement, and feedback. *Assessing Writing, 18*, 132–53.

Lam, R. (2018). *Portfolio Assessment for the Teaching and Learning of Writing*. Hong Kong: Springer.

Lance, D. (1977). What is grammar? *English Education, 9*(1), 43–49.

Lantolf, J. P. (2000). *Sociocultural Theory and Second Language Learning*. Oxford: Oxford University Press.

Lantolf, J. P., & Poehner, M. E. (Eds.). (2008). *Sociocultural Theory and the Teaching of Second Languages*. London: Equinox.

Lantolf, J. P., & Poehner, M. E. (2014). *Sociocultural Theory and the Pedagogical Imperative in L2 Education: Vygotskian Praxis and the Research/Practice Divide*. London and New York: Routledge.

Lantolf, J. P., & Thorne, S. L. (2006). *Sociocultural Theory and the Genesis of Second Language Development*. Oxford: Oxford University Press.

Larsen-Freeman, D. (2014). Teaching grammar. In M. Celce-Murcia, D. M. Brinton & M. A. Snow (Eds.), *Teaching English as Second or Foreign Language* (4th ed., pp. 256–70). Boston: Cengage.

Larsen-Freeman, D. (2018). Mutual empowerment in challenging times. Invited lecture at The New School, New York.

Larsen-Freeman, D., & Cameron, L. (2008). *Complex Systems and Applied Linguistics*. Oxford: Oxford University Press.

Lassonde, C. A., Galman, S., & Kosnik, C. (2009). *Self-study Research Methodologies for Teacher Educators*. Rotterdam: Sense Publishers.

Le, V. C. (2018). Remapping the teacher knowledge-base of language teacher education: A Vietnamese perspective. *Language Teaching Research*, https://doi.org/10.1177/1362168818777525

Lee, I. (2011). Formative assessment in EFL writing: An exploratory case study. Changing English: Studies in Culture and Education, *18*(1), 99–111.

Leung, C., & Morton, T. (2016). Conclusion: Language competence, learning and pedagogy in CLIL: Deepening and broadening integration. In T. Nikula, E. Dafouz, P. Moore & U. Smit (Eds.), *Conceptualising Integration in CLIL and Multilingual Education* (pp. 235–48). Bristol: Multilingual Matters.

Lewis, C. S. (1950). *The Lion, the Witch, and the Wardrobe*. London: England: Geoffrey Bles.

Li, B., & T.B. Tin (2013). Exploring the expectations and perceptions of non-native English speaking students in Master's level TESOL programs. *New Zealand Studies in Applied Linguistics, 19*(2), 21–35.

Li, L., Liu, X., & Steckelberg, A. L. (2010). Assessor or assessee: How student learning improves by giving and receiving peer feedback. *British Journal of Educational Technology, 41*, 525–36.

Lightbown, P., & Spada, N. (2013). *How Languages are Learned* (4th ed.). Oxford: Oxford University Press.

Lindsey, G. (2017). *English after RP*. London: Tequisté TXT.

Loewen, S. (2007). Error correction in the second language classroom. *Clear News*, *11*(2), 1–6.

Lovat, T., Davies, M., & Plotnikof, R. (1995). Integrating research skills development in teacher education. *Australian Journal of Teacher Education*, *20*(1), 30–35.

Lunar, L. (2007). El portafolio: estrategia para evaluar la producción escrita en inglés por parte de estudiantes universitarios. *Núcleo*, *24*, 63–96.

Macaro, E. (2018). *English Medium Instruction*. Oxford: Oxford University Press.

Macaro, E., Curle, S., Pun, J., An, J., & Dearden, J. (2018). A systematic review of English medium instruction in higher education. *Language Teaching*, *51*(1), 36–76.

Mahboob, A. (2017). Understanding language variation: Implications of the NNEST lens for TESOL teacher education programs. In J. Martinez Agudo (Ed.), *Native and Non-Native Teachers in English Language Classrooms: Professional Challenges and Teacher Education* (pp. 13–32). Boston and Berlin: De Gruyter Mouton.

Mahboob, A., & Knight, N. K. (2010). *Appliable Linguistics*. London: Bloombury.

Maley, A. (2009). *Advanced Learners*. Oxford: Oxford University Press.

Mansvelder-Longayroux, D., Beijaard, D., & Verloop, N. (2007). The learning portfolio as a tool for stimulating reflection by student teachers. *Teaching and Teacher Education*, *23*(1), 47–62.

Martin, A. (2016). Second language teacher education in the expanding circle: The EFL methodology course in Chile. *Colombian Applied Linguistics Journal*, *18*(1), 24–42.

Martin, J. R. (1984). Language, register and genre. In F. Christie (Ed.), *Children Writing: Reader* (pp. 21–29). Geelong: Deakin University Press.

Martin, J. R. (2009). Genre and language learning: A social semiotic perspective. *Linguistics and Education*, *20*(1), 10–21.

Martin, J. R., & Rose, D. (2003). *Working with Discourse: Meaning Beyond the Clause*. London: Continuum.

Martin, J. R., & Rose, D. (2008). *Genre Relations: Mapping Culture*. London: Equinox.

Martínez Agudo, J. (Ed.). (2017). *Native and Non-Native Teachers in English Language Classrooms: Professional Challenges and Teacher Education*. Boston and Berlin: De Gruyter Mouton.

Martínez Lirola, M. (2012). Evaluating with a portfolio in the European higher education framework: An example from English studies. *Revista Española de Lingüística Aplicada*, *25*, 147–63.

Martínez-Flor, A., & Alcón-Soler, E. (2005). Pragmatics in instructed language learning. *System*, *33*(3), 381–536.

Mastrogiacomi, F. (2005). The pre-service training of foreign language teachers in CMC learning environments. In P. Kommers & G. Richards (Eds.), *Proceedings of ED MEDIA 2005 World Conference on Educational Multimedia, Hypermedia & Telecommunications* (pp. 762–69). Montreal: AACE.

McCabe, A. (2017). Systemic functional linguistics and language teaching. In T. Bartlett & G. O'Grady (Eds.), *The Routledge Handbook of Systemic Functional Linguistics* (pp. 591–604). London: Routledge.

McDonough, J., Shaw, C., & Masuhara, H. (2013). *Materials and Methods in ELT* (3rd ed.). Malden: Wiley-Blackwell.

McGregor, W. B. (2009). *Linguistics: An Introduction* (2nd ed.). London and New York: Bloomsbury.

McMartin-Miller, C. (2014). How much feedback is enough? Instructor practices and students attitudes toward error treatment in second language writing. *Assessing Writing, 19*, 24–35.

Medgyes, P. (2017). *The Non-native Teacher* (3rd ed.). Callander: Swan Communication Ltd.

Meyer, O. (2010). Introducing the CLIL-Pyramid: Key strategies and principles for quality CLIL planning and teaching. Retrieved from http://www.ccn-clil.eu/index.p hp?name=File&nodeIDX=5219

Ministerio de Educación (2014a). National curriculum guidelines. Retrieved from https://educacion.gob.ec/wp-content/uploads/downloads/2014/09/01-National-Curriculum-Guidelines-EFL-Agosto-2014.pdf

Ministerio de Educación. (2014b). Estándares orientadores para carreras de pedagogía en inglés. Estándares disciplinarios. Estándares pedagógicos. Retrieved from http://www.mineduc.cl/usuarios/cpeip/File/nuevos%20estandares/ingles.pdf

Mukundan, J., Nimehchisalem, V., & Hajimohammadi, R. (2011). Developing an English language textbook evaluation checklist: A focus group study. *International Journal of Humanities and Social Science, 1*(12), 100–06.

Murdoch, G. (1994). Language development provision in teacher training curricula. *ELT Journal, 48*(3), 253–65.

Murphy, R. (2015). *English Grammar in Use: Self-study Reference and Practice Book for Intermediate Learners of English* (4th ed.). Cambridge: Cambridge University Press.

Narita, R. (2012). The effects of pragmatic consciousness-raising activity on the development of pragmatic awareness and use of hearsay evidential markers for learners of Japanese as a foreign language. *Journal of Pragmatics, 44*, 1–29.

Nation, P. (1990). *Teaching and Learning Vocabulary*. New York: Heinle & Heinle.

Nation, P. (2013). *Learning Vocabulary in Another Language* (2nd ed.). Cambridge: Cambridge University Press.

Nava, A., & Pedrazzini, L. (2018). *Second Language Acquisition in Action: Principles from Practice*. London: Bloomsbury.

Nazari, A., & Allahyar, N. (2012). Grammar teaching revisited: EFL teachers between grammar abstinence and formal grammar teaching. *Australian Journal of Teacher Education, 37*(2), 73–87.

Nemtchinova, E., Mahboob, A., Eslami, Z., & Dogancay-Aktuna, S. (2010). Training nonnative English speaking TESOL professionals. In A. Mahboob (Ed.), *The NNEST Lens: Non-native English Speakers in TESOL* (pp. 222–38). Newcastle: Cambridge Scholars Publishing.

Nezakatgoo, B. (2011). The effects of portfolio assessment on writing of EFL students. *English Language Teaching, 4*, 232–41.

Nguyen, M. X. N. C. (2017). TESOL teachers' engagement with the native speaker model: How does teacher education impact on their beliefs? *RELC Journal, 48*(1), 83–98.

Nikula, T., Dafouz, E., Moore, P., & Smit, U. (Eds.). (2016). *Conceptualising Integration in CLIL and Multilingual Education.* Bristol: Multilingual Matters.

Nunan, D. (1998). Teaching grammar in context. *ELT Journal, 52*(2), 101–09.

Nunan, D. (2004). *Task-based Language Teaching.* Cambridge: Cambridge University Press.

Nunan, D. (2013). *Learner-centered English Language Education: The Selected Works of David Nunan.* Abingdon and New York: Routledge.

Nunan, D. (2017). The integrated syllabus: Content, tasks, and projects. In M. A. Snow & D. M. Brinton (Eds.), *The Content-based Classroom: New Perspectives on Integrating Language and Content* (2nd ed., pp. 124–36). Ann Arbor: University of Michigan Press.

Nunes, A. (2004). Portfolios in the EFL classroom: Disclosing an uninformed practice. *ELT Journal, 58*(4), 327–35.

Oranje, J., & Smith, L. F. (2018). Language teacher cognitions and intercultural language teaching: The New Zealand perspective. *Language Teaching Research, 22*(3), 310–29.

Oxford, R. L. (2011). *Teaching and Researching Language Learning Strategies.* Harlow: Pearson.

Oxford, R. L. (2016). *Teaching and Researching Language Learning Strategies: Self-regulation in Context* (2nd ed.). London: Routledge.

Özmen, K. S. (2012). Exploring student teachers' beliefs about language learning and teaching: A longitudinal study. *Current Issues in Education, 15*(1), 24–34.

Özmen, K. S., Çakır, A., & Cephe, P. T. (2018). Conceptualisation of English culture and accent: Idealised English among teachers in the expanding circle. *Asian EFL Journal 20*(1), 8–31.

Paltridge, B. (2012). *Discourse Analysis* (2nd ed.). London: Bloomsbury.

Peachey, N. (2016). *Thinking Critically Through Digital Media.* PeacheyPublications.com

Peachey, N. (2017). *Digital Tools for Teachers.* PeacheyPublications.com

Pennington, M. C., & Richards, J. C. (2016). Teacher identity in language teaching: Integrating personal, contextual, and professional factors. *RELC Journal, 47*(1), 5–23.

Pennycook, A. (2010). *Language as a Local Practice.* London: Routledge.

Perdomo, B. (2010). El portafolio como alternativa de evaluación en inglés para propósitos específicos. *Educare, 14*(3), 32–52.

Phillipson, R. (1992). *Linguistic Imperialism.* Oxford: Oxford University Press.

Phillipson, R. (2009). English in globalisation, a lingua franca or a lingua frankensteinia? *TESOL Quarterly, 43*(2), 335–39.

Phillipson, R. (2016). Additive university multilingualism in English-dominant empire: The language policy challenges. In M. Langner & V. Jovanovic (Eds.), *Facetten der Mehrsprachigkeit. Reflets du plurilinguisme* (pp. 139–61). Bern: Peter Lang.

Porto, M., & Byram, M. (2015). Developing intercultural citizenship education in the language classroom and beyond. *Argentinian Journal of Applied Linguistics*, *3*(2), 9–29.

Porto, M., & Byram, M. (2017). *New Perspectives on Intercultural Language Research and Teaching: Exploring Learners' Understandings of Texts from Other Cultures*. New York/Abingdon: Routledge.

Potter, J. (2004). Discourse analysis as a way of analysing naturally occurring talk. In D. Silverman, D. (Ed.), *Qualitative Research: Theory, Method and Practice* (pp. 200–21). London: Sage.

Purpura, J. E. (2012). Assessment of grammar. In C. Chapelle (Ed.), *The Encyclopedia of Applied Linguistics*. Malden: Wiley-Blackwell.

Purpura, J. E. (2013). Assessing grammar. In A. Kunnan (Ed.), *The Companion to Language Assessment* (pp. 1–25). London and New York: John Wiley & Sons.

Ramos, K. A. (2015). Using genre pedagogy to teach adolescent English learners to write academic persuasive essays. *Journal of Education*, *195*(2), 19–35.

Reardon, V. S. (2017). Alternative assessment: Growth, development and future directions. In: R. Al-Mahrooqi, C. Coombe, F. Al-Maamari & V. Thakur (Eds.), *Revisiting EFL Assessment: Critical Perspectives* (pp. 191–208). Cham: Springer.

Reyes G. (1994). *La pragmática lingüística: El estudio del uso del lenguaje*. Barcelona: Montesinos.

Richards, J. C. (2010). Competence and performance in language teaching. *RELC Journal*, *41*(2), 101–22.

Richards, J. C. (2017a). Teaching English through English: Proficiency, pedagogy and performance. *RELC Journal*, *48*(1), 7–30.

Richards, J. C. (2017b). Teacher identity in second language teacher education. In G. Barkhuizen (Ed.), *Reflections on Language Teacher Identity Research* (pp. 139–44). New York and Abingdon: Routledge.

Richards, J. C., & Farrell, T. (2011). The nature of teacher learning. In J. C. Richards & T. Farrell (Eds.), *Practice Teaching: A Reflective Approach* (pp. 15–30). New York: Cambridge University Press.

Rico, R. J. (2018). Georgia lawmakers push for English-only communication. *US News & World Report* Retrieved from https://www.usnews.com/news/best-states/georgia/articles/2018-01-24/georgia-lawmakers-push-for-english-only-communication

Riestra, N., Goicoechea, M. V., & Tapia, S. M. (2014). *Los géneros textuales en secuencias didácticas de lengua y literatura*. Buenos Aires: NOVEDUC.

Risager, K. (2005). Languaculture as a key concept in language and culture teaching. In B. Preisler, A.Fabricius, H. Haberland, S. Kjærbeck & K. Risager (Eds.), *The Consequences of Mobility: Linguistic and Sociocultural Contact Zones* (pp. 185–96). Roskilde: Roskilde Universitet.

Roberts, J. (1998). *Language Teacher Education*. London and New York: Arnold.

Rogerson-Revell, P. (2011). *English Phonology and Pronunciation Teaching*. London: Bloomsbury.

Rose, D., & Martin, J. (2012). *Learning to Write, Reading to Learn: Genre, Knowledge and Pedagogy of the Sydney School.* Sheffield: Equinox Publishing.

Rose, K. (2001). Compliments and compliment responses in film: Implications for pragmatics research and language teaching. *International Review of Applied Linguistics in Language Teaching, 39*(4), 309–26.

Rose, K. R. (2005). On the effects of instruction in second language pragmatics. *System, 33*, 385–99.

Saavedra, P., & Campos, M. (2018). Combining the strategies of using focused written corrective feedback and keeping a writing portfolio. *Colombian Applied Linguistics Journal, 20*(1), 79–90.

Salcedo, N., & Sacchi, F. (2014). The role of culture in the EFL classroom: A study of teachers' beliefs and practices. In D. L. Banegas, M. López Barrios, M. Porto & M. A. Soto, M.A. (Eds.), *English Language Teaching in the Post-Methods Era: Selected papers from the 39th FAAPI Conference* (pp. 81–91). Santiago del Estero: APISE.

Şallı-Çopur, D. (2008). Teacher effectiveness in initial years of service: A case study on the graduates of METU foreign language education program. Unpublished doctoral dissertation, Middle East Technical University, Turkey.

Sapir, E. (1955). *Language: An Introduction the Study of Speech.* San Diego: Harcourt Brace Jovanovich.

Scarcella, R., & Oxford, R. (1992). *The Tapestry of Language Learning.* Boston: Heinle and Heinle Publishers.

Schall-Leckrone, L. (2017). Genre pedagogy: A framework to prepare history teachers to teach language. *TESOL Quarterly, 51*(2), 358–82.

Scheffler, P. (2009). Rule difficulty and the usefulness of instruction. *ELT Journal, 63*(1), 5–12.

Schegloff, E. A. (2007). *Sequence Organization in Interaction.* Cambridge: Cambridge University Press.

Schmitt, N., & Marsden, R. (2006). *Why is English Like that? Historical Answers to Hard ELT Questions.* Ann Arbor, MI: The University of Michigan Press.

Seferoğlu, G. (2006). Teacher candidates' reflections on some components of a pre-service English teacher education programme in Turkey. *Journal of Education for Teaching, 32*(4), 369–78.

Seidlhofer, B. (2009). Common ground and different realities: World Englishes and English as a lingua franca. *World Englishes, 28*(2), 236–45.

Seidlhofer, B. (2011). *Understanding English as a Lingua Franca.* Oxford: Oxford University Press.

Sheen, Y. (2007). The effect of focused written corrective feedback and language aptitude on ESL learner's acquisition of articles. *TESOL Quarterly, 41*, 255–83.

Sheen, Y., Wright, D., & Moldava, A. (2009). Differential effects of focused and unfocused written correction on the accurate use of grammatical forms by adult ESL learners. *System, 37*(4), 556–69.

Shulman, L. (1986). Those who understand: Knowledge growth in teaching. *Educational Researcher, 15*(2), 4–14.

Shulman, L. (1987). Knowledge and teaching: Foundations of the new reform. *Harvard Educational Review, 57*(1), 1–22.

Smit, U., & Dafouz, E. (2012). Integrating content and language in higher education: An introduction to English-medium policies, conceptual issues and research practices across Europe. *AILA Review, 25*(1), 1–12.

Snow, M. A., & Brinton, D. M. (Eds.). (2017).*The Content-based Classroom: New Perspectives on Integrating Language and Content* (2nd ed.). Ann Arbor: University of Michigan Press.

Spratt, M., & Leug, B. (2000). Peer teaching and peer learning revisited. *ELT Journal, 54*(3), 218–26.

Steiner, E. (1997). Systemic functional linguistics and its application to foreign language teaching. *Estudios de Lingüística Aplicada, 26*, 15–27.

Stern, H. H. (1983). *Fundamental Concepts of Language Teaching*. Oxford: Oxford University Press.

Stirling, J. (2011). *Teaching Spelling to English Language Learners*. Raleigh: Lulu.

Stortch, N., & Tapper, J. (2000). The focus of teacher and student concerns in discipline-specific writing by university students. *Higher Education Research and Development, 19*(3), 337–55.

Swain, M. (1997). The output hypothesis, focus on form, and second language learning. In V. Berry, R. Adamson & W. T. Littlewood (Eds,), *Applied Linguistics* (pp. 1–21). English Language Centre: University of Hong Kong.

Symeonidis, V., & Schwarz, J. F. (2016). Phenomenon-based teaching and learning through the pedagogical lenses of phenomenology: The recent curriculum reform in Finland. *Forum Oświatowe, 28*(2), 31–47.

Tagle, T., Díaz, C., Briesmaster, M., Ubilla, L., & Etchegaray, P. (2017). Pre-service EFL teachers' beliefs about teaching writing: A case study in two Chilean universities. *Electronic Journal of Foreign Language Teaching, 14*(2), 187–200.

Taguchi, N. (2009). *Pragmatic Competence*. Berlin: Mouton de Gruyter.

Taguchi, N. (2011). Teaching pragmatics: Trends and issues. *Annual Review of Applied Linguistics, 31*, 289–310.

Taguchi, N. (2015). Instructed pragmatics at a glance: Where instructional studies were, are, and should be going. *Language Teaching, 48*(1), 1–50.

Taki, S. (2011). The effect of using portfolio-based writing assessment on language learning: The case of young Iranian EFL learners. *English Language Teaching, 4*(3), 192–99.

Tarone, E., & Allwright, D. (2005). Second language teacher learning and student second language learning: Shaping the knowledge base. In D. J. Tedick (Ed.), *Second Language Teacher Education: International Perspectives* (pp. 5–23). Mahwah: Lawrence Erlbaum.

Tatsuki, D., & Houck, N. (2010). *Speech Acts and Beyond: New Directions in Pragmatics*. Alexandria: TESOL.

Taylor, D. S. (1991). Who speaks English to whom? The question of teaching English pronunciation for global communication. *System, 19*(4), 425–35.

Tedick, D. J. (2013). Embracing proficiency and program standards and rising to the challenge: A response to Burke. *Modern Language Journal, 97*(2), 535–38.

Thompson, G. (2014). *Introducing Functional Grammar* (3rd ed.). London: Routledge.

Thorne, S. L., & Payne, J. S. (2005). Evolutionary trajectories, internet-mediated expression and language education. *CALICO Journal, 22*, 371–97.

Thornbury, S. (2006). *A-Z of ELT*. Oxford: Macmillan.

Thornbury, S. (2017). *About Language* (2nd ed.). Cambridge: Cambridge University Press.

Thorne, S. L., & Smith, B. (2011). Second language development theories and technology-mediated language learning. *CALICO Journal, 28*(2), 268–77.

Tomlinson, B. (Ed.). (2013). *Applied Linguistics and Materials Development*. London and New York: Bloomsbury.

Tsang, A. (2017). EFL/ESL teachers' general language proficiency and learners' engagement. *RELC Journal, 48*(1), 99–113.

Upton, C. (2015). British English. In M. Reed & J. M. Levis (Eds.), *The Handbook of English Pronunciation* (pp. 251–68). West Sussex: Wiley-Blackwell.

Van Dijk, T. A. (1993). Principles of critical discourse analysis. *Discourse & Society, 4*(2), 249–83.

Van Dijk, T. A. (1998). *Ideology: A Multidisciplinary Approach*. London: Sage.

Van Dijk, T. A. (2008). *Discourse and Context: A Socio Cognitive Approach*. Cambridge: Cambridge University Press.

Villacañas de Castro, L. S. (2017). "We are more than EFL teachers—we are educators": Emancipating EFL student-teachers through photovoice. *Educational Action Research, 25*(4), 610–29.

Vygotsky, L. (1978). *Mind in Society: The Development of Higher Psychological Processes*. Cambridge, MA: Harvard University Press.

Walker, R. (2010). *Teaching the Pronunciation of English as a Lingua Franca*. Oxford: Oxford University Press.

Wang, Y. (2016). Native English speakers' authority in English: Do Chinese speakers of English care about native English speakers' judgments? *English Today, 32*(1), 35–40.

Watanabe, S. (1983). *Eigo no rekishi* [The making of the English tongue]. Tokyo: Taishukan-shoten.

Wedel, A. (2011). Self-organization in phonology. In E. A. H. Marc van Oostendorp, Colin J. Ewen & K. Rice (Eds.), *The Blackwell Companion to Phonology* (pp. 130–47). Malden: Wiley-Blackwell.

Wei, R., & Su, J. (2012). The statistics of English in China. *English Today, 28*(3), 10–14.

Wells, J. C. (2008). *Longman Pronunciation Dictionary* (3rd ed.). Harlow: Pearson.

Widdowson, H. G. (2002). Language teaching: Defining the subject. In H. Trappes-Lomax & G. Ferguson (Eds.), *Language in Language Teacher Education* (pp. 67–82). Amsterdam and Philadelphia: John Benjamins.

Widdowson, H. G. (2007). *Discourse Analysis*. Oxford, England: Oxford University Press.

Wilson, J. J. (2008). *How to Teach Listening*. Harlow: Pearson.

Wood, D., Bruner, J. S., & Ross, G. (1976). The role of tutoring in problem solving. *Journal of Child Psychology and Psychiatry, 17*, 89–100.

Woodgate-Jones, A. (2008). Training confident primary modern foreign language teachers in England: An investigation into preservice teachers' perceptions of their subject knowledge. *Teaching and Teacher Education, 24*(1), 1–13.

Xerri, D., & Pioquinto, C. (2018). Introduction. In D. Xerri & C. Pioquinto (Eds.), *Becoming Research Literate: Supporting Teacher Research in English Language Teaching* (pp. i–xii). Sursee, Switzerland: English Teachers Association Switzerland.

Xhosakhaya. (2009, January 11). *Xhosa Lesson 2. How to say "click" sounds*. Retrieved from https://www.youtube.com/watch?v=31zzMb3U0iY&t=3s

Yancey, K. B. (2004). Made not only in words: Composition in a new key. *College Composition and Communication, 56*(2), 297–328.

Yates, L. (2014). Learning how to speak: Pronunciation, pragmatics and practicalities in the classroom and beyond. *Language Teaching, 50*(2), 227–46.

Yavuz, A., & Zehir Topkaya, E. (2013). Teacher educators' evaluation of the English language teaching program: A Turkish case. *Novitas-ROYAL (Research on Youth and Language), 7*(1), 64–83.

Yule, G. (1996) *Pragmatics*. Oxford: Oxford University Press.

Yule, G. (1998). *Explaining English Grammar*. Oxford: Oxford University Press.

Zabala, F. (2015). El dictado fonemático en la clase de pronunciación de una lengua extranjera. In P. L. Luchini, M. A. García Jurado, & U. Kickhöfel Alves (Eds.), *Fonética y fonología: Articulación entre enseñanza e investigación* (pp. 153–62). Mar del Plata: Universidad Nacional de Mar del Plata.

Zein, M. S. (2017). Professional development needs of primary EFL teachers: Perspectives of teachers and teacher educators. *Professional Development in Education, 43*(2), 293–313.

Zheng, Y. & Yu, S. (2018). Student engagement with teacher written corrective feedback in EFL writing: A case study of Chinese lower-proficiency students. *Assessing Writing, 37*, 13–24.

Zhu, Y. and Shu, D. (2017). Implementing foreign language curriculum innovation in a Chinese secondary school: An ethnographic study on teacher cognition and classroom practices, *System, 66*, 100–12.

Zubizarreta, J. (2009). *The Learning Portfolio: Reflective Practice for Improving Student Learning*. San Francisco, US: Jossey Bass.

Index